Lessons
That Change Writers

For my students,
who worked hard and made literature

Lessons
That
Change Writers

nancie atwell

*first*hand

Heinemann
Portsmouth, NH

Heinemann
A division of Reed Elsevier, Inc.
361 Hanover Street
Portsmouth, NH 03801–3912
www.heinemann.com

Offices and agents throughout the world

The author and publisher wish to thank those who have generously given permission to reprint borrowed material: "Thirteen Ways of Looking at a Blackbird" from *The Collected Poems of Wallace Stevens* by Wallace Stevens. Copyright © 1954 by Wallace Stevens, renewed 1982 by Holly Stevens. Used by permission of Alfred A. Knopf, a division of Random House, Inc. New York, and by Faber and Faber, London.

"Sestina at 3AM" from *Heroes in Disguise* by Linda Pastan. Copyright ©1991 by Linda Pastan. Used by permission of W.W. Norton & Company, Inc.

Library of Congress Cataloging-in-Publication Data
Atwell, Nancie.
Lessons that change writers / Nancie Atwell.
p. cm.
Includes bibliographical references.
ISBN 0-86709-546-6
1. English language-Composition and exercises-Study and teaching (Middle school) 2. Language arts (Middle school) I. Title.
LB1631 .A725 2002
428'.0071'2--dc21   2002012572

Printed in the United States of America on acid-free paper
06   05   04   03   02   RRD   1   2   3   4   5

CONTENTS

Introduction   ix

Conditions of a Writing Workshop   xvii

Expectations and Rules for Writing Workshop   xx

Mini-Lesson Basics   xxii

A Chronology of the Mini-Lessons   xxviii

SECTION I: LESSONS ABOUT TOPICS

Lesson 1   Writing Territories: Launching the Writing Workshop 3

Lesson 2   Questions for Memoirists   9

Lesson 3   Heart Mapping   12

Lesson 4   Where Poetry Hides   17

Lesson 5   Problems to Explore in Fiction   21

Lesson 6   Twenty Actions   26

Lesson 7   Itches to Scratch in Essays   30

SECTION II: LESSONS ABOUT PRINCIPLES

Lesson 8   What Is Writing?   35

Lesson 9   The Rule of *So What?*   38

Lesson 10   Thoughts and Feelings   44

Lesson 11   The Rule of Write about *a* Pebble, or "No Ideas but in Things"   48

Lesson 12   Narrative Leads   50

Lesson 13   Good Titles   53

Lesson 14   Polishing   56

Lesson 15   Final Copies: What Readers Need   60

Lesson 16   Thinking on Paper: Planning Sheets   62

Lesson 17   Can a Reader See It, Hear It, Feel It?   66

Lesson 18   A Movie behind Your Eyelids   69

Lesson 19   How a Thesaurus Can Help   73

	Troubleshooting: Surefire Ways to Weaken Your Writing
Lesson 20	The Really Bad Words 80
Lesson 21	Too-Long and Too-Short Paragraphs 82
Lesson 22	The Missing *I* 84
Lesson 23	Passive Sentences 86
Lesson 24	Exclamation Points 87
Lesson 25	Hopefully 88
Lesson 26	Stories That End "The End" 89

CONTENTS *continued*

SECTION III: LESSONS ABOUT GENRES

Lesson 27   Ineffective and Effective Memoirs 93

A Course of Study: Fiction

Lesson 28   What's Easy about Writing Bad Fiction? 103
Lesson 29   What's Hard about Writing Good Fiction? 105
Lesson 30   The Main Character Questionnaire 107
Lesson 31   Considerations in Creating a Character 113
Lesson 32   Short Story Structure 115
Lesson 33   Ways to Develop a Character 117

A Course of Study: How Free-Verse Poetry Works

Lesson 34   The Power of *I* 121
Lesson 35   Beware the Participle 125
Lesson 36   Leads: Begin Inside 127
Lesson 37   Conclusions: End Strongly 129
Lesson 38   Breaking Lines and Stanzas and Punctuating 132
Lesson 39   Cut to the Bone 136
Lesson 40   Use Repetition 139
Lesson 41   Two Things at Once 142

Troubleshooting: Some Poetic Forms

Lesson 42   Sestinas and Tritinas 147
Lesson 43   Irregular Odes 151
Lesson 44   Haiku 153
Lesson 45   Thirteen-Ways Poems 155
Lesson 46   Memoir Poems 158

Lesson 47   Gifts of Writing 161
Lesson 48   Effective Book Reviews 166

A Course of Study: Essays

Lesson 49   Effective Essays: Teasing Out Criteria 174
Lesson 50   How Do I Scratch the Itch? 177
Lesson 51   Write with Information 178
Lesson 52   Order the Information 180
Lesson 53   Leads for an Essay 182
Lesson 54   Experiment with Essay Conclusions 184

Lesson 55   Ted L. Nancy Letters and Other Genres for Humorists 187
Lesson 56   Test Writing as a Genre 189

CONTENTS *continued*

SECTION IV: LESSONS ABOUT CONVENTIONS

Lesson 57   The Individual Proofreading List   195

Lesson 58   Business Letter Format and Addressing an Envelope   200

Lesson 59   A Brief History of the English Language   209

Troubleshooting: Spelling Essentials

Lesson 60   Weekly Word Studies   216

Lesson 61   Personal Survival Words   220

Lesson 62   Proofreading for Spelling   223

Lesson 63   The Truth about *I* before *E*   225

Lesson 64   Some Foreign Words Used in English Texts   226

Lesson 65   Root Words and Prefixes   227

Lesson 66   Suffixes: To Double or Not?   229

Lesson 67   Other Suffix Rules That Mostly Work   232

Lesson 68   A Brief History of Some Common Punctuation Marks   234

Lesson 69   Essential Punctuation Information   238
  Period Confusions
  Most Common Comma Omissions
  Reasons for a Semicolon
  Colons Signal Readers
  To Dash or to Hyphen?
  Apostrophe Headaches
  Parentheses: Why Not

Troubleshooting: Convention Confusions

Lesson 70   How to Correct Comma Splices   241

Lesson 71   How to Punctuate Dialogue   244

Lesson 72   Homonyms   246

Lesson 73   Four Capitalization Confusions   248

Lesson 74   Writing Numbers   250

Lesson 75   Indicating Titles   252

Lesson 76   *Me* or *I*?   254

IN THE ACCOMPANYING NOTEBOOK

Section I   Blackline Masters for Reproducibles and Overheads

Section II   Blackline Masters for Reproducibles and Overheads

Section III Blackline Masters for Reproducibles and Overheads

Section IV   Blackline Masters for Reproducibles and Overheads

Appendixes A Student Memoirs
           B Student Short Stories
           C Student Essays
           D Student Book Reviews
           E Resources for Writing Mini-Lessons

INTRODUCTION

The longer I teach, the simpler my teaching becomes. I don't mean that what I ask of kids is simplistic or watered-down or—not very often, anyway—easy. I mean my thinking about teaching has grown less cluttered. Some of the questions of theory and pedagogy that once kept me awake at night feel contrived or beside the point—for example, how to conduct a writing conference without directly teaching the writer, or whether red-inking kids' editorial errors doesn't embarrass them and hurt their feelings, or the inevitable, big question for teachers of writing: Is it possible to teach someone how to write well, or are good writers talented by nature?

Time and experience have given me twin gifts as a teacher. I know what I can expect from my student writers, and I understand how to help them make good on my expectations. Some teaching decisions come so easily these days, I suspect that to an observer they might look like intuitions. But almost nothing I do that works is a function of intuition. When I'm teaching well, a quarter century of knowledge of writing, teaching, and learning propels me from point A to point B, from problem to solution—sometimes, if I'm cooking, to multiple solutions. The clutter of received theories and confused pedagogies has been replaced by a bracing sense of efficiency and productivity, qualities that, as a novice, I never thought to associate with good teaching.

So, these days, in our writing conferences, I teach my students. As an experienced adult, I sit down with less experienced children and make suggestions, give advice, demonstrate solutions, and collaborate with them on pieces of their writing when I think they need to see how something could work. And student writing submitted to me for editing is already so thoroughly hatched up by the writers themselves, whose self-editing shows what they know about making their writing conventional, that my copyediting is just another set of hatch marks. I correct every remaining error I can find and confer with students about them a handful at a time, so that when a final copy goes public, it will do and be what a reader's eyes and mind expect—so it will show respect for readers and actually be *read*. Finally, I know that I can, and sometimes do, teach kids how to write well.

My students' writing knocks me out. It knocks them out. In our writing workshops, they learn how to act deliberately to *create literature* (Shelley Harwayne [1992]). I show them everything I've learned about writing through writing and noticing what I do and need as a writer, through reading literature, through reading about writing and its teaching, and through the accumulated experiences of years of working with young writers. This expertise exists to serve my kids. Sharing it feels satisfying, genuine, and nothing like the tensions and insecurities of the early years of writing workshop, when I worked so hard not to usurp students' "ownership" of their writing, not to advise or instruct or praise writers, not to assign or suggest pieces of writing, not to appear to be teaching.

As a teacher of teachers of writing, I experienced a similar, gradual transformation as I wrestled with comparable issues of direction *vs.* indirection in my approaches. When talking to teachers, should I tell and show what I do in my classroom? Or is it more professional to present theories about teaching, supply the sources that influenced my thinking, and invite teachers to imagine the pedagogy?

Teachers familiar with *In the Middle* (1987; 1998) know which side I came down on. I gave away the blueprints to my classroom. I came to understand that sharing practical knowledge is my responsibility as a classroom teacher who presumes to speak to other teachers. So I shape the descriptions of my practice as specifically as I can, with as much narrative structure as I can weave in, in hopes that teachers who come across my writing will be able to visualize my classroom, then visualize themselves behaving similarly with their own students, just as back in the early 1980's I read Donald Graves's narrative descriptions of the writing workshops at Atkinson Academy and imagined myself as Atkinson teachers Mary Ellen Giacobbe, Judy Egan, and Pat Howard.

Conversation with teachers, like the conversations with the writers in my classroom, feels satisfying, genuine, and *useful*. Rather than trying to guess at and invent procedures and structures, teachers inclined toward writing workshop can lean on the scaffolds I've developed as they teach themselves and as they establish conditions for their kids to produce impelled, excellent writing.

In *Lessons That Change Writers* I narrowed and deepened my conversation with teachers to focus on how mini-lessons can help students improve their writing. And I confess to some qualms about this focus. I recall the crowds of teachers at the "Ideas Exchanges" at conventions of the National Council of Teachers of English, and I cringe. Well-meaning writing teachers happily swapped recipes for their best lessons, as if children's needs, classroom contexts for writing and standards for writing excellence, and a teacher's knowledge and experience were irrelevant to what "works" in teaching writing.

So when readers of *In the Middle* spoke or wrote to me about their desire for a book of writing mini-lessons, I resisted. I knew that when any one of my kids produced a fabulous piece of writing, the end product was inevitably the result of way too many variables—conferences with me, conferences with friends, the significance of the topic, the writer's strong intentions, the pull of the potential audience, the child's previous experiences as a writer and reader, and many, many mini-lessons—to give credit to any one recipe for successful writing.

But I also regularly query my kids about aspects of their learning and my teaching. In self-evaluation questionnaires at the end of each trimester, they assess their growth, strengths, and goals as writers; they also consider my teaching and report about anything I've done that seems useful to their writing. I ask and ask again, "Did any mini-lesson help you? Make a difference in your writing? Change you as a writer?" And when a student answers yes, and explains the lesson and its effect, I document the response.

My kids' answers are the basis for this book. They're also my best argument that writing *can* be taught and learned. Students identified a course of study of writing that allowed them to write well—not isolated recipes, but advice, models, and activities that worked for them as writers in the specific context of writing workshop. Figure 1, "Conditions of a Writing Workshop," (pages xvii–xix) provides a stripped-down description of that context, which is a subject of the second edition of *In the Middle*, and Figure 2, "Expectations and Rules for Writing Workshop," (pages xx–xxi) lists the specific guidelines I establish each September for my seventh- and eighth-grade writing workshops.

In *Lessons That Change Writers* I've narrated the lessons that students in my writing workshops of the past six years most frequently cited as those that helped them change their writing for the better and become different writers—more productive, more purposeful, more literary, and more conventional.

Fine-tuning the role of the mini-lesson in writing workshop has been one of my professional preoccupations for a long time. I know that like many veteran English teachers who became writing teachers in the early 1980's, I jumped at the concept of the mini-lesson. In the student-centered environment of a writing workshop, it seemed a welcome opportunity to regress a little and do what I had trained to do as an English education major: impart information about English.

I loved to teach about English and still do. So the mini-lesson format—leading a meeting of students at the start of each day's workshop—suited me just fine. Subsequent refinements over the next twenty years had little to do with the format of the lessons and everything to do with their content. In the context of the writing workshop, what exactly *is* English? What lessons will have a practical, lasting, positive influence on student writing? And, given every teacher's sense of urgency—we and our kids have just 175 days together—what is worthwhile to teach?

So I pondered the content of mini-lessons and how to make them most effective for my kids. At first I believed that lessons must be responsive—planned day to day in reaction to what I saw kids doing and needing as writers in the workshop. It was exhausting. But then I began to see patterns of needs and information to address in the fall, in winter, and in spring: in short, a course of study of writing. Finally, I recognized that good lessons draw on a balance of ad hoc teachable moments and the teacher's prior experiences with writing and with teaching it.

I also considered sources to tap in planning the lessons. Which resources are too obscure for my kids to relate as writers? Too Mickey Mouse for them to take seriously? Which are honest and accurate, and which are inauthentic and gimmicky? What background information is conducive to effective writing, and what's arcane?

I wondered about how to use pieces of writing in the lessons. What's the best way to introduce and teach from examples of excellent published writing? And what's to be gained by showing successful student writing or students' attempts at solving specific writing problems? By showing pieces of my own writing, the problems that arose, and my attempts at solutions? Or by demonstrating my writing on overhead transparencies, in impromptu, out-loud protocols? And is there merit in documenting, saving, labeling, and filing the materials of good lessons, so that I can teach them again another year?

Then came the genuinely difficult thinking. From the perspective of a writing teacher, *what is English?* What are the conventions of standard edited American English that readers' eyes and minds crave and that writers need to understand and anticipate? Among these, which are priorities for my students? And which conventions are, frankly, a waste of their time? I'm thinking of such school conventions as topic sentences, the four kinds of sentences, identifying and naming grammatical constructions, or the injunctions against starting a sentence with a conjunction, ending one with a preposition, splitting infinitives, and writing sentence fragments. How do I identify the points at which students break the compact between their texts and their readers? And how do I demonstrate conventions so student writers will understand and learn how to conform to a literate reader's expectations?

Then, which genres are worth teaching in middle school mini-lessons? If there are school conventions, there surely are school genres, kinds of writing a reader will never locate in a library or bookstore but which are rampant in English lessons. I'm thinking of book reports as opposed to book reviews and critical essays; personal experience narratives in middle school classrooms instead of memoirs; fiction pieces *vs.* short stories; friendly letters *vs.*, for example, thank-you letters that get sealed, stamped, and mailed by grateful gift recipients; five-paragraph essays instead of op-ed features and letters to the editor; encyclopedia- and Internet-based reports *vs.* arguments and essays based on firsthand research; and compare-contrast themes, descriptive paragraphs, acrostic poetry, 5-7-5 haiku, and the whole host of forms of writing that exist only between the hours of 8:00 A.M. and 3:00 P.M.

Finally, while working to identify what's authentic and important about writing, I tried to find the language that would best convey the essential features of literary, conventional writing to heterogeneous groups of seventh and eighth graders. What are the words that will resonate for preadolescent and adolescent writers?

Kids' brains have frozen before my eyes when I've spoken to them about writing and mentioned concepts like *independent clauses, parallel structure, concrete* vs. *general nouns, imagery, coherence, tone, syntax, compression, pace, reflection,* and, the scariest brain popsicle of them all, the T word: *theme.* I needed to develop language and examples to convey the elements of good, mature writing to a less than mature audience, but one that still deserves a shot at producing literature and needs to understand literary qualities in order to do so.

Today, as a teacher of writing mini-lessons, I move between the course of study my kids defined—the files of lessons and examples that I know, from their answers to my questions about helpful mini-lessons, are likely to change kids' writing— and the pressing concerns that arise during my conferences with students in one day's writing workshop and are ripe to be addressed in the next day's mini-lesson.

For example, I know that by the second or third week of school, my students need to begin gathering ideas for memoirs that will resonate: narratives to capture and explore powerful moments in their lives, to help them know themselves and make sense of who they were, who they are, and who they're becoming. So an annual September mini-lesson revolves around a list of questions for memoirists that pushes kids' memoirs beyond "The Time I Went to Funtown U.S.A."

But last fall, on a Monday morning in early September, I conferred with three seventh graders whose pieces were titled with labels—for example, "My Experience with Our Foreign Exchange Student, Alvaro." So titles became the subject of the Tuesday mini-lesson. With her permission, I made transparencies of drafts of a poem by Erin, and we looked at how brainstorming helped her find an effective title. I went to my files and found, then showed, examples of other students' experiences with brainstorming titles; then, as a group, we created a list of the qualities of good titles and techniques for creating one.

Students took notes on both of these lessons in their writing hand-books, a method I learned from Linda Rief's book *Seeking Diversity* (1992). If I'm concentrated on imparting only useful information in mini-lessons, the information should survive the lesson in a usable form, one that writers can return to and tap throughout a year of writing work-shop. Students bring spiral notebooks to the mini-lesson circle and record lessons chronologically, sometimes from discussions, sometimes by copying my notes from an overhead transparency or chart paper, or sometimes by attaching clean, typed photocopies of notes we created in a previous mini-lesson to the pages of their handbooks. Students create and update tables of contents for the handbooks that allow them easy access to the help they need.

The lessons my students identified as best fall into four categories, which provide the structure for this book:

- Lessons about topics: ways to help writers develop ideas for pieces of writing that will matter to writers and to their readers
- Lessons about principles of writing: ways to think and craft deliberately to create meaningful, literary writing
- Lessons about genres: how to observe and name the qualities of good free-verse poems, formatted poetry, essays, short stories, memoirs, parodies, and book reviews
- Lessons about conventions: what readers' eyes and minds expect from texts, and how marks and forms give writing voice and power and make reading predictable and easy

I've narrated the mini-lessons as scripts: straightforward invitations to teachers to listen to, try on, then adapt my voice and experience. The accompanying Teacher's Notebook provides 95 percent of the materials I use in teaching the lessons, including masters for overhead transparen-cies and reproducibles. You can bet I thought long and hard about approaching mini-lessons in this fashion. The scripted lessons of DISTAR and other programmed instruction give me apoplexy: they take away teachers' professionalism and turn us into mere technicians or, worse, puppets. But I also know how much I learn when I watch and hear an effective, experienced teacher in action.

When I'm lucky enough to observe Mary Ellen Giacobbe conduct a demonstration lesson with young writers, I take notes that create a script of her explanations and responses to kids. Then I debrief after-ward with her about why she behaved as she did. Later, I read and reread the script of Mary Ellen's teaching, and her words, actions, and motivations that resonated for me gradually become part of my reper-toire as a teacher.

So the lessons I've scripted here are my best versions of how I choose to speak to kids about writing. I hope that teachers who use *Lessons That Change Writers* will read a lesson once or several times, take what feels right from my language and experience, and speak directly to their kids about what they understand about good writing and writers.

And I hope that through the scripts, teachers will recognize the power of a mini-lesson—one that's relevant, practical, illustrative, and purposeful—to improve student writing when large classes make daily, individual writing conferences impracticable.

I'm well aware of the writing teachers out there who struggle with huge classes and the pressure they feel to try to confer with every writer every day. In classes of twenty students or more, it is *impossible* to confer with writers frequently enough for conferences to serve as the major vehicle for writing instruction. Regular, rich, extended conversations with individual writers are a wonderful ideal, but the reality of public school classrooms militates against an exclusive reliance on one-to-one conferring. In the context of most K–12 classrooms, the mini-lesson should be at least an equal partner to the writing conference.

When teachers with classes of thirty or more students ask for my advice, I suggest they try to see every writer at least once or twice a week, then focus on making each day's lesson a kind of whole-group conference about problems kids are having as writers, solutions to writing problems that students or the teacher invented, examples of excellent writing, ways to develop topics, genres students want to write in or the teacher wishes them to try, literary techniques, and confusions students have about conventions of writing—in short, I suggest they teach writing.

That final big question—whether it's possible to teach someone how to write well—these days strikes me as particularly irrelevant and pessimistic. I notice how we don't pose comparable questions about our potential as teachers and our kids' as learners in the other disciplines: for example, is it possible to teach someone to do well in math, have a sense of history, read with understanding? Here, words like *talent* and *giftedness* never enter the conversation. But when it comes to writing, teachers and kids too often settle for mediocre—or even no—writing because, well, a few kids have the knack, but most never will. We need to raise our expectations for student writing to a higher literary standard and teach students how to meet them. And we also might rethink the teaching of writing in light of how we approach the other disciplines.

Take reading. It seems as if each fall, the new kindergarten class at the Center for Teaching and Learning included one child who entered school already reading. Of course Nancy Tindal, their teacher, would have been thrilled to pieces if they were all able to enjoy books on their own. But she never talked about talent or giftedness in relation to her students, and she never considered that all of her kids wouldn't eventually learn to enjoy books independently. Instead, throughout the school year, Nancy and her class created a cumulative record of reading strategies—a list on chart paper of the approaches the children might take when they came across words they didn't know. By June there were twelve or thirteen strategies on the chart, and every one of Nancy's kindergartners was reading.

I suspect that all writing teachers have had the experience, over the course of our careers, of one or two or a handful of students whose entry-level writing took our breaths away, and we had nothing to do with it. I'm thinking of the rare student who read a lot, loved literature, invisibly and effortlessly ingested its lessons, and produced literature of his or her own. These kids are often the acknowledged "good writers" in a class, and how we wish other students could be more like them, could intuit their way to texts full of grace, voice, and purpose.

The real question for writing teachers is, how do we help our students develop a repertoire of approaches to writing comparable to the reading strategies Nancy Tindal taught her kindergartners? How do we help all writers identify problems, solve them, and take charge of their writing and thinking?

The qualities of good writing *are* complex and nuanced. But they can be named, and I'm convinced they can be taught. Of all the arts, writing should be among the most democratic: all one needs is paper and a pen—and, I would suggest, a teacher or two along the way who work to make the intangible tangible, so every student might know the joy of writing well.

CONDITIONS OF A WRITING WORKSHOP

■ **A Predictable Structure**
Writing workshop begins with a mini-lesson (typically, 5–25 minutes); continues with independent writing/teacher and peer conferring, during which the teacher circulates among writers and meets with individuals; and may conclude with a group meeting (e.g., response to a piece of student writing; a group discussion of what writers accomplished or problems that emerged; the teacher's observations; follow-up to the mini-lesson).

■ **Regular Time**
Teachers schedule three–five writing workshops a week of at least forty-five minutes each.

■ **Choice**
Students develop most of their writing projects. Teachers push for *authority* and *purpose*: students writing with passion about what they know and care about, for reasons they believe in. During genre studies, students choose their own subjects, themes, and approaches, and the genre work becomes another project a writer might engage in during the workshop.

■ **Workmanlike Atmosphere**
The writing workshop is quiet and productive: writing is thinking, and teachers insist on silence so writers may think well. There is no talking during independent writing time, except in peer conference areas or when a teacher and a writer confer. Teacher and students whisper during their conferences: if the teacher's volume is louder than a whisper, the noise level in the workshop will rise to emulate it, and the teacher's voice will distract writers from their thinking.

■ **Response During Writing**

Teacher Conferences
Teachers move during writing conferences. They meet with individuals at students' tables or desks, and they try to meet with every student often. Individual conferences last anywhere from one minute to ten. Teachers either listen to the writer read aloud, or they read the writing silently to themselves. They focus on content, style, and structure: information, organization, language, reflection, direction, significance, purpose, character development, leads, conclusions.

Typical teacher entrées to the conference:
■ How's it going?
■ How may I help you?
■ Tell me about your writing.
■ What are you working on?
■ What do you have so far?
■ What part can I help you with?

Typical questions that focus on information, direction, reflection, and purpose:
■ Why are you writing this?
■ Where are you going with this?
■ What are you trying to do here?
■ Tell me more about X.
■ I don't understand Y.
■ Does this make sense?
■ What's this piece of writing really about?

Figure 1

- How did you feel or what did you think when X happened? Are there other places where a reader will wonder about your thoughts and feelings?
- As a reader, I can't see, feel, or hear X. What can you do?
- Is the pace too fast here? Can you make a movie, then expand this part?
- What would happen if you tried to do X here?
- May I show you how I'd handle the problem of Y?
- What will you do next?

Peer Conferences

The teacher designates two or three spaces apart from the writing tables or desks for students to confer. To initiate a peer conference, the writer tells what he or she needs. Students use peer-response forms attached to clipboards. Peer conferences are about content/information only: students don't edit each other's writing.

■ Mini-Lessons

Mini-lessons grow from teachers' observations of what students don't know or will need to know to produce excellent, literary writing. Teachers research mini-lessons. For example, they learn about different genres and their features, poets' and authors' experiences and processes, poetic and literary features and techniques, kinds of writing for kids to try, writing-as-process, pieces of writing that demonstrate different techniques, how different punctuation marks cue readers, format conventions, usage conventions, techniques for organizing information and argument, elements of fiction, character development, theme, purpose, and so on.

Most mini-lessons in the first weeks of school are procedural, as students get the hang of workshop routines. Mini-lessons are presented on overhead transparencies or easel pads, so the information is visual *and* oral *and* participatory. Students take notes on mini-lessons. Teachers save and collect plans and materials for future use.

■ Demonstrations

In mini-lessons teachers present their ideas for writing and their processes as planners, drafters, revisers, polishers, editors, and proofreaders. They show students *how* to create literature. Examples of demonstrations:

- The teacher's list of territories: potential and favorite topics, genres, audiences
- How to punctuate, capitalize, and paragraph prose; how to quote and paragraph dialogue
- Brainstorming titles
- Trying alternative leads and conclusions
- Different kinds of narrative leads
- Brainstorming solutions to a writing problem
- Writing an ineffective memoir or essay/writing, or at least beginning, a good one
- Options for poetry: how to use the white space, create line breaks and stanza breaks, cut to the bone, use a rhyming dictionary
- Poetic forms: haiku, sestina, tritina
- Different kinds of correspondence: thank-you letter, letter of condolence, letter of complaint
- Collaborative poetry (teacher and students contribute lines, and the teacher formats these on the chart or overhead)
- Generating and organizing data for an essay, writing a lead, creating transitions, experimenting with conclusions
- Using a thesaurus to find strong verbs
- Composing on the computer
- Proofreading for spelling errors

Figure 1, *continued*

■ **Work in Genres**
Teachers push for variety and teach about, show, and demonstrate memoirs, poetry, short fiction, essays, book reviews, parodies, a variety of business and friendly letters, and plays, plus other genres as a need or interest emerges.

■ **Conventions and Editing**
Students spell, punctuate, capitalize, form letters, and format as well as they can as they draft. Students self-edit formally when the content of a piece of writing is set, using individual proof-reading lists as a guide; then the teacher edits and corrects any errors that writers missed. The next day the teacher teaches the individual writer a few conventions at a time, based on the errors the teacher observed when editing the student's writing. Students add the new conventions to their individual proofreading lists and check for these the next time they edit.

■ **Publication/Going Public**
Students write to be read, not to complete pieces of writing for inclusion in their folders. Teachers look for and present both in-house and professional publication options, and they edit student writing with an eye toward preparing it for real readers.

Figure 1, *continued*

Expectations and Rules for Writing Workshop

Expectations for Writing Workshop

- Find topics and purposes for your writing that matter to you, your life, who you are, and whom you want to become.

- Keep a list of your territories as a writer: the topics, purposes, audiences, genres, forms, and techniques that are your specialties or that you'd like to experience and explore.

- Try new topics, purposes, audiences, genres, forms, and techniques.

- Make your own decisions about what's working and what needs more work in pieces of your writing. Be the first responder to your writing, and read yourself with a critical, literary eye and ear.

- Listen to, ask questions about, and comment on others' writing in ways that help them move their writing forward, toward literature.

- Take notes and create a handbook of information presented in writing mini-lessons, recorded chronologically, with a table of contents (Rief, *Seeking Diversity*, 1992).

- Produce *at least* three to five pages of rough draft each week, and bring *at least* two pieces of writing to completion every six weeks (Rief, *Seeking Diversity*, 1992). Recognize that good writers build quality upon a foundation of quantity.

- Work on your writing for at least an hour every weekend.

- Maintain a record of the pieces of writing you finish, and file finished writing (including all drafts, notes, etc.) chronologically in your permanent folder.

- Sometime during this academic year, produce a finished piece of writing in each of the following genres:

  A memoir
  Three to five poems or songs
  A short story
  A book review
  An essay

- Attempt professional publication.

- Recognize that readers' eyes and minds need your writing to be conventional in format, spelling, punctuation, and usage. Work toward conventionality and legibility, and use everything you know about format, spelling, punctuation, and usage *as you compose*.

- Keep an individualized proofreading list that you check your writing against when you edit and proofread.

- Take care of the writing materials, resources, and equipment I've provided for you.

- Each trimester, establish and work toward significant, relevant goals for yourself as a writer.

- In every writing workshop, take a *deliberate stance* (Harwayne, 1992) toward writing well: try to make your writing literature, and use what you've been shown in conferences and mini-lessons to help you get there.

- Work as hard in writing workshop as I do. Re-create happy times from your life, work through sad times, discover what you know about a subject and learn more, convey information and request it, parody, petition, play, explore, argue, apologize, advise, sympathize, imagine, look and look again, express love, show gratitude, and make money.

Figure 2

Rules for Writing Workshop

1. Save everything: it's all part of the history of the piece of writing, plus you never know what you might want to come back to later and use. On the computer, either label and save multiple versions *or* print a copy of each draft to save.

2. Date and label everything you write to help you keep track of what you've done (e.g., *notes, draft #1, brainstorming*). On the computer, label multiple versions as D.1, D.2, etc.

3. Write on one side of the paper only. *Always* skip lines or type double-spaced. Both will make revision, polishing, and editing easier and more productive. Professional writers *always* double space. You may wish to draft single-spaced on the computer, so you can see more text at a time, then shift to double-space when you print and revise and edit the text.

4. Draft your prose writing in sentences and paragraphs. Draft your poems in lines and stanzas. Don't go back into a mess of text and try to create order. Format as you go: real writers do this, too.

5. Get into the habit of punctuating and spelling as conventionally as you can *while* you're composing: this is something else writers do.

6. When composing on the word processor, print a double-spaced version *at least* every two days. Then read the text with a pen in your hand, away from the computer, and consider and work with the whole text, rather than one part at a time on the screen.

7. Understand that writing is thinking. Do nothing to distract me or other writers. Don't put your words into our brains as we're struggling to find our own. Instead, find your private, internal, writing place, lock the door, and listen to your voice.

8. When you confer with me, use as soft a voice as I use when I talk to you: *whisper*.

9. When you need to confer with peers, use a conference area and record responses on a peer conference form, so the writer has a reminder of what happened. Limit peer conferences to occasions when you have a specific problem that could benefit from a friend's response.

10. When you're stuck or uncertain, use the resources available to you in this room, including your writing handbook and your lists of writing territories, and tap the techniques you've been shown in conferences and mini-lessons.

11. Maintain and update your proofreading list, and refer to it when you self-edit.

12. Self-edit as completely as you can in a color different from the print of your text, and complete an editing checksheet to show what you know about conventions of writing. On the computer, spellcheck only at the very end, as part of the editing process.

13. When a piece of writing is finished, clip or staple everything together, including drafts, notes, lists, editing checksheet, and peer conference form, and file it in your permanent writing folder, with the final copy on top.

14. Record every piece of writing you finish on the form inside your permanent writing folder. Collect data about yourself as a writer, look for patterns, and take satisfaction in your accomplishments over time.

15. Write as well and as much as you can: work hard and make literature.

Figure 2, *continued*

MINI-LESSON BASICS

Every student will need a lined, 8½-by-11-inch spiral-bound notebook of at least one hundred pages in which to generate, record, and include mini-lesson information, and something to write with. In August my school sends a letter to parents that details what students should purchase for the coming school year. At my level the list includes two dozen new pencils and the notebook. The school provides folders for writing, because teachers want uniformity of color and style: my kids' daily writing folders are recognizable at a glance by color, and they come with pockets for storing works in progress and grommets for clasping permanent data, such as "Expectations for Writing Workshop," "Rules for Writing Workshop," and each student's proofreading list (see Lesson 57).

I collect all the pencils on the first day of school and put them in storage. Twenty-five at a time they become the source for a communal supply, which I keep in a jar in the classroom materials center. Students borrow pencils as they enter the classroom; mostly they return them when they go. This means there are always writing utensils available in the room.

In the fall I teach students to get a pencil from the materials center as they enter the room, come to the mini-lesson circle with their pencil and writing handbook, and sit down. I would say I teach this lesson, easily, ten times every fall. As soon as I announce to the gathered circle, "Please turn to the next clean page in your writing handbook," some kid asks, "Can I go to my locker and get mine?" *Yes.* A student who has left his or her handbook at home takes the day's notes on a sheet of plain paper, then tapes them onto the appropriate page the next day.

The appropriate page is always the next right-facing page in the notebook. I ask kids not to write on the backs of pages because it makes for less readable notes. Students number pages in the upper right-hand corners, starting with the fourth sheet of notebook paper as page 1; the first three pages are left blank to become a table of contents, so that as writers create their handbooks, they have a way to document where the entries are and can refer to them as they need them.

The basic materials and equipment I use to conduct mini-lessons include an overhead projector, blank transparency film labeled for use in plain paper copiers, fine-point permanent markers in a range of colors, regular markers, five desk-type tape dispensers, a paper cutter, pads of lined easel paper (Staples #24717), a low easel, and a low stool. When I write on the overhead, I use a transparency of a blank notebook page (see the Teacher's Notebook for a master). I make numerous copies of this transparency to have on hand as we collaborate on documents or I demonstrate my writing. Ken Maxim built the first easels that CTL teachers used for mini-lessons; I thank him for allowing me to include his plans here, as Figure 3.

The low easel is great because I can save lessons on the pages of the pad for future reference and because it's close to the ground, where I insist my students sit during mini-lessons. It's a major hassle at the start of each class to push back the desks and chairs and create a space on the floor for the mini-lesson circle, but it is essential.

Sometimes I feel like the kids are a football team, I'm the coach, and we're huddling in that circle before the big game. Pulling the group in creates intimacy. It allows the mini-lesson to feel like a conversation among writers or, again, an opportunity for straight talk from the coach. And the circle makes it possible for students to make eye contact and converse with each other. Gathering here feels collegial and comfortable, especially since kids are seated on pillows and whistle cushions (Highsmith #L21-27443), an item so popular I make schedules for kids to share the eight I've been able to purchase.

In the mini-lesson circle, students raise their hands, and I call on them to speak. This is a time-honored school convention that continues to make good sense to me. Raised hands allow turntaking and opportunities for everyone to participate; for me it's especially important that I get to call on the speakers, because some of my boys would run the show if I let them, and many of my girls, already in the process of going underground, would become voiceless.

Students often take notes in their writing handbooks from my notes on the easel pad, an overhead, or the discussion. Other times I tell them to hold off on notetaking and wait for tomorrow and a typed, clean copy from me of the material we generated in a lesson. These are sessions that involve the group in extensive theory building, for example, techniques writers use when they polish their writing, characteristics of an effective essay, or considerations in creating a fictional character.

For some lessons I've already prepared the document we're going to discuss, for example, models of different kinds of narrative leads, a copy of the Rule of *So What?*, or tips on how to keep troublesome homonyms straight. I type these data for discussion and reference, run copies, trim the edges with a paper cutter so they'll fit nicely within the pages of the spiral-bound handbooks, circulate five tape dispensers around the circle, ask students to tape the document to the next clean page of their handbooks, and instruct them way too many times, "Will you please just *take four pieces* of tape and pass it along?"

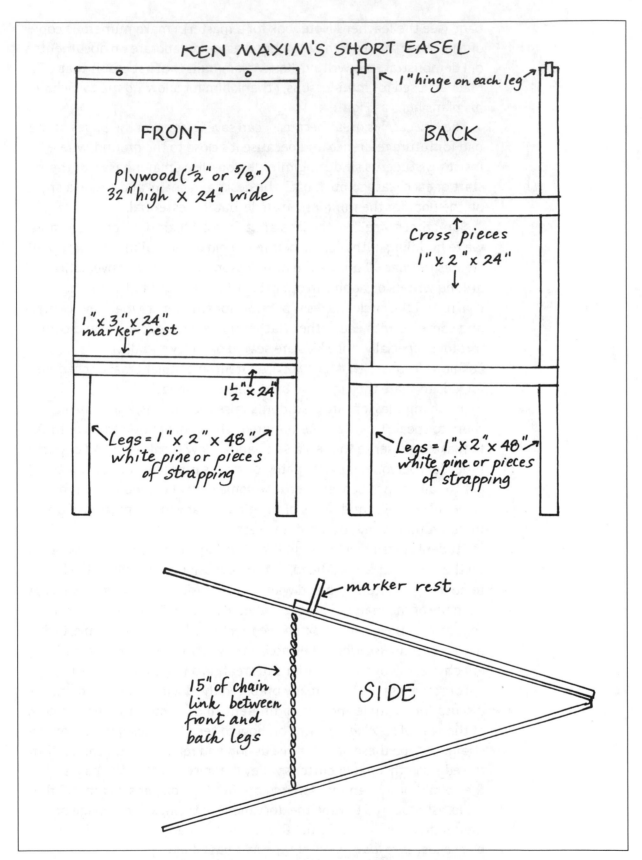

Figure 3

Some of the mini-lessons require homework, to follow up or extend a discussion. I have become a dragon about homework; students who don't do it or have it can't participate in the subsequent activity, and it's important to me that every writer be engaged—available to act and learn. So each student begins the year with a homework pass: one day on which I'll excuse missing homework. After that, any time an assignment isn't there or completed, I keep the student in at noon recess, the CTL version of detention, and I mail home a form letter to the student's parents explaining what was missing and asking for their help. After three letters I schedule a meeting with the student and his or her parents to discuss the child's failure to do schoolwork and to involve the family in making a plan for homework to get finished and be checked by parents. Again, I have become a dragon about homework—fierce and consistent with kids *and* with parents, because I want every student to get all he or she can out of every day of writing workshop.

This seems an appropriate place to talk about who my students are. The Center for Teaching and Learning is a non-profit demonstration school founded in 1990, using the royalties from the first edition of *In the Middle*. The idea was to create a school where my colleagues and I could teach kids and teachers at the same time. Since 1991, through our intern program, CTL has hosted classroom teachers from twenty-two states. They spend a week with us, closely observe teachers and students in action, meet with the faculty, and make plans for changes back home.

All of us who work at CTL are former public school teachers, committed to supporting and improving public education. Most of the interning teachers come to us from public school classrooms. Back in 1990 we knew that if our demonstration school was to have any credibility, our students must be representative, that is, not a private school population of children of the wealthy and well-educated. So our policy is to set tuition rates extremely low (that first year, tuition was $2,900), handpick a student body as diverse and balanced as we can find in midcoast Maine, and work hard to raise the rest of the money it takes to run a school, fund salaries, and pay the mortgage.

A location in rural Maine means we serve no ESL students. Otherwise our kids look and sound much like the students of the public school teachers who intern at CTL. We have a slightly higher than average population of children with identified learning disabilities; they are mainstreamed into our classrooms, along with students who live with ADHD, depression, divorce, and the always tough socioeconomics of rural Maine.

My colleagues and I did give ourselves two advantages. In grades 1–8, no group has more than twenty kids. In the past we've taught classes of as many as thirty-two students. We know it can be done, and we know it's bad for kids. So we maintain class sizes that are reasonable but not, we think, unrealistic.

The other advantage we gave ourselves was permission to teach as well as we could—to read research and conduct our own, develop methods that make sense and help kids move forward as learners, implement others' approaches that fill the bill, and change our minds as we learn more or when a method doesn't help kids as we wish it to. In this thoughtful, purposeful setting, as a teacher responsible for curriculum development and for classes of regular kids whom I adore, I have the power to pose questions about how lessons might help writers, develop the lessons, teach and refine them, consult with my students, and refine them some more.

Because I teach a grades 7–8 combination, my students are with me for two years. This means there's some repetition of lessons, especially

MINI-LESSON BASICS

at the start of the year, as I'm establishing the routines and requirements of the workshop, and when it comes to teaching about genres. My eighth graders have been generous and understanding about the need for repetition, and I try to vary the specific content and examples I use from one year to the next.

"Lessons That Change Writers, September – June: A Chronology" (Figure 4) shows a typical year of writing mini-lessons. I've also included, in Appendix E, the works I read aloud to writers and the poets we read and discuss each day before the mini-lesson. These whole-group literary experiences play a central role in the writing workshop and in support of mini-lessons. The short stories, essays, parodies, and memoirs I read aloud, and the poetry we read together, forge the best possible understandings of what literature is and is good for as students attempt to create literature of their own.

I packed this book with examples of excellent or illustrative student writing. I want teachers to reproduce or read aloud the pieces that I included as overheads and reproducibles, as well as the student memoirs in Appendix A, short stories in Appendix B, essays in Appendix C, and book reviews in Appendix D. For my kids, observing how someone close to their age and experience solved writing problems and produced important work has proved a major inspiration. Students need to see, hear, and talk about what writing is good for, what's possible for kids as writers, what's possible for *themselves* as writers.

Including follow-up lessons, this book describes more than a hundred of the lessons that kids selected as most valuable to them as writers. For each lesson I describe my rationale for teaching it, and I indicate when I conducted it during the school year. I hope it might be helpful for teachers to know my writing priorities in September and throughout the fall and winter, *vs.* the lessons I was comfortable to put off until spring.

At the end of each mini-lesson meeting with my kids, I conduct a status-of-the-class conference and record each student's plans for the independent writing time that follows the lesson. Then I close the meeting and send individuals off to fulfill their plans by offering the best benediction I know: "Off you go. Work hard, and make literature." And they do.

A CHRONOLOGY OF THE MINI-LESSONS

This chronological listing of the *Lessons That Change Writers* reflects the quirks of my school calendar—we have two weeks off in December, a week in February, and another in April—as well as CTL's rituals and evaluation procedures. The school devotes considerable class time to student self-evaluation and portfolio preparation in late November-early December, March, and June. In addition, every eighth grader writes and delivers a graduation speech, which is another focus of June instruction that doesn't show up here.

I want to be careful not to suggest that this is *the* order to conduct the lessons described in the book. At best, it's a rough timeline of one year in my life as a writing teacher. But there are constants. I conduct versions of the lessons that appear in boldface type every year, and I present them pretty much on this schedule, with an emphasis on memoir and free-verse poetry in September and October, fiction in November, holiday gifts of writing in December, book reviews in February, punctuation in March, essays in April, and humor writing and Mother's Day poems in May.

▪ September

Writing Territories: Launching the Writing Workshop .... (Lesson 1)
What Is Writing? .... (Lesson 8)
Ineffective and Effective Memoirs .... (Lesson 27)
Weekly Word Studies .... (Lesson 60)
Questions for Memoirists .... (Lesson 2)
A Brief History of the English Language .... (Lesson 59)
The Rule of *So What?* .... (Lesson 9)
Good Titles .... (Lesson 13)
The Individual Proofreading List .... (Lesson 57)
Final Copies: What Readers Need .... (Lesson 15)
Heart Mapping .... (Lesson 3)

▪ October

Polishing .... (Lesson 14)
Stories That End "The End" .... (Lesson 26)
Personal Survival Words .... (Lesson 61)
Thinking on Paper: Planning Sheets .... (Lesson 16)
Narrative Leads .... (Lesson 12)

Figure 4 Lessons That Change Writers, September–June: A Chronology

Thoughts and Feelings .... (Lesson 10)

Proofreading for Spelling .... (Lesson 62)

Where Poetry Hides .... (Lesson 4)

The Rule of Write about *a* Pebble .... (Lesson 11)

The Power of *I* .... (Lesson 34)

Beware the Participle .... (Lesson 35)

Breaking Lines and Stanzas and Punctuating .... (Lesson 38)

Leads: Begin Inside .... (Lesson 36)

Conclusions: End Strongly .... (Lesson 37)

Cut to the Bone .... (Lesson 39)

■ **November**

Two Things at Once .... (Lesson 41)

Can a Reader See It, Hear It, Feel It? .... (Lesson 17)

What's Easy about Writing Bad Fiction? .... (Lesson 28)

What's Hard about Writing Good Fiction? .... (Lesson 29)

Problems to Explore in Fiction .... (Lesson 5)

The Main Character Questionnaire .... (Lesson 30)

Considerations in Creating a Character .... (Lesson 31)

Short Story Structure .... (Lesson 32)

Ways to Develop a Character .... (Lesson 33)

■ **December**

Use Repetition .... (Lesson 40)

A Movie behind Your Eyelids .... (Lesson 18)

Gifts of Writing #1 .... (Lesson 47)

How a Thesaurus Can Help .... (Lesson 19)

The Really Bad Words .... (Lesson 20)

■ **January**

Sestinas and Tritinas .... (Lesson 42)

Too-Long and Too-Short Paragraphs .... (Lesson 21)

Exclamation Points .... (Lesson 24)

The Truth about *I* before *E* .... (Lesson 63)

Passive Sentences .... (Lesson 23)

Hopefully .... (Lesson 25)

Figure 4, *continued*

■ February

Effective Book Reviews .... (Lesson 48)
The Missing *I* .... (Lesson 22)
Irregular Odes .... (Lesson 43)
Memoir Poems .... (Lesson 46)

■ March

Twenty Actions .... (Lesson 6)
A Brief History of Some Common Punctuation Marks .... (Lesson 68)
Essential Punctuation Information .... (Lesson 69)
Some Foreign Words Used in English Texts .... (Lesson 64)

■ April

Effective Essays: Teasing Out Criteria .... (Lesson 49)
Itches to Scratch in Essays .... (Lesson 7)
How Do I Scratch the Itch? .... (Lesson 50)
Write with Information .... (Lesson 51)
Order the Information .... (Lesson 52)
Leads for an Essay .... (Lesson 53)
Experiment with Essay Conclusions .... (Lesson 54)
Thirteen-Ways Poems .... (Lesson 45)

■ May

Ted L. Nancy Letters and Other Genres for Humorists .... (Lesson 55)
Gifts of Writing #2 .... (Lesson 47)
Root Words and Prefixes .... (Lesson 65)
Suffixes: To Double or Not? .... (Lesson 66)
Other Suffix Rules That Mostly Work .... (Lesson 67)

■ June

Haiku .... (Lesson 44)

Figure 4, *continued*

SECTION 1:
Lessons about Topics

One of my overriding goals as a teacher is that after the first day of writing workshop, no student will complain, "I don't know what to write about." My job is to teach them how to discover and act on their intentions as writers, not give them my intentions or devote precious conferring time to trying to nudge a rudderless writer toward a topic.

This means the workshop environment needs to be a rich, fertile context for writers to identify ideas for writing. So I read aloud to them and we read together poetry, memoirs, short stories, essays, parodies, profiles, and book reviews relevant to students' lives. I demonstrate my own writing ideas and intentions. I structure and encourage peer writing conferences, so students can demonstrate their ideas for each other. I provide information about publication options, from *Acorns*, the school literary magazine, to poetry and essay contests, guidelines for letters to the editor, short fiction competitions, places to submit book and CD reviews, gifts of writing for people we love, and options for guest editorial columns in local papers. And we stage informal readings of students' finished writing. At every step I remind students: "You could do this."

In addition to working to establish a vital environment, I extend explicit invitations to writers to name their ideas. Starting on the first day of school, students use topic mini-lessons as occasions for generating and recording different kinds of writing ideas they can explore in a range of genres.

For example, I launch the workshop by demonstrating my territories as a writer—subjects, genres, audiences—and asking students to begin to make a record of theirs. I hope kids will leave the first day's workshop with too many places to begin, feeling overwhelmed by a wealth of personal material. I stress the personal in my own list of territories because this is where I'll ask students to begin in September, with poems and memoirs, as opposed to fiction or exposition. The chances that kids will produce literature early on are seriously enhanced if they're working in genres that are manageable, compact, personally significant, and based on data they know well, in other words, their experiences and feelings. So poetry and memoir writing is where we start.

As the year progresses, I teach about other genres—short fiction, book reviews, essays, thank-you notes, parodies, profiles—in brief courses of study. In addition to helping kids learn the features of each genre, I teach separate topic mini-lessons for each literary form and invite students to identify the themes, problems, works of literature, and individuals they might wish to write about.

I instruct students to reserve the first fifteen pages of their writing handbooks (after the three pages set aside for a table of contents) for capturing and recording ideas they come up with in response to the topic mini-lessons, as well as projects and subjects that occur to a writer independently. In my own writing life and those of my kids, I've witnessed the many ways that informal writing—notes, plans, outlines, lists, even single words—can aid thinking and memory. So I instruct kids to create a separate territories section in the first fifteen pages of their writing handbooks, and to use it. My job is to invite specific entries throughout the year, in the form of lessons aimed at helping kids find meaningful, worthy ideas for their writing.

Topic lessons were cited again and again by writers as useful and important to their development. As Tyler put it, "My territories section of my handbook is like my security blanket. I never panic about ideas because I have all these plans. It makes me feel confident. But mostly it reminds me of how much I have to say."

Writing Territories: Launching the Writing Workshop

Preparation

✔ Overhead transparency of your writing territories—a list that's personal, specific, diverse, and unpretentious, so your ideas help students generate ideas of their own

✔ Overhead transparencies of Jed Chambers' and Marnie Briggs's first day writing territories lists, as examples for your kids of what's possible

✔ Trimmed photocopies of "Collecting Your Writing Territories" for students to tape into their handbooks

✔ Tape dispensers

What I Was Thinking I've started writing workshop in different ways, but a launch that focuses on writing territories, mine and kids', works best to set a tone for a year of personal, purposeful writing and to start student writers working from quantity. At the end of the first workshop I want them to feel overwhelmed by the possibilities that await them as writers, and I want the possibilities to be concrete and specific: named and recorded in the pages of the writing handbook. I've included here my own list of writing territories, as well as two student lists that might prove useful as models.

> "Maybe the most important thing for you to know about me is that I write, and I write for lots of different reasons. I call the range of things I do as a writer my *territories*. They include genres that I write in or would like to try, subjects I've written about or would like to, and real or potential audiences for my writing.

This summer I revised my profile of myself as a writer and copied it for you on overhead transparencies [see Figure 1-1 for a sampling of mine]. I'll ask you to begin our year of writing workshop the same way—by brainstorming your territories as writers.

My territories list gives me a window on who I am as a writer, citizen, woman, teacher, learner, mother, wife, daughter, and friend. It also gives me a place to go when I'm trying to figure out what I'm going to write next. It's my ideas bank. It's my big prompt, to remind myself, "Oh, yeah, I wanted to do that as a writer." And when I have an idea, which I know I'll lose if I don't write it down, this is where I capture it.

Keeping a list like this one helps me be more organized, productive, and focused as a writer. It's my constant reminder of who I am and what I know and care about.

I'm going to talk from my list for ten minutes about the ideas I came up with when I brainstormed my writing territories. I'm going to ask you to write that phrase

My Writing Territories

right now at the top of the *fourth* page of your writing handbook and to write the number 1 in the upper right-hand corner of the page. Later on, the first three pages, which you're leaving blank today, will become a table of contents for your handbook.

While I'm describing my territories to you, if anything I say rings a bell and makes you think of a topic that's part of your repertoire as a writer, or something you think you'd like to try someday, jot it down here, on page four of your handbook. When I'm done, you'll have ten minutes to continue your lists and then a chance to talk with each other. I'll ask you to make your lists as long and complete as you can before you leave here today. Don't lose any germ of an idea that comes to you while I'm talking. Listen and write at the same time. Ready?

One of the things I write about a lot are my students, what you do and what I think it means. Right now I'm writing about mini-lessons that students say helped them become better writers. I hope it will do good—help other teachers plan useful writing mini-lessons for their students. I'm endlessly fascinated by what my students do as writers. You and your work have been a topic on my territories list for more than twenty years.

Poetry is another professional subject on my list. Today we started class by reading and discussing a poem together; I promise that's how we'll begin every writing workshop between now and June. I love poetry. It's so generous—it's the genre that can do and express anything—and the form is so compact, compared with prose, that the poet's challenge and delight is to do and express anything, but in a nutshell. Poetry is beautiful, difficult, and barely taught in American schools. So another project on my professional plate is thinking and writing about how to help teachers not be threatened by poetry, but to embrace it and love it. Someday I'd like to put together an anthology of poems that my students have loved and would recommend to other kids and their teachers.

My daughter, Anne, is on my list because I have tons of memories of watching her grow up. The one on my mind right now—I think it'll be a poem—is about riding with her this summer. She got her learner's permit

My Writing Territories

- My students—how they learn to be great writers: scripts of the lessons they identified as best for other teachers
- Poetry—how to teach it so it isn't scary (to teachers) and is inviting (to kids)
- Toby—thirty years of adventures, working things out, plus how we met; for Anne?
- Anne—watching her grow up; riding with her this summer
- Rosie—this summer: my shadow, finally
- Rosie in the car with the windows open, fantasizing that she's flying
- The heron that comes to our pond each evening; his sound; finally seeing him at summer's end
- My mother—the changes in our relationship and in her as she ages; "I love you" on the phone; our week together in August
- My brother—the conversation with him about our family; his genius at everything (*now* I see it)
- The eternal search for the perfect pen
- Earl Grey tea
- Being older than everyone by at least twenty years at the Area:One Festival
- Books for teenagers; short stories for teenagers; my arguments with proficient reader research and strategies
- Songs that speak to me and for me in pop music; VH1's "Rock 'n' Roll Jeopardy" is my goal

- Adult female friendships *vs.* the friends of my youth; how the Bluebirds shaped who I am more than anyone (including my parents?); Mary Harris' book
- CTL—its philosophy, history, methods, curriculum, accomplishments
- School business—parent handbook, reports on students, grant proposals
- Candy corn, fireballs, chocolate Necco wafers, candy cigarettes, and Mary Janes: the gourmet foods of my childhood
- Earrings: how buying a pair never fails to lift my spirits
- Collecting—Staffordshire spaniels, shells, antiquing in London, Victorian *smalls*, and the aesthetic pleasure they bring to my life
- Exercise and why I HATE it; dusting off the abandoned exercycle yet again
- Finally forgiving my face and body for not being "perfect;" my angst about young girls who can't love their faces and bodies
- How I love bare legs in summer
- How I learned to love reading: bedridden with rheumatic fever in fifth grade with nothing else to do
- The proposed Wiscasset bypass
- My summer addiction to cable movies
- Greenhouse gas emissions, global warming, the abandonment of the Kyoto agreement
- Bush administration's assault on reading instruction

Figure 1-1 A Sampling from Nancie's Writing Territories List

in May. After four months of riding with her, I still double-take when I glance to my left and realize that this grown-up, concentrated profile is my daughter's—that she's in control of the car, and a lot more, too.

My springer spaniel, Rosie, means the world to me. She just turned three and is finally responding as if the humans at our house are in charge. When I stepped down as director of CTL, so I could write more, a gift certificate for a springer spaniel puppy was my thank-you present from CTL families and teachers. One of them, Justine, said, "We can imagine you writing away, with your puppy curled up at your feet." Well, for the first two years, Rosie bit my feet, along with fingers, shoes, woodwork, furniture, socks, books, sticks, and rocks. But this summer, when I wasn't taking a break outside and throwing tennis balls for her, I was in my blue room writing, and Rosie was asleep across the threshold or, indeed, curled up at my feet. I've started one poem about how this dream came true—my cozy spaniel shadow—and another about what may be going on in her rich fantasy life when Rosie rides in the car, with her head out the window and her face wearing an expression of ultimate fulfillment. I know she likes to watch the birds fly over our pond. So does she pretend she's a bird when her ears are flapping in the breeze? I think so. That's a poem.

This summer my family watched—or tried to watch—the heron who visits the pond behind our house. Every evening at dinnertime we heard his loud, ugly honk above our roof, but no matter how quick we were, we could never catch sight of him. Finally, last weekend, he landed in a low branch of a tree by the shore and perched there for a long time. He was still there when I finally tired of looking. His presence felt like a gift, like a glorious way to say good-bye to summer. There's a poem here, too, or maybe a memoir.

My mother and brother are on my territories list because no matter how sure I am that I've figured out our relationships, something shifts, and I see them from new perspectives. With my brother it was a conversation we had this summer about the Dalai Lama, one of his heroes, and the idea of compassion as a way of life. With my mom, it's the way she tells me she loves me every chance she gets these days, after seldom saying it when I was growing up. I want to ask her, *Why now?* I think I'll scratch these itches in letters to Glenn and to Mom.

My passions are scattered throughout my territories list: finding just the right pen (because I still write everything longhand and hand it off to Ron to type), rock music (at the Moby concert this summer, I looked and felt like a dinosaur, but *I didn't care*), my love of young adult literature, my addiction to Jackson Brothers Earl Grey tea, and my obsession with my roses and the other perennials in the gardens I've been making over the past few summers.

I've listed the romance of the penny candy of my childhood, my theory that a woman can't have too many earrings and that buying a new pair is the best antidepressant on the market, my fussy collection of Victorian bric-a-brac, my powerlessness to resist watching movies—*any* movie—on cable TV, and my delight each summer in baring my legs and abandoning uncomfortable, itchy tights and stockings for three months. I'm thinking that good genres for these topics would include memoir, poetry, or personal essays.

Other topics on my list definitely call for essays, some in the form of letters to politicians, newspaper editors, or state officials—for example, my fear about what a Route 1 bypass might do to Edgecomb and Westport, my anger that our government abandoned the Kyoto agreement to stop global warming, my distrust of the aliterate, politically motivated approaches to teaching and testing reading that the Bush administration and its cronies in the world of publishing are mandating for American kids and teachers, and my strong feelings about women's and girls' health and body images.

Do you get my drift? My writing territories are jam-packed full of my ideas, obsessions, experiences, itches, aversions, and feelings. My writing about these subjects will take many forms—poems, memoirs, book reviews and literary criticism, essays, articles, letters, notes, speeches, guidelines, lists, proposals, and plans.

And I'll direct the writing to many different readers: my family, my friends, you and your parents, CTL teachers, the midcoast community, elected officials, the teachers and other people who read my books or attend my speeches. Something will happen with almost everything I write: I write to be read.

Now it's your turn. Please take ten minutes to begin—or continue—a list of your territories. Concentrate on ideas for topics. Go for quantity, and try not to censor yourself. See how many writing ideas you can capture, and watch how new ideas will piggyback off old ones. Use the next ten minutes to sketch as detailed a self-portrait as you can of yourself as a writer. When you get stuck, consider this list of ideas, "Collecting Your Writing Territories." See if these subjects strike chords in your dreams, your memories, your identity. And check out these two lists of territories compiled on the first day of school by eighth graders Jed and Marnie. They may inspire you, too.

In Collecting Your Writing Territories, Consider . . .

memories: early, earlier, and recent	favorites, now and then
obsessions	pets, now and then
idiosyncrasies	teachers, now and then
problems	places: school, camp, trips, times away with friends and relatives
dreams	hobbies
itches	sports
understandings	games
confusions	music
passions	books
sorrows	poems
risks	songs
accomplishments	movies
fears	writers and artists
worries	food
fantasies	pet peeves
family, close and distant	beloved things—objects and possessions—now and then
friends, now and then	all the loves of your life
fads	

© 2002 by Nancie Atwell from *Lessons That Change Writers* (Portsmouth, NH: Heinemann)

COLLECTING YOUR WRITING TERRITORIES   LESSON 1

Reproducible
Collecting Your
Writing Territories

Will you partner up with two other writers, preferably friends of yours, and take turns reading aloud your territories? If you're inspired by an idea a classmate recorded, add it to your own list of territories: that's the reason you're sharing. So make sure you have pencils before you head off to your small groups. And if a friend of the writer hears something missing from the list, please suggest that he or she include it.

FOLLOW-UP WITH THE WHOLE GROUP

I invite you to add to your list of writing territories throughout the school year *whenever* an idea for a piece of writing occurs to you. Don't count on remembering it if you haven't written it down. Do take responsibility for ideas for your writing and for developing projects that matter to you. Please circulate the tape dispensers, take four pieces of tape, and affix the list of territory ideas I gave you to your writing handbook, on the back of the page that faces page 1, so you may be inspired by it when you need inspiration.

For homework, please select a subject from your territories list, one that especially interests or pleases you—and *one that can be written as a memoir or a poem*. These are the two genres we'll start with this fall. As I teach about fiction, book reviews, essays, and profiles, you'll have opportunities to add new ideas to your territories lists and to try these genres, too.

Draft for at least half an hour tonight, and see where the writing takes you. Tomorrow we'll have our first status-of-the-class conference and discuss your options as independent writers for the first, official workshop.

Comments or questions?

Overheads
Jed's and Marnie's
Writing Territories

My Writing Territories
- Watching Hannibal with Jimmy.
- Driving the riding mower.
- Plowing the drive way will D.J.
- Televangelists.
- The Simpsons.
- Spreading Lucy's
- My broken CD pl
- Shortbread dough.
- Watching professional
- The Warren library.
- The school/county
- The movie The Ma
- My green Yo-Yo.
- Bis— the new tr
- Monopoly with Jimm
- Vampires.
- The girl at the Lo
- My life plan.
- Catch 22.
- Nick and Jonathan
- Dilbert on my loc
- Red Pilot precise
- Scotland.
- My father and mot
- My "parental advis
- Soccer at recess/
- My Tekken2 expert
- How I go to the
- Steel-toed boots.
- Slave Zero.

© 2002 by Nancie Atwell from
Lessons That Change Writers
(Portsmouth, NH: Heinemann)

My Writing territories
- Making marshmallow taffy
- Roasting marshmallows
- Iris and my cat (Fatty-Lumpkins)
- The carpool
- Orange juice
- Atomic fire balls
- Socks
- Cable at my dad's office
- Sunglasses— I can never find the perfect pair and when I do they break
- Television rules
- Movies that make me cry
- Our fish— they always die
- Walter Dean Myers
- Music— how it always seems that if you don't like the "right" music people will hate you
- Marco Polo in the pond w/ Katie, Kelsey Duncan, and Charlotte
- Iris swimming in the pond.
- Singing— what it means to me
- the fizziness of soda
- My fear of snakes
- Cape Cod potato chips
- My swingset
- Soccer
- How we go to Moosehead every year but last time I got sick
- The stars at night
- The reading zone— what it's like
- Lemonade and lemons— my obbsession
- bonfires
- Solstice celebration— am I getting too old?
- Passats and Jettas
- Colleen thinking my name was Mario
- Zoey's ashes

© 2002 by Nancie Atwell from
Lessons That Change Writers
(Portsmouth, NH: Heinemann)

MARNIE'S FIRST DAY WRITING TERRITORIES LIST   LESSON 1

1

Questions for Memoirists

Preparation

✔ Trimmed photocopies of "Questions for Memoirists" for students to tape into their handbooks

✔ Transparency of Jimmy Morrill's list of memoir-worthy experiences as an example of what's possible

✔ Wall poster of Willa Cather quotation

✔ Tape dispensers

✔ Optional: Photocopies of the student memoirs in Appendix A for reading aloud to your students

What I Was Thinking Students said this lesson helped them follow "The Rule of *So What?*" (Lesson 9) by focusing right from the start on theme and significance in their memoir writing. When I wrote the list of questions for memoirists to consider, my goal was to move young adolescents beyond personal experience narrative ("and then we did this and then we did that and it was all so much fun") into the realm of memoir. Answering big, specific questions pushed writers to look at their lives both broadly and deeply, to identify meaningful events and incidents, and to learn about themselves through the art of memoir.

> "Memoir is one of my two favorite genres to teach—poetry is the other. These forms resonate most for me because I've seen how writers use them to consider and shape their experience and recast it as literature. Adolescents' memoirs are especially important and beautiful to me because they're so useful to the writers. It's thrilling to watch students use writing to figure out who you are, through glimpsing and reflecting on who you were.

Which doesn't mean that writing about an event from your life is automatically an exercise in literature. I've read some *bad* memoirs; I've written some, too. These narratives suffered from a host of correctable problems and one big, uncorrectable one. If the memoirist's heart isn't in his or her subject, if the personal experience isn't one that intrigues the writer, if there's no *itch* to find out how and what a memory signifies in a writer's life, then the writing will be empty and flat. Then it's not even a memoir—just a string of events laid end-to-end in narrative form.

I'm going to argue that when you've read—or written—a boring description of "and then we did this and then we did that and it was all so much fun," the boredom you feel is at least partly the result of a writer having settled on a safe, superficial subject. Where's the emotional or intellectual risk in writing a memoir about "The Time I Went to Disney World" or "My Summer Camp"? I think kids settle for topics like these because they feel easy—lots of incidents and details to string together, without much call for personal investment or reflection.

Today I want you to begin the process of investing in and reflecting on your lives through memoir. We'll start by identifying events of each of your lives that signify—meaty moments that help to define the person you are and the one you're becoming. This list of "Questions for Memoirists" is designed to help you uncover memories that matter to you, events in your life that make you itch to capture and consider them. Please circulate the tape dispensers, take four pieces of tape, and affix this list to the back of page 3 of your writing handbook, in other words, right after the section you headed "My Writing Territories." Then read through the questions with me. . . .

For homework, please use these questions as tools to help you mine your memories. On the next clean page in the territories section of your handbook—that is, page 4 or 5—copy this heading:

Memoir-Worthy Experiences

Then, for at least half an hour tonight, sit quietly with the list of questions, a pen or a pencil, and your handbook. Consider each question thoughtfully. I know that some won't ring any bells for you tonight—that's okay. You're looking for the ideas that do jog your memory in intriguing ways. Capture the topics that

---

QUESTIONS FOR MEMOIRISTS

- What are my earliest memories? How far back can I remember?
- What are the most important things that have happened to me in my life so far?
- What have I seen that I can't forget?
- What's an incident that shows what my family and I are like?
- What's an incident that shows what my friends and I are like?
- What's an incident that shows what my pet(s) and I are like?
- What's something that happened to me at school that I'll always remember?
- What's something that happened to me at home that I'll always remember?
- What's an incident that changed how I think or feel about something?
- What's an incident that changed my life?
- What's a time or place that I was perfectly happy?
- What's a time or place that I laughed a lot?
- What's a time or place when it felt as if my heart were breaking?
- What's a time with a parent that I'll never forget?
- What's a time with a grandparent that I'll never forget?
- What's a time with a brother or sister that I'll never forget?
- What's a time with a cousin or another relative that I'll never forget?
- Can I remember a time I learned to do something, or did something for the first time?
- What memories emerge when I make a time line of my life so far and note the most important things that happened to me each year?

© 2002 by Nancie Atwell from
Lessons That Change Writers
(Portsmouth, NH: Heinemann)

QUESTIONS FOR MEMOIRISTS   LESSON 2

Reproducible
Questions For
Memoirists

emerge as a bulleted list under that heading "Memoir-Worthy Experiences." Don't feel compelled to go into detail. Use just as many words as you need to preserve the gist of each memory, so you have a list to use as a reference when you begin to consider the stuff of your memories. Check out this overhead, "Jimmy's Memoir-Worthy Experiences," to see how he used the questions.

The novelist Willa Cather said something wonderful about writing topics. Read along with me: "Most of the basic material a writer works with is acquired before the age of fifteen." I absolutely believe this to be true of narrative or story writing. The themes of my life emerged in my childhood and adolescence; the themes of your life are developing right now.

Don't waste this opportunity to begin to name and follow the threads of your life themes. Spend serious time tonight brainstorming in response to the questions. Come in tomorrow with an excellent list of important topics—the big ideas of *you*. I'll give you a chance at the start of class to meet with other writers and discuss what you uncovered in your search for memoir-worthy experiences.

Comments or questions?

FOLLOW-UP LESSON

Overhead
Jimmy's List of Memoir-Worthy Experiences

[At the start of class the next day, I ask students in the mini-lesson circle to open their handbooks to the homework assignment. I circulate quickly around the inside of the circle and check that everyone has a list/did the homework. Then students gather in groups of three (definitely no more than four) with their handbooks and a pencil, take turns describing to one another the memories they recorded, and also jot down new memories that emerge as they listen to their peers' recollections. I circulate among the small groups to listen, enjoy the material, and keep them on task. I give the groups ten minutes or so and let them know when they have a minute left, so they can be sure to get to each member. Then I reconvene the mini-lesson circle and lead a discussion among the whole group.]

Take a moment to look again at the list of "Questions for Memoirists." I'm curious about which questions helped you dig deep and come up with interesting memories. Can you identify one or two and talk about them, about where they sent you as a researcher of your own life?. . .

Now, take a moment to look at your list of memoir-worthy experiences. I'm curious if you surprised yourself with what you found. Let's talk about the unexpected nuggets that surfaced when you mined your past. . . .

One of the things I hope you're discovering is the value of using writing to generate writing ideas and of having a handy, organized place to capture them. What are your observations or questions?

Heart Mapping

Preparation

✔ Overhead transparency of your heart map, packed with obsessions, memories, people, places, and comforts

✔ Trimmed photocopies of "Questions to Help Mine Your Heart," for students to tape into their handbooks

✔ Tape dispensers

✔ Optional: Transparency of Peter Wilde's heart map as an example for your kids

✔ Optional: Photocopies of the poems "Emerald Memories" (Audrey Stoltz), "Table Tennis" (Nick Miller), and "Sour Patch Kids" (Forrest Carver), as examples of what's possible

LESSON 3

SEPTEMBER

What I Was Thinking

I was fortunate to attend one of poet Georgia Heard's workshops held in conjunction with the publication of *Awakening the Heart: Exploring Poetry in Elementary and Middle School* (1998). I loved the workshop and I adore the book, because of Heard's knowledge, her passion, and the usefulness of the tools she develops for teachers who want to invite good poetry.

After the workshop, at home that evening, I tried an activity that she suggested to help poets "sharpen our inner visions": I drew a map of the contents of my heart, of "all the things that really matter" (108). In an hour I had more ideas for poems than I knew what to do with. In the morning I revised my lesson plans and devoted the next mini-lessons to the creation of students' heart maps. Many of my kids' best ideas for poems and much of their best poetry began as locations on the maps of their hearts. As Jimmy observed, "My most personal poems began in my heart map."

"I think many of you already know the poet Georgia Heard, through her collection *Creatures of Earth, Sea, and Sky* (1992) and from poems of hers that we've read at morning meeting. Heard has written a new book, for teachers, about how to help students read, write, understand, use, and *love* poetry. It's filled with good ideas—sensible and inspiring invitations to poetry—and I think you'll find this approach especially helpful to you as a poet. But hold on a second. Let's begin by thinking about a problem that Heard's idea addresses.

When I ask kids, "What are good subjects for poems?" what do you imagine some of the typical responses are?. . .

You've got the idea. Poems are "supposed" to be about subjects like the four seasons, rainbows, snowflakes, flowers, falling leaves, smiles, tears, puppies and kittens, and love. Why do you think kids feel this way?. . .

I think one problem is there's not a lot of poetry to *be* exposed to in most elementary school classrooms and, when there is, it's often cute or clichéd. It kills me when poetry for children is written to a lower standard than the beautiful, resonant poems I read for my own pleasure. I also have a pet theory about how the poetry in greeting cards helps ruin a lot of us for the good stuff. I'm afraid that in America, Hallmark messages pass for poems.

So, how to break out of the cute-and-clichéd syndrome and write deep, beautiful, resonant poems? Georgia Heard says, "Look in your heart."

Of all the genres, poetry is the one that's made for feelings. More than any other, this genre exists to help us name and know and say what we care about. It's why I love it so much—because it expresses my needs, dreams, and emotions, and because it connects me with other people at the most essential level: one heart and mind touching another heart and mind.

Georgia Heard suggests that we literally draw the place where our feelings reside: create maps of our hearts and explore the territory of our feelings.

On the overhead you'll find my map of my heart [Figure 3-1]. I've placed the most important elements in the middle of my heart: Anne, Toby, and our dog, Rosie. Then, around them, I captured all kinds of feelings.

Look on the edges for some of my obsessions: with natural, beautiful things, like seashells and roses and beachglass, and with unnatural things like Barbie dolls and the computer—which gets wavy lines because it *scares me*. More serious obsessions are scattered closer to the center, like my need for shoes—many, many shoes—and my physical dependency on the most delicious substance in the world, dark chocolate. I added my comfort foods, too, the foods I crave when I'm feeling low: white rice with gravy, mashed potatoes, root beer floats, and chocolate cake with chocolate frosting and a tall glass of milk.

My Heart Map

STAFFORDSHIRE DOGS
LONDON · CAPTIVA
ROSES · BEACH GLASS · Expresso Extra Fines

Movies
A Wrinkle in Time

My blue room

Having a washer and dryer: a blessing

Traveling with my pillow (all I have in common with George W.)

Watching Anne run cross-country

Rosie's tennis balls

COMFORT FOODS: rice & gravy, mashed potatoes, root beer floats, chocolate cake

My chair at the kitchen table

Rosie in the car, her ears as wings

My shoe obsession

First crushes: Robert H. & Jeff M.

· Springsteen
· Dylan
· Lennon

RIDING WITH DAD ON HIS MOTORCYCLE

DARK CHOCOLATE

Grandma Lang's body

DAYS I DON'T GET DRESSED

Dad's wild fantasies when he was dying

Shells

Pregnant with Anne: missed her after she was born

Anne

Hendricks Head beach: know it by heart—don't even need to look

Dams on the creek in Clarence

Toby ♡— the moment we knew—

GLENN'S ELABORATE SNOW FORTS

Anne's piano

Rosie

Rosie in the a.m.: kisses & more kisses

OUR FAMILY DINNERS

Shopping: my favorite form of meditation

"Dancing" with Bonnie at Mark's wedding

Lemon ices with Mom, Bonnie, Kate, and Anne

Toby's snoring

Walking/stalking the fields with Lizzie

Anne walked at Maya's 1st birthday party

SLAP WARS w/ MY BROTHER

Bike-riding, no hands, down Main St.

THE COMPUTER—

Barbies

Lillith Fair with Anne, Maya, Kath.

Learning cat's cradle

Figure 3-1
Nancie's Heart Map

3

My heart's crowded with special memories. Some are about my father—sitting behind him on his motorcycles, always 850's or bigger, scared to death and thrilled to pieces at the same time, no matter how old I was. And I remember the last week he was alive, when the brain tumor that took his life induced wild, wonderful fantasies that everyone in my family went along with because they made him—and us—so happy at such a sad time. Other memories that have stayed in my heart come from my childhood—stalking the fields behind our house when I was a kid with my mutt dog, Lizzie, and pretending I was Francis Marion the Swamp Fox; building snow forts and dams with Glenn, my ambitious older brother, that were feats of engineering; and also engaging in scarily furious slap wars with him: nobody before or since has made me *so angry*. I remember bike riding down the main street of my little hometown, coasting no-handed as I stood on the pedals and soared through the village, and I remember my first two crushes, one in middle school and one in high school, both unrequited, that shaped forever what I find attractive in a guy.

Some memories that stay in my heart are more recent, like the first time Anne walked. We were at her friend Maya's first birthday party, and Anne pushed herself to her feet and toddled across the room, to get at the dish of ice cream I was holding.

Years later, Anne, Maya, her mother Katherine, and I had one of the best mom–daughter girls-just-wanna-have-fun days ever at the Lillith Fair music festival. Last fall my sister and I had another wonderful girls' night at our cousin's wedding, inventing goofy dances to challenge the macarena.

And one scorching day last summer, Anne, my mom, my sister, her daughter Kate, and I walked to the ice cream parlor at the corner of my mother's street and treated ourselves to lemon ices. I have a happy, primal memory of the five of us walking home, bumping sticky shoulders, laughing, and slurping our ices.

Places have stayed in my heart, too. London is the biggie—my favorite place in the world. When we're there together, Toby and Anne tease me unmercifully because at least ten times a day I announce, "At this moment I am perfectly happy." I can't help it. The bookstores, museums, gardens, and restaurants, the plays, the *history*, all knock me out. Plus it doesn't hurt that my special place is an ocean away from my real life and its responsibilities.

But right behind London are other beloved places, like my chair at our kitchen table. It's not even particularly comfortable, but it's mine. I love to read the papers here, drink my tea, and stare into space. Then there's the blue room where I write, which I love and hate equally—its presence reminds me that I need to get to work, but once I get down to it, it's a perfect place to write. Everything I need is there, including boxes of Expresso Extra Fine Point pens and three doors I can close between me and the rest of the world. I can make a mess here and walk away from it. Nobody else enters the blue room.

And the beach at Hendrick's Head is a longtime special spot for me— it's where Toby and I were sitting in the summer of 1975, watching the waves, when we decided to move to Maine. Later it was where Anne spent her childhood and Rosie her puppyhood. I know that beach and the walk down there so well I don't even look at the vista anymore—just putter around looking for seaglass or sit on a rock and close my eyes to the sun. My heart is at peace there.

Another place I found peace was in my Grandma Lang's lap—she was built like an overstuffed chair, and I loved to hug her and sink into all that flesh and affection. And our dining room table—the ritual of Toby, Anne, and me together there every single night, eating, arguing, teasing, laughing, and sharing our days—is a spot that will stay in my heart forever.

Do you see what happened when I mapped my heart? There are so many poems waiting here to be written, and I think they're poems with the potential to *matter*. There's little that's clichéd or cute in my heart, but lots of specific things, people, places, and experiences that matter to me. Drawing and filling in my heart helped me to name them.

For homework I'd like you to spend a half an hour or more mapping your heart. These questions may help. Please tape them onto the lower-

3

left-hand corner of the next clean page in the territories section of your writing handbook. Draw a heart shape on the same page, above and to the right of the questions. Make it big—fill the page, so you can fill your heart. . . . Now, read along with me:

Reproducible
Questions to Help
Mine Your Heart

Questions to Help Mine Your Heart

What has stayed in your heart? What memories, moments, people, animals, objects, places, books, fears, scars, friends, siblings, parents, grandparents, teachers, other people, journeys, secrets, dreams, crushes, relationships, comforts, learning experiences? What's at the center? The edges? *What's in your heart?*

Spend serious time with this assignment at home tonight: at least half an hour. You may want to take breaks and come back to it. Give your long-term memory time to do its work. Don't labor over drawing a perfect heart; do sweat over the contents. Fill your heart with as much personal meaning as you can. [Peter Wilde's heart map might be shown to the group at this point as an example of the contents of a student's heart.]

Comments or questions?

FOLLOW-UP LESSON

[The next day, I ask students to gather in groups of three, with pencils and their writing handbooks, and take turns teaching one another about what has stayed in their hearts. I remind them that a purpose of sharing writing ideas is to listen for new inspirations, then record ideas prompted by friends' discoveries. I circulate to listen, enjoy the ideas, and keep kids on task.

Then I reconvene the mini-lesson circle and conduct a fast whip around the circle, asking each student to respond to the question, "What's something that has stayed in your heart that surprised you?" Again, the point is for writers to hear and learn from the ideas of their peers.]

FOLLOW-UP ASSIGNMENT

[For weekend homework students draft poems about one of the subjects that has stayed in their hearts. I stress the importance of choosing a topic they love and feel excited to write about, because ideas that stir the writer lead to the best poems, always.

Your students might be inspired by three poems by eighth graders— "Emerald Memories," "Table Tennis," and "Sour Patch Kids." Audrey's first pair of pierced earrings found a place in her heart, as did Nick's memories of Ping-Pong and Forrest's obsession with a particular candy and his, er, unique approach to enjoying it.]

3

Where Poetry Hides

Preparation

✔ Overhead transparency of your list of "Where Poetry Hides"—concrete objects, places, and moments in your life in which poems are hiding

✔ Transparency of Anne Atwell-McLeod's list of "Where Poetry Hides" as an example for your kids

✔ Wall poster of William Carlos Williams quotation

✔ Optional: Photocopies of four poems inspired by this activity: "Sandy's Joy Bin" (Ashley Sherman), "Indulgence" (Tristan Durgin), "Durable" (Peter Wilde), and "Living in Rings" (Anne Atwell-McLeod), as examples for your students of what's possible

What I Was Thinking This is another idea from Georgia Heard's book *Awakening the Heart: Exploring Poetry in Elementary and Middle School* (1998). As Heard notes, "Discovering where poems come from is an essential part of the poet's process" (47). Too often, it seemed, my students' poems were coming from the sources I described in the previous lesson—safe, stock notions of what poems could be about. I was also concerned about student poetry that didn't limn kids' experiences and observations; instead, these poems spoke in grand, general terms about large, philosophical topics: loneliness, conformity, family, change, death, growing up. The poetry was banal and impersonal, even though the poets' feelings were genuine and strong.

This mini-lesson helped students go deep as poets by beginning with concrete objects and grounding their ideas and feelings in palpable experience. Lesson 11, "The Rule of Write about *a* Pebble, or 'No Ideas but in Things,'" addresses the same need from a different angle. When he cited this mini-lesson as important to his growth as a writer, Tristan observed, "It made it okay to write poems about the small things, and then you realize you're really writing about something bigger."

"Today I want us to think about poetry and subjects for poems from another perspective. This one, too, is an approach suggested by Georgia Heard. Heard joked that she has "never heard a poet describe the origin of a poem by saying it came from an assignment about pretending to be a grass blade blowing in the wind or from a poetry contest about health safety." She knows the truth about being inspired to poetry: "finding where poems hide from us is part of the process of being a poet and of living our lives as poets" (47).

Where do poems hide? Sometimes, when I write poetry, I still get bogged down in a mistaken belief that poems should define the big emotions or ideas—what I call billboard topics, like motherhood, marriage, or aging. But the poems I write when I suffer from this misapprehension are awful—clichéd, generalized, voiceless. No matter how many words I write around a billboard topic, the poems don't evoke the real sensations, feelings, and connections that I'm after.

WHERE POETRY HIDES

In the blue crock full of yellow onions on the kitchen counter

In the WWI model biplane Dad carved from balsa wood when he was a kid

In microwave popcorn

In the conversations among the kids in my morning carpool

In Toby's nightly vigil at the kitchen table with his coffee and the *New York Times*

In the tangle of boots in the mudroom—mine, Toby's, Anne's of all ages

In the slumber parties Anne and I have before Toby comes to bed and carries the sleeping Anne off to her room

In avocadoes, artichokes, and asparagus

In the trinket box on my dresser—the junky treasures of thirty years

In the framed family photos of a century, especially of my grandparents and of Glenn, Bonnie, and me when we were little

In Rosie's mouth

In a package of M&M's

In the spines of my books, especially my special collection of novels

In our dinner table conversations

In the way Toby sets the breakfast table and decorates Anne's plate with a face made of strawberries and banana

In my ridiculous earring collection

In Anne's piano playing—like honey in the air

In the mass of shoes on the floor of my closet

In our tennis ball sessions with Rosie

In my jars of beachglass

Figure 4-1 A Sampling from Nancie's List of Where Poetry Hides

I'm learning that when I ground my big feelings and ideas in small moments from my real life, I can write poems that resonate for me—and for the people I want to read them. It's noticing the small moments that's the tricky part—being alert to people, things, times, and places that have the potential to become poems that resonate.

So last night I grabbed an Expresso Fine Point and a pad of my favorite narrow-lined paper and went looking for specifics, for the objects, places, and moments where my poems might be hiding. It was like a treasure hunt of my life, and I plucked so many jewels I don't know where to begin [see Figure 4-1]. More important, I saw that the billboard topics of my life—family, love, domesticity, motherhood, food, marriage, death—can be explored and revealed as poems about small moments.

As I said, I don't know where to start writing, the possibilities are so inviting. I want you to gather ideas from your life with this level of specificity and to know this feeling of excitement as poets. So your assignment for tonight is to make a similar list of your own.

Right now turn to the next clean page of the territories section of your writing handbook and head it

Where Poetry Hides for Me

Take your handbook home with you tonight and spend serious time—at least half an hour—searching your house, family, and life for places where poems are hiding. Go for quantity and specificity—as many things, places, occasions, and people as you can observe or recall that matter to you and that might hold the seeds of the poems of your life. It may help you to see another student's list of where she found poems hiding—here's Anne's on the overhead.

William Carlos Williams was insistent that poems be grounded in everyday experience—that we be able to see, hear, taste, touch, and smell the stuff of our real lives in poetry. He wasn't exaggerating when he wrote about so much depending on that red wheelbarrow. His mantra for writing poems was this: "Say it, no ideas but in things." My question for you tonight is, What are your things?

Comments or questions?

Overhead
Anne's List of Where Poetry Hides

> "Say it, no ideas but in things."
>
> – William Carlos Williams

FOLLOW-UP LESSON

[The next day, as the mini-lesson activity, I ask students to gather in groups of three with their pencils and writing handbooks and teach one another about where they found poems hiding. I remind them that a purpose of sharing is to listen for and capture new inspirations, then I circulate to listen, celebrate the ideas, and keep kids on task.

Then I reconvene the mini-lesson circle and conduct a fast whip around the circle, asking each student, "What's one surprising or pleasing place, object, or occasion where you found a poem hiding?" I tell the group, "Listen to and learn from these good ideas."]

FOLLOW-UP ASSIGNMENT

[For weekend homework students draft a poem about one of the places they found a poem hiding. Again, I stress the importance of each poet choosing an idea he or she feels excited to write about: poetry that matters begins with an itch. Your students might be inspired by Ashley's poem about her dog's toy basket, Tristan's poetic process for eating ice cream, Peter's observation of his boots, worn by his dad during the Vietnam War, and Anne's reverie about her ring collection.]

4

Problems to Explore in Fiction

Preparation

✔ Students' individual records of their reading (or a group list, created in class, of some of the novels that kids in the class have read over the previous year)

✔ Overhead transparency headed "Problems We Found in Published Fiction" for brainstorming with students

✔ Overhead transparencies of Tyler Cadman's and Erin Witham's "Potential Problems in Fiction" lists, as examples for your students of what's possible,

✔ Wall poster of Roald Dahl quotation

✔ Optional: Photocopies of the short stories Tyler and Erin eventually produced (in Appendix B)

What I Was Thinking

I've attempted to teach short story writing from so many angles over the years I've lost track. I struggle with fiction—and my kids struggle with it—because of all the genres, it is the most difficult to write well. The successful writer of fiction creates a world, one so complete, plausible, and seamless that readers slip into its rhythms and feel as if they live in the text. It takes a *lot* to pull off this feat.

In the past I relied on a character development questionnaire (see Lesson 30), which kids filled out before they started drafting, as the way to push them to begin short fiction with people, *vs.* plot. And although it did make a big difference in the character and plausibility departments, issues of theme still hung fire: main characters enjoyed elaborately detailed inner and outer lives that didn't add up to anything. I knew many of my students had a hard time thinking about theme; I also knew from my reading about writing that many authors of published fiction weren't aware of the themes threading through their stories. So where did theme come from, and how could I help student writers find that place?

I decided to try a dual focus: development of the main character was still crucial, but now development of the problem of the story came first. Professional novelists and short story writers might not be conscious of the themes of their fictions, but they are impelled by the problems they create for their characters and how a character will confront—or avoid—a particular challenge. Theme—not to mention plot—emerges from the *what if?* of a problem.

To teach students what I meant, I sent them back to the short stories I'd been reading aloud (listed in Appendix E) and to the fiction they'd been reading: the young adult and transitional novels in our classroom library. My kids keep records of the books they read. By early November, when I conducted this mini-lesson, individual students had recorded anywhere from three to thirty titles, with a heavy emphasis on fiction.

By stepping back from each novel and imagining the *what if?* in the mind of its author, students came to their own attempts at short fiction with a clearer sense of purpose, a stronger imagination, and a feeling of engagement. Starting a short story with a specific problem to develop also provides a touchstone to help young writers keep focused through the long weeks and months of the fiction writing process. I conduct this lesson as part of a course of study of fiction described in Lessons 28–33. Chronologically, it comes after two introductory discussions, about the qualities of bad student fiction and good fiction in general.

It took Marnie, a seventh grader, two months to finish her short story "Betrayal." I think her stamina, not to mention the success of the story, had everything to do with Marnie's interest in the problem she created for her main character. As she put it, "My short story this year was the first good piece of fiction I've ever written. Jenni had to decide between following her own values or standing by her big sister, while Ellie was becoming someone who did bad stuff and was growing apart from their family. It was an interesting problem to me, about how far you should take loyalty."

> " It seems to me that most published novels and short stories are *about* two things: a particular person or group of people, and the particular problems that one or more of them are facing. Have you noticed this?
>
> For example, how many of you have read S. E. Hinton's *The Outsiders* (1967)? I think we can agree: Ponyboy Curtis is the main character. What are the problems Hinton gives Ponyboy to confront? . . . Stereotyping, kid-on-kid violence based on social class, the death of his parents, the death of his best friend, terrible tensions with Darry, the brother who's acting as his surrogate father. Whew. Ponyboy is practically the y.a.—or young adult—Job, Hinton has given him so many problems.
>
> Do you see what I'm getting at? I'm not talking plot or theme; I'm talking *difficulty*: what will a particular character do, faced with a particular challenge?

Can you name other novels that many of you have read? Let's tease out the *problems* the authors were exploring. . . . [Some examples to prime the pump might include *Tangerine* by Edward Bloor (1997): a dark family secret needs to be exposed and dealt with; Sarah Dessen's *Keeping the Moon* (1999): an insecure girl has a mother with a strong identity and national celebrity; *Tomorrow When the War Began* (1995) by John Marsden: kids see if they have what it takes to confront an enemy invasion; *Running Loose* (1983) by Chris Crutcher: a star football player is asked by his coach to do something the boy knows is wrong.]

For homework tonight, your assignment is to consider the novels you've read over the past months and the short stories I've read aloud to you so far this school year. You'll need to take home your reading record and your writing handbook. Please write this heading on the next clean page of the territories section of your handbook:

Problems in Published Fiction

Then, tonight, list the problem or *what if?* of each title you've read.

It's not necessary to record book or story titles—what you're doing here is gathering data about *problems* or *plot premises* that have served as the foundations of fictions. Tomorrow we'll create a group list from your individual lists, and I'll ask each of you to begin a new list, this time of the problems you might wish to explore as an author of fiction.

Comments or questions?

FOLLOW-UP LESSON

[Students come to the mini-lesson circle the next day with their individual lists. On the easel pad or a blank overhead transparency, I write the heading "Problems We Found in Published Fiction," ask students to volunteer the answers they found, and record a group list. (A group response I recorded appears as Figure 5-1.)]

FOLLOW-UP ASSIGNMENT

Please check out this quote from author Roald Dahl. It's from a note he wrote to himself about a problem that intrigued him: "What about a chocolate factory that makes fantastic and marvelous things—with a crazy man running it?" That *what if?* jotting was the seed from which Dahl grew *Charlie and the Chocolate Factory*.

Tonight for homework I'd like you to brainstorm a list of problems or *what ifs?* that intrigue you as an author of fiction. On the next clean page of the territories section of your writing handbook, record this heading:

Potential Problems in Fiction

Problems We Found in Published Fiction: Sample Class List

Troubled relationship with a grandparent

Looking for an adult role model

Changes in a friendship

Kids with different religious views

Adult censorship of kids

Peer pressure to do something dangerous

Peer pressure at school

Figuring out one's identity

Competition with a friend/jealousy

Gender stereotyping

First love

Finding love

Facing the past and trying to make a new life

Seeking revenge

Trying to fit in

Pressure to fit in

Death of a pet

End of a friendship

Moving away from friends

Parents' divorce

Teen pregnancy

Physical appearance issues

Class issues

Interracial relationship

Troubled friend

Ghost encounter

Homophobia

Troubled sibling relationship

Fighting evil

A parent's or sibling's death

Disfunctional family

Peer pressure to win

Survival against the elements

Getting beyond stereotypes/first impressions

Facing a fear

AIDS

Gun violence

Drug experimentation

Friend becomes ill/dies

Solving a crime/mystery

Proving one can do something

Deciding to make a big change

Telling the truth

Fighting an enemy

Nuclear holocaust

Child abuse

Childhood friends who change in high school

Kidnapping

Influence of childhood friends on rest of one's life

Traveling in time

Recovering from an accident

Figure 5-1

Then, under that heading, write

What if . . . ?

Tonight at home, imagine and list dilemmas that interest you as a writer. What problems inspire your imagination? What *what ifs?* intrigue the writer in you? Go for quantity *and* quality of ideas.

But first let me give you one piece of advice: Although many of you have read novels in which characters die, can I ask you to resist using death as a short story problem? Death is so huge, as a subject, that it requires pages and pages of the main characters' thoughts and feelings, reacting to such an overwhelming loss and trying somehow to come to terms with it. You won't have the physical space in a fifteen- to twenty-page short story to do death justice or make it convincing. So my suggestion as you brainstorm tonight is this: don't go there.

It may help you to see a couple of student lists of *what ifs?* for short stories. Check out these overheads of Erin's and Tyler's ideas. [See Appendix

B for the stories Erin and Tyler eventually produced based on ideas from the lists.]

Try to spend at least an hour tonight poking into the corners of your imagination and experience. Comments or questions?

FOLLOW-UP LESSON

[The next day at the start of class, I ask students to gather in groups of three with their writing handbooks and pencils and take turns describing to one another the fictional problems they imagined. I circulate among the small groups, listen to and discuss their ideas, and keep them on task. I allow ten to fifteen minutes for kids to share ideas, help one another refine them, and come up with new possibilities. I let the groups know when they have a minute left, then reconvene the mini-lesson circle.

Then I ask, "Who already knows the problem you're going to explore in your short story?" and call on volunteers and discuss their ideas. For homework students narrow down to one problem they'd like to create, explore, and resolve in a piece of short fiction. The follow-up lesson to this one, Lesson 30, "The Main Character Questionnaire," appears in the section "A Course of Study: Fiction."]

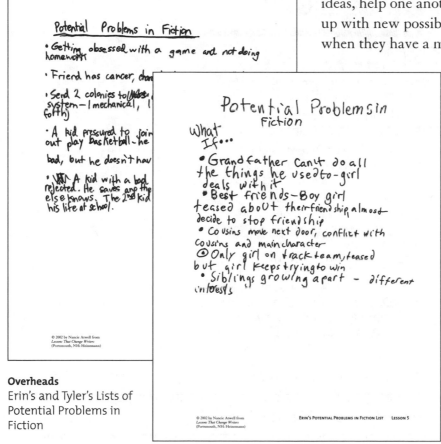

Overheads
Erin's and Tyler's Lists of Potential Problems in Fiction

Twenty Actions

Preparation

✔ Overhead transparency of your "Twenty Actions"—a list of your everyday actions over one weekend that could become poems

✔ Overhead transparency of a poem about one of the actions on your list

✔ Transparency of "Twenty Actions That Could Become Poems: A Sampling of Student Ideas" as examples for your kids

✔ Optional: Photocopies of action-inspired poems: "Beach in Winter" (Erin Witham), "The Perfect Opportunity" (Meg Benton), "Soccer Again" (Jacob Miller), "Still" (Jed Chambers), "Mirage" (Marnie Briggs), and "Ode to Ovaltine" (Siobhan Anderson) as examples for your students of what's possible

What I Was Thinking

As I write, Billy Collins is the eleventh poet laureate of the United States. Collins became a favorite of my students in a heartbeat: his poems make them feel welcome like no others.

Five of my kids bought, or received as requested holiday gifts, Collins' book *Sailing Alone Around the Room: New and Selected Poems* (2001). When I assigned students to read an essay by Collins about "the companionship of a poem"—about the joys of memorizing poems and carrying them with us—they decided they wished to do this, and among the poems they memorized were "Snow Day," "Morning," "Budapest," "Introduction to Poetry," "Walking Across the Atlantic," and "Afternoon with Irish Cows," all by Billy Collins. And in what struck me as the oddest and funniest outcome of their fandom, the word *accessibility* showed up on numerous individual spelling lists. It's the term students learned to use to describe what they like best about poems by Billy Collins.

So when I photocopied and asked them to read a profile of Collins that appeared in *The Washington Post*, they were struck by a poetry assignment he gave to his adult students at Lehman College—to make a list of twenty actions from their everyday lives that could become poems. The profile cited two examples Collins gave of actions from his own life: he moved his dog's head off his pillow, and, by mistake, he drove over an American flag.

I told the kids I was interested in trying this, as another way to generate topics for my poems. So that weekend I observed my everyday life, kept a running list of things I did that might be the stuff of poetry, and showed the twenty actions to my kids as Monday's mini-lesson. Clearly, here was another way to add to our lists of territories as poets.

"Billy Collins has written an American best-seller. By itself that's not a startling statement—not unless you know that Billy Collins is a poet. Not to mention a good poet. Not to mention the poet appointed by the Library of Congress to the post of poet laureate of the United States.

There are lots of theories about why Collins' poetry is so popular with ordinary Americans. Highbrow critics say it's because his poems are cute, a novelty act. One critic wrote, "Collins writes like a man with a pile of those poetry refrigerator magnet sets who happened to get pretty handy with them," and he even compared Collins to Jerry Seinfeld.

But other critics and many readers love Billy Collins' poems. They're simple and inviting to enter, often funny, frequently moving, sometimes startling, and generally deeper and more mysterious than they first appear, with the serious and the trivial mixed together—just like in real life.

Last week I read a profile of Billy Collins in the *Washington Post*. The reporter described a poetry class Collins taught at Lehman College in the Bronx. He read to his students a list of twenty actions he'd taken the day before. They included running over an American flag by mistake and moving his dog's head off his pillow. Collins assigned his students to keep a list of twenty of their everyday actions that could become poems.

Last weekend I tried Collins' assignment, to see if and how it might inspire me as a poet, and I love where it led me. Here's my list of twenty actions, twenty things I did last weekend that could become poems. . . . [See Figure 6-1 for my list and 6-2 for the poem I wrote.]

The exercise showed me moments in my life that are raw material for personal poems. Even better, I think many of the moments have the potential to go beyond the personal and to matter to others, too. I don't know where to start, there are so many ideas that intrigue me.

Because making a list of twenty actions gave me so much material to mine, I learned it's something I want you to do, too. Turn to the next clean page in the territories section of your writing handbooks and record this heading

Twenty Actions of Mine That Could Become Poems

This weekend take your writing handbook home. Fold it open to this page and leave it, along with a pen or a pencil, in a conspicuous spot—maybe on your desk, the kitchen counter, the living room sofa. Observe yourself. If you notice yourself engaged in an action that might have poetic potential, jot it down. If you're away from home and do something that has potential, make a mental note to remember it, so you can record it when you return. Don't limit yourself to twenty actions, but you must observe and record at least that many, because twenty will push you beyond the obvious to the quirky, the deep, the surprising, and the intensely personal moments of your days.

By way of example, the overhead shows a sampling of the actions that a group of seventh and eighth graders observed over a weekend in March. Read along with me. . . .

Can you envision how these everyday actions might contain the seeds of interesting poems? In many of them there's already a tension between what was expected and what was delivered. Some of the actions fix a moment of beauty or satisfaction. Others suggest a possibility, or bring a

---

TWENTY ACTIONS THAT COULD BE POEMS

Watching Toby teach Anne how to parallel park, feeling glad it's not me

Walking on Salt Pond Road with Anne and reciting "Stopping by Woods" by Robert Frost for about the millionth time

Examining my face in the mirror in the morning—the lines, pores, broken veins, age spots

Adding a sixth tea mug to the collection of dirty ones on my writing desk—a sign of a good writing week

Reading in bed again at 1:30 A.M., unhappily wide awake

Holding my calf stiff for half an hour because Rosie's napping on it and I love being her pillow—the feeling of her trust

Sophia's parents calling: they'll pick Anne up, so for once we don't have to carpool to Damariscotta: the moment of greatest joy of my day

Looking at frozen rose bushes for signs of life

Dining on take-out shrimp pattay in winter on an island in Maine: 21st century America

Awakening Anne from a late afternoon nap—her face like baby Anne's for just that moment

Removing toenail polish I applied before Captiva: waving good-bye to February vacation

Not getting dressed on Sunday 'til 4:00: my definition of weekend

When the week's laundry is done: *the feeling of fresh laundry*

Lying across our bed with Anne on Sunday afternoon, both of us reading poetry (Mary Oliver and Heaney's *Beowulf*)

Being told by an airline phone recording that I'll have to wait seventeen minutes for a live person, and waiting

Anne trying to curl into my lap, all sharp knees, elbows, hip bones, and ankles, both of us trying so hard to cuddle

Figure 6-1 Nancie's Twenty Actions List

Overhead
Students' Twenty
Actions List

smile of recognition. All of them find art in the everyday. Let me show you a handful of the poems that resulted. . . .

Have fun with this assignment. Look hard at the mundane world around you. Make sure these are your actions, rather than an observation of others in action, so your *I* voice can be strong. Bring your lists of twenty actions to the mini-lesson on Monday. Questions?

FOLLOW-UP LESSONS

[After walking the inside of the circle and checking their homework, I ask students to meet in groups of three or four and talk to one another about the actions they captured. Then I reconvene the circle, ask writers to skim their lists and select one or two ideas that seem to offer the best potential as art, and do a quick whip around the group, asking kids to share their best ideas. New homework, due in two days, is a draft of a poem about one of the twenty actions.]

6

ON SALT POND ROAD WITH FROST

I know whose woods these are.
A thousand visits made them mine,
a thousand visits and Robert Frost.

Anne's first summer I strolled her down the
    shaded lane
and said the words to the woods and her,
a lullaby for a baby
from the country of white houses.

Other days I passed alone, head down, hands in
    pockets,
walking hard to beat the blues
'til shocked out of myself by the emerald of the
    forest floor—
a reminder I could stop, breathe,
keep the promises tomorrow.

Once I walked this way in winter with my mother,
who doesn't live among poems or woods.
I said Frost's words and told her I knew the urge—
to disappear among dark and lovely trees,
to rest on the snow forever—
and stopped her short.
So it's a poem about death?
Maybe. And choosing life, I think.

Today I hiked by the woods with my grown-up
    girl.
We didn't stop—she had places to go.
But we said the words together and marched to
    their beat—
a reflex on this road like wishing on a star.
Whose woods whirled past us, as we walked
Frost's truth: Earth is the right place for love.

—Nancie Atwell

Figure 6-2

Itches to Scratch in Essays

Preparation

✔ Overhead transparency of "Sample List of a Student's Essay Ideas," from a seventh grader's handbook

✔ Trimmed photocopies of the questionnaire "What Itch Needs Scratching?" for students to tape at the top of a page in their writing handbooks

✔ Wall poster of Donald Murray quotation

✔ Tape dispensers

✔ Optional: Photocopies of the student essays in Appendix C, as examples for your students of what's possible

What I Was Thinking I've only started teaching essay writing in a serious, sustained way in the past five years. Before that I was so discouraged by the school stereotype of essays—topic outlines, five paragraphs, topic sentences to start each paragraph, and assigned subjects—that I didn't see the potential of essays to be useful to my students in the ways that poetry, memoir, and short fiction informed their lives.

But I also recognized that most of the writing I do in my real life is nonfiction prose—arguments, explanations, persuasions, descriptions—and that most of the writing my kids produce after they leave eighth grade will be nonfiction prose. The challenge was to find a way to invite student essays that inform kids' lives—essays that do something for them as individuals, teens, girls, boys, learners, citizens, consumers, fans, artists, and activists.

The question that best invites my students to generate useful, meaningful ideas for their essays has proved to be, "What itch needs scratching?" I ask them to delve into the realm of problems, opinions, issues, choices, and passions in search of the intellectual itches worthy of scratching as essays. In identifying this lesson as one that changed him as a writer, Colby, one of the student essayists whose work is collected in Appendix C, wrote, "There's political and sociological stuff I'm always thinking about and talking about in a vague way. Writing an essay and thinking on paper really helped me know my opinions and get them across to other people. It's my new favorite genre."

"Effective Essays: Teasing Out Criteria" (Lesson 49) comes before this lesson on ideas for essays: students need an orchestrated introduction to the genre, since it's unlikely that many will have read essays on their own.

> One of my favorite writers and writing teachers is Donald Murray. He writes a weekly column of essays about his everyday life, which appears in the *Boston Globe*, and he has written a ton of books about writing. I quote him a lot because his advice to writers is specific, practical, and true. Today's Murray quote is his assertion "Problems make good subjects."
>
> As you've gathered from the essays we've been reading and discussing, this is the genre that invites you to write about what you know, what you think, what you can observe, what you can find out. And as with all the genres you've tried this school year, we'll begin the process of writing essays by searching for the topics that motivate you as a writer: the mental itches you're interested in scratching.
>
> Turn to the next clean page of the territories section of your writing handbook, tape this invitation—"What Itch Needs Scratching"—at the top of the page, so there's room below for writing, then read along with me. . . .
>
> Tonight for homework your assignment is to consider these questions and brainstorm, in the space below, a list of at least six itches that intrigue you—topics that make you happy, sad, curious, furious, confused. Go for quantity. And go for idiosyncrasy—a list of potential essay topics that no one but you could have written.
>
> For example, the overhead shows a list of itches brainstormed by a seventh grade girl. These are the problems, questions, and issues that she discovered mattered to her. . . .
>
> Tonight, as you make your own list of itches that need scratching, try to spend half an hour poking into the corners of your ideas and experiences. And take breaks, to let your long-term memory do its work.
>
> Comments or questions?

"Problems make good subjects."

– Donald Murray

WHAT ITCH NEEDS SCRATCHING?

("Problems make good subjects."   Donald Murray)

What problem needs solving?

What situation needs correcting?

What issue needs explaining?

What phenomenon needs exploring?

What choice I've made/stand I've taken/personal preference needs to be understood by others?

What area of my expertise needs sharing?

What subject that's close and familiar to me needs to be viewed and considered from a distance?

What point of view needs my powers of persuasion?

© 2002 by Nancie Atwell from *Lessons That Change Writers* (Portsmouth, NH: Heinemann)

WHAT ITCH NEEDS SCRATCHING?   LESSON 7

Reproducible and Overhead
What Itch Needs Scratching? and
Sample List of Students' Essay Ideas

[I ask students to gather in groups of three with their writing handbooks and pencils and take turns describing to one another their ideas for essay topics. I circulate among the small groups, listen, ask questions, respond to their ideas, and keep them on task. I allow ten to fifteen minutes for kids to talk together about their ideas and record any new possibilities that emerge, then let the groups know when they have a minute left. I reconvene the mini-lesson circle and ask, "Who already knows the itch you're going to scratch in your essay?"

I call on volunteers, discuss their ideas, and, as necessary, respond to overly broad topics—for example, war, religion, censorship—with questions that push students to uncover the specific, personal concerns at the heart of their interest in a topic and to narrow to manageable subjects: Was the nuclear attack on Hiroshima necessary? What's the status of spirituality among kids today? Should video games be rated, and if so, how?

For homework, kids choose the itch they'd like to scratch in an essay by writing it in the form of a *statement* or a *question* at the top of the next clean page of their writing handbooks. Figure 7-1 shows a list of essay topics developed by the kids in one of my classes. I follow up with "How Do I Scratch the Itch?" (Lesson 50).]

SAMPLE ESSAY TOPICS CHOSEN BY ONE CLASS: THEIR STATEMENTS AND QUESTIONS

How many animal species have become extinct because of human actions?

Fad diets are harmful to girls' bodies and health.

CAFE standards should be raised for all vehicles.

How is airport security since 9/11?

Do grades help students learn?

Fishing quotas are not the best tool to manage groundfishing.

Fast-food restaurants—McDonald's and Burger King—are bad for Americans' health.

Humans should be more aware of breakthroughs in chimp intelligence and communication abilities, because they are our closest genetic relatives.

Are there health benefits to eating beef?

It's time to pass a gay rights bill in Maine.

What are the effects of school uniforms on a student population?

Gambling casinos don't belong in Maine.

What is stopping us from using hydrogen as an energy source?

Dark chocolate: maybe it's not as bad for us as we've been told.

The Afghan prisoners in Cuba should be treated according to International Law (i.e., the Geneva Convention).

Is an annual mammogram really helpful in detecting breast cancer?

Parents should be allowed to spend state/town funds on tuition to religious schools.

What are the root causes of animal abuse, and what can be done to stop it?

Adoption of foster children is needlessly difficult in Maine.

Teen magazines inundate adolescent girls with distorted body images.

Figure 7-1

SECTION II:

Lessons about Principles

At the same time we help students generate and focus on ideas for writing that matter to them and motivate them to want to produce good writing, the other tough job is to show them *how* to write well. I want students to write deliberately: to understand that good writing isn't an accident and to draw on a repertoire of techniques and approaches in their attempts to write well. The lessons in this section are those most frequently cited by my kids as activities and discussions that showed them how to craft their texts as literature.

In some lessons about principles, the group, including the teacher, collaborates in creating definitions, procedures, and techniques. In others the teacher presents guidelines for writing well, along with relevant models of excellent writing—and sometimes weak writing, too, so the differences are clear. And some lessons involve demonstrations of the teacher's writing: I draft in front of students on overhead transparencies or bring in and show them writing I crafted at home, explain what I was thinking and trying to do, and answer students' questions about my choices. Lessons about principles are directed toward one of two ends: making productive use of process—using writing as a tool to plan and generate writing—and writing to satisfy a reader.

In these lessons I try to shoot straight with my kids about qualities of good writing, process and product, and avoid clichéd labels and jargon. Kids aren't helped by teacher exhortations to be original, develop a logical organization, compose with imagery, have a voice, write concretely, create mature sentences, include vivid details and descriptions, consider tone and point of view, and draft in support of a theme.

Instead, the language I use is as stripped-down and evocative as I can make it: the Rule of *So What?*; the Rule of Write about *a* Pebble; four ways to organize essay information; the Rule of Thoughts and Feelings; can a reader see it, hear it, feel it?

Lessons about principles of writing help kids take on the perspective of insiders. They don't wait around as writers, hoping that lightning will strike and they'll produce something brilliant. Instead, they consult their own repertoires of knowledge about effective writing, captured in the pages of their writing handbooks, and they take action: get themselves unstuck and work purposefully to move their writing into the realm of literature.

I pack the first month of school with lessons about principles, to lay a foundation for a year of literary writing and, more important, to help kids produce good writing ASAP, so they know the satisfaction that comes from writing well and the level of thinking-on-paper work it takes to get there.

One September a returning eighth grader, Forrest, asked if he could speak to me after class. He looked concerned. I said sure. Later, when the rest of his group had moved on to their next class, Forrest unloaded.

"You *have* to do the Rule of *So What?* and you have to do it soon," he said. "Some of these seventh graders don't have a clue how to write a memoir that has meaning, and I just feel sorry for them. They have good topics, but they can't get inside them. They really need that mini-lesson."

I laughed and showed Forrest my planbook. Tomorrow's mini-lesson was the Rule of *So What?* "I should have known you wouldn't let them down," he said. I responded, "Thank you, anyway. It's good to know you're looking out for these guys and their writing."

Lessons about principles invite novice writers into the club that Forrest was eager for his seventh-grade classmates to join. And lessons about principles convince young writers that their teacher is there to teach them—that when it comes to techniques and ideas that help every student write well, they can trust we will not let them down.

What Is Writing?

Preparation

✔ Overhead transparency headed "What Is Writing?" for brainstorming with students

✔ Wall poster of Kurt Vonnegut Jr. quotation

What I Was Thinking Although writing is taught, and taught well, in all the grades at CTL, September's incoming group always represents a range of writing experience. It includes seventh graders brand new to the school, kids who entered CTL during the previous year or two, and students who have been writing with us since kindergarten. At the start of a year of writing workshop, I need to bring everyone to the same page. So together every September we collaborate on a definition of writing process that's generous, true, and focused on the behaviors of effective writers: thinking on paper, generating, selecting, and reading.

I was surprised by the number of students who cited such a basic lesson as crucial to their writing. One of them, Noah, said, "It's reassuring to know there's not one right way to do it, to write. At the same time it helps to remember everything that's involved in writing well and focus on the parts that make the most difference, especially the idea of thinking on paper, then taking your thinking further."

❝ You can tell, from the question on the overhead, the focus of today's minilesson. Please write

What Is Writing?

at the top of page 16 in your writing handbooks; this is the first non-territories lesson you'll be capturing as notes. . . .

I want you to help me answer this question. As I record your answers on the transparency, please copy them into your handbook. When the lesson is over, you'll have a record of what we thought about and discussed today, for your future reference as a writer. I'll begin by giving you a crucial piece of background information. Please write it under the lesson heading:

> Writing is a process, not a single activity. It involves lots of activities, steps, behaviors, and changes. These include:

This is where I want us to start, with the notion of writing as a continuous series of changing activities. Writing is complex, rich, and messy. It isn't *just* handwriting or spelling or drafting, although these are part of what a writer does. So let's brainstorm. What are *all* the activities involved in the process of writing?. . . [See Figure 8-1 for one class's response.]

You made a great, thorough list: writing *is* complicated. My contribution was to point to the bottom line: good writing is thinking on paper. This means that like serious thought about any subject, writing is disorderly, demanding, frustrating, satisfying, and definitely nonlinear. A writer doesn't move smoothly from point A to point B to point C, no matter what my English teachers told me back in high school. Writers circle among all these activities until, at some point, you *have* to stop, you have to let a piece of writing go out into the world and stand on its own.

My job this year is to help you get better at everything on the list, but especially thinking on paper: getting ideas down, jotting half-formed

Overhead
What Is Writing?

WHAT IS WRITING?

Writing is a process, not a single activity. It involves lots of activities, steps, behaviors, and changes. These include:

drafting words and ideas	*thinking on paper*	punctuating
thinking of a topic	cutting and taping	capitalizing
brainstorming ideas	making spider legs	paragraphing
deciding on a genre	listing	line breaking and stanza breaking
thinking on paper	making priorities	
revising	considering audience	*thinking on paper*
editing	organizing	proofreading
polishing	handwriting	final-copying
researching	typing	*reading what you've already written*
planning	spelling	
notetaking	*thinking on paper*	

Figure 8-1 Nancie's Class's Brainstorming about What Is Writing? (Items in italics indicate my contributions to the list, which emphasized writing as thinking on paper and reminded kids that reading over what's been written is a crucial, often-overlooked part of the process of writing well.)

notions, going back and thinking about the captured thoughts, and thinking them anew. Writers aren't necessarily smart people, but they are patient. As Kurt Vonnegut Jr., one of our best contemporary writers, wrote, "We have discovered that writing allows even a stupid person to seem halfway intelligent, if only that person will write the same thought over and over again, improving it just a little bit each time. It is a lot like inflating a blimp with a bicycle pump. Anybody can do it. All it takes is time."

What are your comments and observations about the process of writing?

FOLLOW-UP LESSON

[Later that fall, after a mini-lesson in which I drafted a business letter on transparencies in front of the group—a demonstration of working from a planning sheet—a student surprised me by observing, "I can't believe how much time you spent going back and reading over what you'd already written."

When I asked the class, "Don't you do this when you write?" fewer than half the kids said yes. It explained a lot about the nonliterary prose of many in the group. So at the start of the next day's mini-lesson I wrote on the easel pad: "Writing is as much an act of reading over what you've already written as it is drafting new writing. *Why?*"

The list we brainstormed, which kids recorded in their handbooks, got at many of the problems that weaker writers in the group were struggling with:

- You hear redundancies.
- You hear ineffective repetitions.
- You catch weak verbs.
- You refind your voice—your attitude and tone.
- You build up a sense of flow, so new writing can join the flow.
- You catch contradictions.
- You remember which tense—past or present—or voice—first or third—you're writing in.
- You can build or gather momentum when you're stuck.
- You catch things that are in the wrong place.
- You remind yourself of what you haven't said yet.
- Your old ideas inspire new ones.]

The Rule of So What?

Preparation

✔ Overhead transparency of a bereft draft (i.e., events described with no *So what?*) of a memoir about a significant time in your life

✔ Photocopies of an alternative version of the same incident, in which you pushed your thinking toward meaning and theme

✔ Trimmed photocopies of "The Rule of *So What?*" for students to tape into their handbooks

✔ Wall poster of Robert Frost quotation

✔ Tape dispensers

LESSON 9

What I Was Thinking

I took a hiatus from teaching to raise my daughter and build the Center for Teaching and Learning. I was ecstatic in 1994 when the first group of CTL students was finally old enough for seventh grade and I could return to the classroom as their teacher of writing, reading, and history.

That first year back was the genesis of the second edition of *In the Middle*. I learned so much about what kids can do as writers, and I rethought almost everything about my role in writing workshop. One of the biggest changes was a conviction that students' writing had to matter to them, had to instruct or engage them in some way, had to be good for something. By 1994, it wasn't enough any longer to get students writing and "experiencing the process." We'd done that; we knew kids could do that. What was the point of asking kids to choose their own topics if the writing they produced wasn't important to them?

Questions I found myself asking a lot in writing conferences that fall and winter were, "Why are you writing about this?" and "What's the point?" I tried to nudge students to use writing to find the themes of their lives. When I broached this idea in a mini-lesson, I said something like, "When you write about the day your father told you there was no Santa Claus, you have to do more than relate the conversation and the order of events. You need to step back and look for what the experience means to you, how it signifies, what its themes are. Is anyone catching my drift?"

The group looked at me blankly. Finally Joe spoke up. "It's like, 'Okay, so now I know there's no Santa, *so what?*'"

As usual, Joe went straight to the point. The question *So what?* became a shorthand phrase that stood in for the literary language—theme, purpose, motif, guiding principle, central idea, motivation—that did not resonate for middle school students as potential writers of literature. In my conferences with writers, in their conferences with each other, and in students' assessments of their own emerging drafts, we learned to ask, "Okay, so this happened and this happened and this happened: *So what?*"

I present this mini-lesson in a big way over several days in September and illustrate it with versions of one of my memoirs, since memoir is one of the two genres students are crafting at this point; again, poetry is the other. Throughout the year I return to the Rule of *So What?* and we discuss how to apply it to other genres—how to find and shape meaning in poems, short fiction, and essays.

The Rule of *So What?* is annually cited by more students, as a lesson that changed them as writers, than anything else I do as a writing teacher. It helps kids find their footing as intentional, deliberate writers of substance.

> Today we're going to look at a piece of my writing that's just terrible. [See Figure 9-1.] It's bad on so many levels we could spend a week finding its faults. But I'm bringing it to you today with one big idea in mind: this draft doesn't begin to answer the most basic, most important question to be asked of any piece of writing: *So what?* Read along with me. . . .
>
> As I said before, *so what?* My bout with rheumatic fever is one of the

MY BAD MEMOIR

I remember that when I was in fifth grade I got really sick. My throat was raw, and all my joints ached. The family doctor said I had rheumatic fever.

I had to stay in bed for six months. I couldn't walk up and down stairs or even go to the bathroom by myself.

When my dad came home from work at night, he'd carry me downstairs so I could watch television and be with the rest of the family, then carry me back upstairs at bedtime. Otherwise it was a lonely, boring time. All I could do was read. During the six months I had rheumatic fever I practically ate books. I made my poor mother go to the library almost every day for new ones.

Finally the doctor said I could go back to school. It was one of the happiest days of my life, even though I couldn't run or play sports for a long time.

Figure 9-1 Nancie's Deliberately Bereft Memoir

big experiences of my childhood, but in this draft I haven't begun to get at *why*, to discover why it intrigues me enough that I want to write about it. As it stands, the memoir is a description of a string of events. You don't know why I'm writing about it, because I haven't figured out the reasons it stands out for me as a memoir-worthy experience.

Please turn to the next clean page of your writing handbook and tape in "The Rule of *So What?*" Then follow along with me as I read. . . .

Do you understand? Every time you write, there should be an itch you're trying to scratch—something in the topic that intrigues you for some reason, whether you can name it or not, and your job as a writer is to find out why.

I haven't done my job as a writer in this memoir. I need to find and make a point about this time in my life. And if I can't, I probably need to abandon this topic, at least for now, and move on to a subject about which I can feel a sense of purpose and find my *So what?*

Stay tuned. I did not give up on this topic. I knew there was a *So what?* Tomorrow I'll show you how I looked for and found it.

Reproducible
The Rule of *So What?*

FOLLOW-UP ASSIGNMENT

[In the next day's mini-lesson I distributed copies of an alternative version of my memoir (Figure 9-2), read it aloud, then discussed it with the group. I asked, "What are your observations and impressions of this version of the memoir? What did you notice happened to the writing when I pushed the story toward finding a meaning and answering the question, *So what?*" I concluded:]

This is your challenge as a writer for the rest of the school year: as you select topics from the various territories lists that you generate this year, as you feel that pull or itch inside of you that says *this is a subject that matters to me*, can you go below the surface, use writing to push your thinking, and find the meaning in your experiences, ideas, and feelings? Can you ask yourself *So what?* And in your conferences with me and with each other, can this be one of your agendas in asking for help: "Is there a *So what?* Can you tell, yet, as a reader, why I'm writing about this?"

Now, what are your comments or observations?

MY SECRET GARDEN

Mr. Ioanne told great stories, and his fifth graders loved to hear them—especially after we figured out that once we coaxed him into story-telling mode, he'd forget about the chapter from the social studies book, the spelling test, or the new vocab list, lean back in his chair, and narrate his life for us.

The boys liked stories about the rough neighborhood where Mr. Ioanne grew up: the more fights the better as far as they were concerned. And the girls—or, at least, this girl—ate up tales about his early poverty, close-knit family (Catholic, like mine), and childhood illness.

He could always squeeze a few tears out of us by launching into the story about the disease that had attacked his heart and left him bedridden for months—and then, when he finally returned to school, unable to run or play or even climb stairs. One of his brothers had carried him up and down the flights of stairs at his school, and on the days when his brother forgot him, Mr. Ioanne sat down on the top step and waited. I pictured him perched there in the waning sunlight, long after the bells had sent the other children laughing and shouting from the building, nursing a sick and broken heart and wondering when someone in his family would realize they were a child short and delegate a brother to fetch him. Of all his stories, I remember this one best because of what happened to me that winter.

I caught a cold that stayed forever. When I coughed it hurt deep inside, and I rumbled like a car that couldn't start. I'd never had such a long cold. One day after school, when I ran into the house from playing with my sister, my cough kicked in and wouldn't stop. Rose, my mother's friend, was sitting at the kitchen table drinking coffee as I barked and rumbled to and from the bathroom. "That doesn't sound good," she said to my mother.

Mom sighed. "Does it hurt?" she asked.

"Where?"

"Your *throat*."

I stood still and thought. Did my throat hurt? Well, no—not unless I swallowed. "Nope," I shook my head. "Can I go back out now?"

"Yes—but only for another half hour. Then I want you in here to set the table. Did you hear me?"

"Okay." Released from the attention of the mothers—never a good thing—I tore out the back door and down to the creek, to help Bonnie finish the new dam before dinner. Later I would replay the throat conversation a hundred times. Much later, when my own child looked feverish, I'd pose the question the way I needed Anne to answer it: "Does it hurt *when you swallow*?"

Two weeks later, when the cough was even worse and my knees and elbows hurt so much I couldn't sleep at night, my mother called the doctor. He diagnosed rheumatic fever.

I was horror struck. Mr. Ioanne's romantic fever had claimed me as a victim. While the doctor explained the ramifications of rheumatic fever to my mother, I imagined my future: lying alone in my bed in my room, no school friends, no gang of neighborhood kids, no skating at Dieners' Pond, no sledding at the Town Park, no snow fort in the front yard, no snowball fights with the Boodies, no life as I knew it.

And no television. These were the days when every family had one TV set,

Figure 9-2 Nancie's Better Version of Her Memoir; continued on page 42

a console that took up half the living room. When my father came home from his job at the post office at 5:00, he carried me downstairs to the sofa, where I ate off a tray, watched television, and listened to my family having dinner in the next room. At 9:00 he heaved me back upstairs to my room, where I faced another twenty hours of seclusion and self-pity.

At first I slept a lot. I was exhausted from my symptoms and didn't have the energy to be bored. But after a few weeks, when the prescribed aspirin and penicillin kicked in, I began to feel okay. Then it was hard to keep still, hard to remember that this was more than a cold and that I needed to lie here and protect my heart until the doctor said otherwise. I missed school, but I grieved for play. Playing had been my life—outside in all seasons, inside with Barbie dolls and games with my sister and brother. Now what?

One morning, desperate with boredom, I asked my mother if she could please go to the town library and see if they had any good books. I wasn't able to say what I meant by that or give any examples besides the World Book Encyclopedia, Nancy Drew, Cherry Ames, Trixie Belden, and comic books, which up 'til then had comprised my meager experience as an independent reader.

At school I was an A student, but my reading was from textbooks. Every year from third grade on I had a science book, an English book, a reading book, and a social studies book. There were no shelves of story books in my classrooms. Once a week the teacher did take us to the school library for twenty minutes to choose books, and among the dusty volumes, mostly with copyrights from the 1930's, I had found Nancy, Cherry, and Trixie.

Later that day, my mother returned from the town library with two books. I don't remember what they were; I do remember that by 5:00, when my father came home from work, I'd finished both of them.

The next morning, as I lay in bed waiting for breakfast, I rehearsed how I'd break the news to my beleaguered mother. She worked hard at the usual, grueling mother tasks, but in addition there was always a renovation project in the works as she and my father tried to fix up the terrible house they'd bought for its good neighborhood. Now she also served me meals on a tray and heaved me back and forth to the bathroom.

She slid the breakfast tray onto my lap, and I popped the question. "Do you think you could get me some more books today?"

"Are you kidding? What happened to the ones I borrowed yesterday?"

"I finished them. I'm sorry. I couldn't help it."

She stared at me. "Do you think I have nothing to do here all day but go to the library?" She rolled her eyes. "All *right*. What do you want?"

"I don't know . . . something good?"

And so began my mother's education as an authority on children's literature circa 1960, and my life as a reader of literature. She combed the shelves of our tiny public library and, over time, borrowed more than a hundred books for me to read. That winter she lugged home all of Beverly Cleary, even *Jean and Johnny*. I worked my way through the entire series of Landmark Biographies for Children and met Lotta Crabtree, Jenny Lind, Tom Paine, Annie Oakley, and, my personal favorite, Francis Marion the Swamp Fox. I read *Little Women* many times, *Little Men*, and all the Little House on the Prairie books. And then my mother found *The Secret Garden*.

continued on page 43

This one I had shifted again and again to the bottom of my book pile until the day before it was due for return to the library. The cover was practically moldy it was so old, and the title sounded silly. Finally, when I'd read and reread everything else in the pile, I cracked open *The Secret Garden*.

To this day I can close my eyes and bring back the feeling of pleasure and excitement that book gave me. It was just the story I needed—a feisty, unhappy girl hero, an invalid child who recovers and becomes strong, and a magic place that heals them both. "Mom," I said. "This book was so good. It was perfect. Please, can you find more like this one?"

She sighed, and she tried. *The Little Princess* was good, but there was only one *Secret Garden*. My mother renewed it four times for me that winter and spring.

Finally, in May, the doctor said I was well enough to go to school. I remember the first day back—the bear hug from Mr. Ioanne, the yellow dress I wore, the way the other kids weren't sure how to act toward me. It only took a few days to ease back into my friendships and the give-and-take of the classroom.

Outside of the classroom was harder. When we had gym, I stayed behind in the room and helped Mr. Ioanne. When he took us out to the playground for kickball, I sat on the bench and watched. I remember a day in June when I walked away in tears from a class party at a girl's swimming pool. It was too hard to sit in an aluminum folding chair with the chaperones and watch my friends splashing. I stumbled to a swingset in the girl's yard, sat on a swing, and cried.

The creaking of the chains of the other swing told me Mr. Ioanne had followed me. "I know you're sad," he said. "I know how hard this is."

"I know you know," I snuffled. He was the only one.

"It won't last forever. You can learn from this how to be patient—to get through something hard with the understanding that it *will* pass. This is something some people never learn. And sometimes, when you're enduring a hard time, you find other consolations, new things that can make you happy. For me it was reading."

"Really?" I asked him. He nodded *yes*. "Me too. I read a ton of books. And I found this great one, *The Secret Garden*. What did you read when you were sick?"

I wish I could remember the titles he named. What does stay with me is the comfort I took from his words about patience and a feeling of solidarity deeper than our mutual victimhood. We were two readers, together.

"Come on," he said. "Let's go back." He put his hand on my shoulder and walked me over to the pool and my friends and an event I would get through.

Although in time my recovery from rheumatic fever was complete, I emerged from the experience a different girl. Maybe I was more patient, but for sure I was a reader. Rheumatic fever gave me three gifts that have lasted my lifetime: a sense of how my mother did her best for me, a passion for books, and the ability to read fast and with feeling.

All that quiet time alone to read, all those good books chosen by an adult who loved me, changed me forever—made me happier, smarter, and, unexpectedly, more in touch with life and history and the world beyond than if I had never endured that bedridden winter.

Thoughts and Feelings

Preparation

- ✔ Overhead transparencies of Tyler Reny's first draft and annotated draft of "Christmas Eve"
- ✔ Photocopies of Tyler's final draft: "The Perfect Christmas Eve"
- ✔ Trimmed photocopies of "The Rule of Thoughts and Feelings" for students to tape into their handbooks
- ✔ Tape dispensers

What I Was Thinking

My husband teases me about my use of the phrase *thoughts and feelings* in teaching kids how to be reflective as writers. He's amused because the language is 1960's clichéd, but I continue to talk to kids about thoughts and feelings because it works.

Decades into my own life as a writer, I'm still not sure what *voice* is, and my kids struggle to understand terms like *reflection, perspective,* and *personal style.* But I find they begin to write with voice, reflection, perspective, and personal style when they discover and describe their thoughts and feelings—or, in short stories, those of their main characters. A writer's thoughts and feelings give readers a way inside the writing and the writer's experience.

More important, for writers who struggle to find a *So what?*, approaching revision as an act of remembering or discovering thoughts and feelings pushes them toward theme. And, perhaps most important, describing thoughts and feelings is the surest-fire way I know to transform a mediocre narrative into a story that resonates, for both the writer and the reader. As Krystin said, "My memoirs were pretty boring until you taught us about T and F. When I thought about and told my thoughts and feelings, then I found out *why* I was writing about a memory and I could make other people feel like I did. My memoirs this year were 100% better. They were interesting, and they really show what I was like. I'll keep them forever, to remember."

"I have permission from Tyler, a seventh grader, to show you the drafts of his memoir about a Christmas Eve he and his family spent in, of all places, Fiji. Tyler did something important to begin to transform his memoir. It's a technique for you to consider when you write stories—memoirs and short fiction—because it can transform your narratives, too.

Let's face it. Nobody *wants* to write boring stories. We want to be interesting, to ourselves and to others. But what are the bottom-line differences between a lifeless narrative and one that resonates, for the writer and for our readers? That's the challenge. One answer is *thoughts and feelings*.

When I read a memoir in which the writer doesn't tell along the way what she's thinking and feeling, to me it's just a string of events. I can't care because the writer hasn't figured out why she cares. Now, this could be a memoir about something as over-the-top as winning the lottery, getting lost on a mountain, or being reunited with a long-lost twin, but it won't excite or move me as a reader unless I can go inside the writer, unless I can become her, unless I can think and feel what she's thinking and feeling during her adventure.

Conversely, some of the best, most interesting memoirs I've ever read were about such seemingly mundane topics as a fort kids built at recess, getting separated from parents in a store, picking blueberries, and fishing with grandparents. It's not the nature of the experience being described that guarantees an effective memoir. It's the *intensity of the writer's reflections*—her willingness to figure out and convey what's going on inside her.

In my own experience as a writer of stories, and in the experiences of kids I've taught, sometimes it's hard to include thoughts and feelings in the first draft, we're working so hard to get the events and details right. But if you find that descriptions of your thoughts and feelings aren't there, in an early draft of a narrative, one thing you can do when you revise is step back from the incident and its details, go inside yourself, and discover and capture your responses to the unfolding events of the story. In the process you'll often find the reason you're writing about this memory—you'll find your *So what?*

Look with me at the transparency of Tyler's first draft of his Fiji memoir, "Christmas Eve," and read along as I read aloud to you. . . .

TYLER'S FIRST DRAFT OF "CHRISTMAS EVE"

The damp sand squished between my toes. The humid breeze slicked back my hair. It was my first Christmas Eve spent away from home. My sister, mother, father, and I walked down the beach. The sun, dwindling below the horizon, transformed the sky into a three-dimensional painting. The thin streak of clouds, a crooked stroke, a painter's final touch, transformed Fiji's evening sky.

The faint hum of Christmas carols drifted across the sand from the dining hall, where the local children and community held candles and celebrated Christmas Eve by singing their traditional songs. We, on the other hand, were not so graceful with our voices at the time, belting out any lyrics that came to mind about Christmas.

"I bet I could sing that good if I really wanted to," my father claimed. "Rudolf the red-nosed . . . " he belted out of tune.

"Thanks, Dad, but I think I'll stick with listening to the kids, or, of course, Marlie," I said.

"FALALALALA . . . !"

Okay, not Marlie—just the other children.

The sun had now vanished beneath the horizon and there was nothing left but the vast rolling ocean and a few emerging stars.

It was peaceful and the night was beautiful. The air was weighed down with humidity and the smell of salt.

When we reached the end of the beach, we turned around and started back to the dining hall. When we arrived at the dining hall we watched the kids sing. It was amazing that they had come there that night to sing to the people at the resort.

TYLER'S FIRST DRAFT OF "CHRISTMAS EVE" LESSON 10

Overhead
Tyler's First Draft

This was as far as Tyler got. When I stopped at his desk to confer, and asked how it was going, he said, "I don't know why I'm writing about this. I think I'm going to abandon it. There's no *So what?*" I skimmed the memoir and agreed with Tyler: so far there didn't seem to be a *So what?*

"But," I continued, "writers often find their theme or *So what?* during the writing, if they know how to look. One place to look is inside you. As beautiful as your descriptions of the Fiji landscape are, your readers need your emotional landscape—and so do you—for this memoir to resonate. They need to know your thoughts and feelings.

"Tyler, do you know what an asterisk is? Here's what I'd like you to do. Read through your story with a pen in your hand. At every point in the draft where a reader might wonder what you're thinking and feeling, put an asterisk. For example, at the end of the fourth sentence, when you're walking down the beach with your family, I'm dying to know what you're feeling. Was this fun? Strange? Was it sad, to be so far away from home on Christmas Eve? It's your take on this experience, your thoughts and feelings about it, that will give it life and meaning."

Look at the next transparency. Tyler found five places for his thoughts and feelings. Since he was composing this piece on a word processor, I asked him to go back and type descriptions of what he was thinking and feeling at each of the five asterisks, then tell the rest of the story and this time to try to include his reflections as he drafted.

Now take a look at your own copy of Tyler's final draft. Read it to yourself and *mark it up*: find and underline the lines in which he tells his thoughts and feelings. . . .

Can you see and feel the difference? In this version readers can be with Tyler. His story is deeper—more personal to him and more interesting to us. And all he did was find the points where he decided we needed to think his thoughts and feel his feelings, starting with his title.

Thoughts and feelings is a technique for both drafting and revising stories. From now on, try to include your thoughts and feelings as you go. Later, when you come back and read what you've written, use asterisks at the points where you need to go inside yourself and tell what's going on there.

If the draft is handwritten and there's not room on the page to include

TYLER'S ANNOTATED DRAFT OF "CHRISTMAS EVE"

The damp sand squished between my toes. The humid breeze slicked back my hair. It was my first Christmas Eve spent away from home. My sister, mother, father, and I walked down the beach. * The sun, dwindling below the horizon, transformed the sky into a three-dimensional painting. The thin streak of clouds, a crooked stroke, a painter's final touch, transformed Fiji's evening sky. *

The faint hum of Christmas carols drifted across the sand from the dining hall, where the local children and community held candles and celebrated Christmas Eve by singing their traditional songs. * We, on the other hand, were not so graceful with our voices at the time, belting out any lyrics that came to mind about Christmas.

"I bet I could sing that good if I really wanted to," my father claimed. "Rudolf the red-nosed . . . " he belted out of tune.

"Thanks, Dad, but I think I'll stick with listening to the kids, or, of course, Marlie," I said.

"FALALALALA . . . !"

Okay, not Marlie—just the other children.

The sun had now vanished beneath the horizon and there was nothing left but the vast rolling ocean and a few emerging stars.

It was peaceful and the night was beautiful. The air was weighed down with humidity and the smell of salt. *

When we reached the end of the beach, we turned around and started back to the dining hall. When we arrived at the dining hall we watched the kids sing. It was amazing that they had come there that night to sing to the people at the resort. *

© 2002 by Nancie Atwell from *Lessons That Change Writers* (Portsmouth, NH: Heinemann)   TYLER'S ANNOTATED DRAFT OF "CHRISTMAS EVE"   LESSON 10

Overhead
Tyler's Annotated Draft

TYLER'S FINAL DRAFT: "THE PERFECT CHRISTMAS EVE"

The damp sand squished between my toes. The humid breeze slicked back my hair. It was my first Christmas Eve spent away from home. My sister, mother, father, and I walked the beach. It was weird. I wouldn't get to be with my mother's or father's parents, their brothers and sisters, or my cousins.

The sun dwindled below the horizon, transforming the sky into a three-dimensional painting. The thin streak of clouds, a crooked stroke, a painter's final touch, transformed Fiji's evening sky, resulting in the most beautiful sunset I have ever seen, clearly a work of art.

The faint hum of Christmas carols drifted across the beach from the dining hall, where the local community and children held glowing candles and celebrated Christmas by singing their traditional songs. It amazed me that they would assemble here on this night and sing to the people staying at the resort.

We, on the other hand, were not so graceful with our voices, belting out any lyrics that came to mind relating to Christmas.

"I bet I could sing that good if I really wanted to!" my father claimed. "Rudolf the red-nosed . . ." he sang out of tune.

"Thanks, Dad, but I think I'll stick with listening to Marlie," I replied.

"FALALALALA . . ." my sister screamed.

"Okay, not Marlie."

The sun had disappeared now below the horizon, and nothing was left but the vast rolling ocean and a few emerging stars. It was peaceful, and the night was beautiful and dense with humidity and the smell of salt. I missed home.

When we reached the end of the beach, we turned around and headed back to the dining hall. When we got there, we watched the islanders sing. I was happy, yet it felt awkward to be so far away from home on such a special evening. Their voices echoed around the room. They were dressed in beautiful native robes. After a couple minutes we walked back in the dark to the thatched burre where we were staying.

Reproducible
Tyler's Final Draft

THE RULE OF THOUGHTS AND FEELINGS

In a narrative, the reader needs *someone to be with*. If the narrative is a short story, the someone is the main character. If it's a memoir, the someone is you, the writer.

Knowing your—or your main character's—thoughts and feelings is crucial if a reader is going to be able to participate in your story. Personal reflections—thoughts and feelings—help make a story engaging: interesting to read and vicariously experience. And personal reflections in narratives are often the source of the best *so what's?*—the themes and significances of your experiences or those of your main characters.

From now on, try to include thoughts and feelings as you draft. But if you discover that you needed your first draft to get the details of the narrative right, then revise for thoughts and feelings by going back inside the story and discovering and capturing your or your main character's responses to unfolding events.

When you revise for thoughts and feelings, you can insert asterisks at the points where readers might wonder, use a numbered list for creating notes of thoughts and feelings on a separate sheet of paper, or attach spider legs: strips of paper on which you've written thoughts and feelings to be included in the text in the next draft of the story.

Reproducible
The Rule of Thoughts and Feelings

additional text, this is an appropriate place to cut and paste, use a number code to write numbered additions on a separate sheet of paper, or try spiderlegs—write your additions on strips of paper that you staple or tape to the side of the page, then incorporate into the text when you write your final copy.

I've written up this lesson as a principle for you to include in your handbooks. Please turn to the next clean page of your writing handbook, tape in "The Rule of Thoughts and Feelings," and follow along with me as I read it to you. . . .

Comments or questions?

10

The Rule of Write about a Pebble — or "No Ideas but in Things"

Preparation

- ✔ Overhead transparencies of Nathan Bonyun's first draft of "Pebbles" and final draft of "Pebble"
- ✔ Trimmed photocopies of "The Rule of Write about *a* Pebble" for students to tape into their handbooks
- ✔ Wall poster of William Carlos Williams quotation
- ✔ Tape dispensers

What I Was Thinking This lesson grew out of a writing conference with Nathan, a seventh-grade poet. When I sat down beside him to confer about his latest effort, and read the first draft of "Pebbles," I had a familiar, sinking feeling. Here was another apparently sincere but ungrounded paean to something. It reminded me of several decades' worth of bad student poems with titles like "Dogs," "Fall," "Mothers," "Soccer," "Books," "Flowers," and "Rain." These poets wrote badly because they wrote broadly about general topics instead of specifically about concrete things.

By the time Nathan was my student, I knew to ask him *why*: "Nathan, *why* are you writing about this?" Nathan didn't disappoint me. He had an interesting intention, even if this draft didn't deliver on it. He said, "Because I think pebbles and blades of grass and small things we don't think much about and take for granted are neat."

I responded, "That's an interesting theme. Here's the problem: as a reader, I'm not convinced by this draft. I can't see or hear or feel these pebbles. I can't think about them as important, as mattering, the way you want me to. Do me a favor. Go outside, find a pebble you like in the driveway gravel, and write about *your* pebble."

Nathan's final version of his poem, "Pebble," is a small miracle. He presented the first draft and the final one on overhead transparencies in a mini-lesson, and the Rule of Write about *a* Pebble was born.

variety of names, but we're going to call it the Rule of Write about *a* Pebble.

A couple of years ago, Nathan Bonyun, a seventh grader, wrote this first draft of a poem about pebbles. Read along with me. . . .

Nathan said he decided to write about pebbles because "pebbles and blades of grass and small things we don't think much about and take for granted are neat." The problem with this draft is that a reader isn't convinced that each pebble is important, that each small thing *matters*, because we can't see or hear or feel these pebbles. The concrete, palpable details that would bring pebbles to life and give them the meaning Nathan intends aren't here.

So what did Nathan do next? He went outside, chose a pebble from the gravel in the driveway, brought it back into writing workshop, observed it with almost all his senses (not taste — Nathan did not put the pebble in his mouth), and wrote about his observations. I think the final version, "Pebble," is just an amazing poem. Read along with me. . . .

Hence the rule. We could call it the Rule of Concrete Details or the Rule of Writing from Firsthand Experience, but I like the Rule of Write about *a* Pebble because the name itself is concrete and evocative: it suggests *how* the rule means. Tape this definition of the rule into your handbooks, then read along with me. . . .

William Carlos Williams, famous to you as the author of "This Is Just to Say" and the poem about the red wheelbarrow, expressed the Rule of Write about *a* Pebble this way: "Say it, no ideas but in things." Let that be a mantra for the poems you write this year, as you try to follow the Rule of Write about *a* Pebble. Comments? Questions? Observations?

11

Overheads
Nathan's Bonyun's Drafts of "Pebbles" and "Pebble"

Pebbles
A minniral
a rock
a quiet inocent little thing
that comes in all shapes and sizes.

That you find on the beach
outdoors or on your floor

You think it's just another ordinary thing
but if you think hard it's something that's
special.

Where would all the beaches sand, and
gravel driveways be if it weren't
for that one tiny quiet inocent
ordinary pebble.

NATHAN'S FIRST DRAFT OF "PEBBLES"   LESSON 11

Reproducible
The Rule of Write about *a* Pebble

THE RULE OF WRITE ABOUT A PEBBLE

Don't write about a general idea or topic; write about a specific, observable person, place, occasion, time, object, animal, or experience. Its essence will lie in the sensory images the writer evokes: observed details of sight, sound, smell, touch, taste; and strong verbs that bring the details to life.

Don't write about _____ . Write about *a* _____ .
　　　　　　　　(pebbles)　　　　　　　　　(pebble)

Don't write about *fall*. Write about *this fall day.* Go to the window; go outside.

Don't write about *sunsets*. Write about *the amazing sunset you saw last night.*

Don't write about *dogs* or *kittens*. Observe and write about *your dog, your kitten.*

Don't write about *friendship*. Write about *your friend*, about what he or she does or has done to be a good friend to you.

Don't write about *love*. Write specifically about *someone or something* you love: these are the greatest love poems.

Don't write about *sailing*. Remember and write about *a time you went sailing.*

Don't write about *babies*. Write about *your baby sister, your baby cousin.*

Don't write about *reading*. Write about *your experience reading one book.*

Don't write about *pumpkins*. Write about *the pumpkin you carved last night, the pumpkin you grew from seeds, your family's jack-o'-lantern that the bad high school boys smashed on the road.*

THE RULE OF WRITE ABOUT A PEBBLE   LESSON 11

Narrative Leads

Preparation

- ✔ Students' copies of the individual novels they're currently enjoying during reading workshop
- ✔ Overhead transparency of "Colleen's Alternative Leads"
- ✔ Trimmed photocopies of "Narrative Leads" for students to tape into their handbooks
- ✔ Tape dispensers

12 LESSON

OCTOBER

What I Was Thinking

Good writers sweat their leads. The lead gives shape to the piece, to the experience of writing it, and to the experience of reading it. Beginning writers have particular trouble with story leads. Most often they begin at what they perceive as the beginning, which means they can provide anywhere from a paragraph to several pages of background information and previous developments before they enter the action of the story.

Instructing my kids not to start with background but, instead, to launch into the incident was not particularly useful advice because they didn't know *how* to launch. So I regrouped and spent an evening pulling novels off my shelves at home and investigating how authors of fiction and memoir entered their stories.

I found three basic types of narrative leads: action, dialogue, and reaction. My findings may be simplistic, lit-crit wise, but I can apply them pretty consistently, I can demonstrate them for kids, and kids can put them to good use as they consider and craft leads for their memoirs and short stories.

"If I had to name *the* most important part of a piece of prose writing, I'd have a hard time deciding between the lead and the conclusion. The lead is critical because it sets the tone, determines the content and direction of the piece, establishes the voice and verb tense, and beguiles—or doesn't—the potential reader. Most important, the lead grounds the writer. A good lead fuels writing: it makes the rest of the piece easier to write. The bad news is that a good lead can be hard to write.

Often, beginning storytellers have trouble starting their stories *in* the story. Instead, they produce a paragraph or two—or ten—of background information, before they feel justified in launching into the good parts. I think they see beginning at the beginning as being faithful to the experience. But story *readers* don't want a catalog of details; they don't need a timeline. They want an inviting story. I think there are three basic ways to start one.

Tape a copy of "Narrative Leads" onto the next clean page of your writing handbook, and I'll show you what I mean.

NARRATIVE LEADS

Typical

It was a day at the end of June. My mom, dad, brother, and I were at our camp on Rangeley Lake. We arrived the night before at 10:00, so it was dark when we got there and unpacked. We went straight to bed. The next morning, when I was eating breakfast, my dad started yelling for me from down at the dock at the top of his lungs. He said there was a car in the lake.

■ **Action: A Main Character Doing Something**

I gulped my milk, pushed away from the table, and bolted out of the kitchen, slamming the broken screen door behind me. I ran down to our dock as fast as my legs could carry me. My feet pounded on the old wood, hurrying me toward my dad's voice. "Scott!" he bellowed again.

"Coming, Dad!" I gasped. I couldn't see him yet—just the sails of the boats that had already put out into the lake for the day.

■ **Dialogue: A Character or Characters Speaking**

"Scott! Get down here on the double!" Dad bellowed. His voice sounded far away.

"Dad?" I hollered. "Where are you?" I squinted through the screen door but couldn't see him.

"I'm down on the dock. MOVE IT. You're not going to believe this," he replied.

■ **Reaction: A Character Thinking**

I couldn't imagine why my father was hollering for me at 7:00 in the morning. I thought fast about what I might have done to get him so riled. Had he found out about the way I talked to my mother the night before, when we got to camp and she asked me to help unpack the car? Did he discover the fishing reel I broke last week? Before I could consider a third possibility, Dad's voice shattered my thoughts.

"Scott! Move it! You're not going to believe this!"

When beginning a story, craft several leads. Experiment. A lead you love will fuel you as a writer. Choose the way in that makes you happiest; it will make your readers happy, too.

© 2002 by Nancie Atwell from *Lessons That Change Writers* (Portsmouth, NH: Heinemann)

NARRATIVE LEADS LESSON 12

Reproducible
Narrative Leads

Scott, a seventh grader, had a great story to tell about how a bunch of teenagers drove a car into Rangeley Lake, near his family's camp, and how he and his dad hauled it out the next day. Under the heading "Typical" you'll find Scott's first lead. Read along with me. . . .

Scott has almost written a newspaper lead here. He gives us the who-what-where-when-why information but not a voice, not a direction for the rest of the memoir, and not a sense of *him*, Scott, so we can see, feel, and participate in his memory.

So together Scott and I tried three new ways into his story. First we wrote a lead that jumped into the action of the story with the main character—Scott—*doing* something. Read along with me. . . .

Then we started again, this time with dialogue, with people in the scene speaking: a different kind of action. Read along. . . .

Finally, we went inside Scott's head and wrote his reactions. We started with a main character in mid-thought. Again, read with me. . . .

I think each of these three leads does what a lead should do. And having three alternatives helped Scott choose a starting point he liked and felt inspired to pursue, *vs.* the sinking feeling a writer gets when he tries to stick out a dull lead to the bitter end.

Overhead
Colleen Connell's
Alternative Leads

12

Do me a favor. Open the novel you're reading these days, skim the lead, and notice what the author did to launch the story. Did she move right into the action, begin with characters talking, or start the novel with a main character's thoughts about something? Let's go around the circle and describe the kinds of leads in our books. If you're not sure, read the lead aloud, and we'll help you decide. . . .

So, what practical use can you make of this information? I think you can write good leads deliberately. First, when beginning a memoir or a short story, craft several leads. Experiment with different ways in. A lead you love will fuel you as a writer. *Choose* the way in that makes you happiest; it will make your readers happy, too.

On the overhead, check out the transparency of Colleen's alternative leads for a memoir about Country Town, an imaginary village she and her friends created in the school's woods when they were first graders. She played around with leads—first reaction, then dialogue, then action—until she felt her beginning, until she found the way in that she was itching to pursue.

And let me end with a hint. You'd be amazed how often kids have already written their good lead, but it's buried in the draft. If you're working on a memoir right now and find it has one of those who-what-where-when-why leads, see if you can cut that opening paragraph—or even the first page. Is there a point where the action of the story begins? That's your lead. You can embed—weave in—the background information as the rest of the story unfolds.

Questions or comments about leads?

Good Titles

Preparation

✔ Overhead transparencies of Erin Witham's and Hallie Herz's poems

✔ Overhead transparencies of the lists of titles that Erin and Hallie brainstormed

✔ Overhead transparency headed "A Good Title . . ." for recording your students' ideas

What I Was Thinking A title is the smallest part of a piece of writing—just a few words at the top of the first page, easy to ignore or forget if it's not effective. But a good title is memorable, and it cues a reader. It prepares us, whets our appetites, opens a door into the world of the piece. Title writing is an accessible occasion for kids to practice craft—to generate options and make deliberate choices.

I teach about how to craft a title because beginning writers' titles are so often labels—"When I Tried Out for *The Wizard of Oz*," "The Day at the Common Ground Fair," "Going Bowling," "My Dog"—or clichés—"The Best Christmas Ever," "Fall Leaves," "The Winning Goal." It's fascinating to me how often a student's entrée into the notion of crafting writing will come via what would seem to be a minor act: finding the right few words of an effective title.

When Nora abandoned the working title of her first memoir, "The Bike Accident," in favor of "Uh-Oh," a title she found by brainstorming possibilities, something clicked for her as a writer: Nora could be funny, she could be intriguing, she could be deliberate.

> "Let's talk about titles: why they matter, what makes a good, memorable title, and how a writer develops one. We'll begin by looking at a poem by Erin Witham. Read along with me. . . .
>
> The first title, or working title, of this poem was "The Box in the

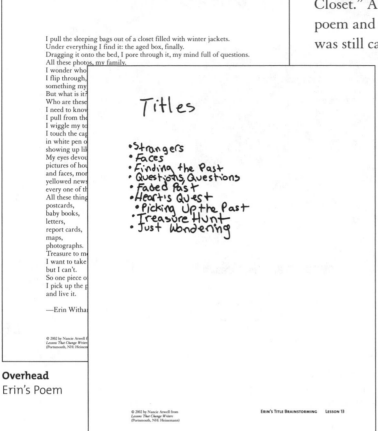

I pull the sleeping bags out of a closet filled with winter jackets.
Under everything I find it: the aged box, finally.
Dragging it onto the bed, I pore through it, my mind full of questions.
All these photos, my family.
I wonder who
I flip through,
something my
But what is it?
Who are these
I need to kno
I pull from the
I wiggle my t
I touch the ca
in white pen o
showing up li
My eyes devou
pictures of ho
and faces, mor
yellowed news
every one of th
All these thing
postcards,
baby books,
letters,
report cards,
maps,
photographs.
Treasure to m
I want to take
but I can't.
So one piece o
I pick up the
and live it.

—Erin Witha

© 2002 by Nancie Atwell f
Lessons That Change Writers
(Portsmouth, NH: Heinem

Overhead
Erin's Poem

Titles

- Strangers
- Faces
- Finding the Past
- Questions, Questions
- Faded Past
- Heart's Quest
- Picking Up the Past
- Treasure Hunt
- Just Wondering

© 2002 by Nancie Atwell from
Lessons That Change Writers
(Portsmouth, NH: Heinemann)

ERIN'S TITLE BRAINSTORMING   LESSON 13

Overhead
Erin's Title Brainstorming

13

Closet." After Erin revised and edited the poem and submitted it for teacher editing, she was still calling it "The Box in the Closet."

Now, that title does fit: the poem is, in fact, about a box of memorabilia Erin found in a closet at her house. But does it do for the poem what a good title should? Is it memorable? Distinct? Does it intrigue a reader—whet our appetites for the writing to come? And is it deliberate? Or is it a handy label that stuck?

After a teacher conference that nudged her to brainstorm possibilities for titles that both fit and invited, Erin came up with the list of possibilities on the overhead. You can see how she pushed her thinking, away from a handy label and toward a crafted, meaningful title. Erin stopped shortly after she reached

A Good Title . . .

- Fits the whole piece of writing

- Isn't a label or description (e.g., "When I Went Skiing for the First Time")

- Attracts a reader's attention—even creates a bit of mystery

- Is grounded in the piece; isn't too obscure

- Gives a hint or taste of the topic or theme to come

- Is memorable

- Generally doesn't come first: the author looks back on finished writing for a sense of the focus and *So what?* that emerged during drafting and revising

- Is a strong or beautiful combination of words and sounds

- Can replace a working title that the writer uses while the piece is in process

- Is often the result of brainstorming: of moving to a fresh piece of paper, removing the mental censors, and writing down as many possibilities as the writer's brain can devise

Figure 13-1 Nancie's Class's List of Characteristics of a Good Title

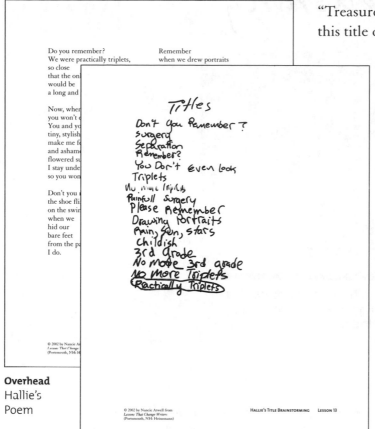

Overhead
Hallie's Poem

Overhead
Hallie's Title Brainstorming

"Treasure Hunt," when she recognized that this title did what she intended. As readers of poetry, what do you think of the difference between "The Box in the Closet" and "Treasure Hunt"? . . .

Let's take a look at another piece of student writing that was made stronger through a revised title. Here's a poem by seventh grader Hallie Herz. . . .

Hallie's initial title for this was "The Shoe Flinging Game." Now, that's an intriguing title, but does it fit what the whole poem is about? This is a seven-stanza poem that describes, from various angles, the friendship of a threesome and its ending; the shoe flinging game they played appears in just one stanza, and its function seems to be to illustrate the kinds of adventures the former friends enjoyed.

After a teacher conference, Hallie brainstormed, too. The overhead shows her list of possibilities. From among these, Hallie settled on "Practically Triplets." She said, "That's really the theme of the poem—we *were* almost as close as identical sisters."

I think we can draw on these examples to begin to describe what a good title does and how a writer gets there. Please write this heading on the next clean page of your writing handbook:

A Good Title

Then talk to me about what you observed in Erin's and Hallie's work with titles, plus your own theories and understandings. As I write your ideas and mine on the transparency, please copy them down into your writing handbook, so you'll have a record of our criteria and the procedures you can use to help you craft strong, meaningful titles [see Figure 13-1 for a sample class list].

Polishing

Preparation

✔ Overhead transparencies headed
"Polishing Prose" and "Polishing
Poems" for brainstorming with your
students

What I Was Thinking One fall evening, as I edited student writing, I was troubled by a host of minor and, to me, obvious problems that strangled the literary potential of the writing.

I found sentences with four *and*'s, rampant examples of ineffective repetition, small but crucial bits of information that had gone missing in action, way too many uses of *really* and *very*, and strings of participles that suffocated the actors and the action.

These pieces had been revised and edited, but they hadn't been *polished*. The writers hadn't yet taken that deliberate stance toward making their final products flow and satisfy as literature does. Rather than give the class a checklist of stylistic flaws to avoid in their writing, I asked them to become researchers of polishing and to generate two lists of techniques to focus on—one for prose and one for poems—with my collaboration along the way.

"We talked last month about the range of activities involved in the writing process. Can you remember what some of them are? . . .

Today I'd like to focus on a less familiar but crucial behavior of good writers. In my own writing, especially writing that's going public, there seems to me to be a stage that comes between revision and copyediting, one that I call *polishing*.

When I draft and revise, I work on figuring out what I think. I try to cast my thoughts as writing that's complete, logical, and convincing. Then, once the content is set, I polish. I approach my text as a reader of literature and ask, "Is it smooth? Does it flow? Is it beautiful, or at least clear and strong? Does it sound like language from a good book?"

For example, when I read over and study my final draft—when I slow down and attend to the sound, flow, and sense of it—I might hear an ineffective repetition. Do you know what that is? Here's an example, from the class highlights newsletter that I wrote last week for your parents:

> Our poems last week were about dogs. The dog poems we read were written by . . .

Finding and fixing ineffective repetition is one activity involved in the act of polishing writing. Other examples might be listening for too many *and then*'s, or, if there's dialogue, making sure it's written the way people would speak in real life. There are many ways to polish.

Please turn to the next clean page of your writing handbook and copy this heading at the top:

What I Do When I Polish My Writing

Then, underneath, write the subheadings *Prose* on one side and *Poetry* on the other.

Tonight for homework, under the two genre subheadings, list everything you can think of that you do when you polish your writing—when you step back and consider it as a reader of literature who wants to write literature. I've separated prose and poetry because although some approaches to polishing will find a place in both columns, other considerations will be particular to poems or prose. For example, when I polish poems, I pay attention to each line break; when I polish prose, I notice my paragraphs: are they too long and dense? Too short and choppy?

Have your daily writing folder open in front of you when you make your lists. It will help you be more specific and productive if you look at actual pieces of your writing as you conduct your research tonight.

Questions?

FOLLOW-UP LESSONS

[We discuss prose and poetry in separate lessons. After I walk the inside of the circle at the start of the next lesson, to be certain that every student wrote *something*, even if it was just the examples I'd given in class, I take suggestions from individuals and we create collaborative lists on the overhead.

We start with prose polishing. This is an occasion when I ask students *not* to copy my overhead notes into their writing handbooks. Instead, I gather their ideas and record them as fully and quickly as possible. Later, I use the overhead notes as the basis for an organized, typed list of the activities of prose polishers. I photocopy it, trim the copies with a paper cutter, and return them to students to be taped into their handbooks and annotated for homework. Then we do the same for poetry. (Figures 14-1 and 14-2 feature versions of the two lists.)

After students tape the lists into their handbooks, they take turns around the circle, each reading an item, and we have another quick discussion of anything that's not clear.

Then, for homework, I ask kids to highlight the areas they know they need to attend to. This activity begins the goal setting that takes place more formally at the end of each trimester, during writing self-evaluation. More important, it's an invitation to students whose writing verges on the literary to read their work with a more critical eye and ear.]

POLISHING PROSE

Either picture a reader or pretend you are the reader, read the writing, and ask:

- Does the writing flow and make sense like published text?
- Does the title fit the whole piece? Does it invite a reader?
- Is the lead inviting and purposeful? Does it set the tone for the rest of the piece?
- Does the conclusion resonate and satisfy? Is it deliberate?
- Is there any information left out that a reader needs to know?
- Is there any information that should be cut, because it isn't pertinent or doesn't move the piece along?
- Does the writing convey a *So what?* to the reader?
- Are there enough thoughts and feelings to take a reader into your own or your main character's heart and mind?
- Is the writing visual? Can a reader see the story happening?
- Does the dialogue sound the way the people would talk? Does it show what they're like?
- Is there a balance of dialogue and narrative? Does the dialogue ever overwhelm the narrative?

- Have you said something more than once?
- Are there places where dashes, colons, or semicolons might give the writing more voice?
- Have you listened for ineffective repetitions?
- Is the pace of the action effective—not too fast or too slow?
- Is the verb tense consistent, past *or* present?
- Are there participles that can be converted to active constructions?
- Are the verbs and nouns strong? Can a reader see, hear, feel, taste the writing?
- Can you get rid of any adverbs (*-ly* words) or adjectives?
- Have you cut Ken Macrorie's bad words: *really, very, kind of, sort of, just*?
- Have you listened for too many *and*'s and *then*'s?
- Do the paragraphs break where they need to? Are any too long and tiring? Too short and choppy?
- Have you read the writing over and over again to yourself and listened to it with a critic's ear?

Figure 14-1 Nancie's Class's List of Considerations in Polishing Prose

POLISHING POEMS

Either picture a reader or pretend you are the reader, read the writing, and ask:

- Does everything in the poem fit and belong here?

- Does the title fit the whole poem? Does it invite a reader?

- Have you begun the poem *inside* the subject or experience?

- Does the conclusion resonate and satisfy? Is it deliberate?

- Is there a human presence, an *I* or *he* or *you*?

- Is there a *So what?*

- Can a smart, anonymous reader get your poem?

- Are the shape of the poem and the use of white space satisfying or stimulating to the eye?

- Do the lines break at points that support the sound and meaning of the poem: ideas, phrases, sentences, meaning chunks? Are significant words or combinations of words emphasized by putting white space around them? Does each line end with a strong word (e.g., a verb or noun *vs.* an article, preposition, or conjunction)?

- Are the stanza breaks effective, deliberate, and helpful to a reader?

- Did you stick with the free-verse form you invented and use it consistently?

- Is the language sensory? Can a reader feel it, taste it, see it, hear it?

- Is the language nonpompous: the kinds of words people might use in a reasonably articulate conversation?

- Is the language cut to the bone? Are unnecessary words deleted?

- Is each word the right one?

- Is every verb strong and imageful (*vs.* forms of *go, come, make, take, do, get, have*)?

- Are there participles that can be converted to active constructions?

- Does the verb tense stay consistent, past *or* present?

- Have you avoided the overuse of commas at line breaks?

- Have you listened for ineffective repetitions?

- Is there too much or too little coded language?

- Have you used any poetic techniques (e.g., alliteration, personification, metaphor, simile, effective repetition)?

- If there is figurative language, do the metaphors match the tone or feeling of the poem?

- Have you read the poem over and over again to yourself?

14

Figure 14-2 Nancie's Class's List of Considerations in Polishing Poems

Final Copies: What Readers Need

Preparation

✔ Trimmed photocopies of "Considerations for Final Copies" for students to tape into their handbooks
✔ Tape dispensers

What I Was Thinking The success of writing workshop is predicated on students understanding that they're writing *to be read*. If the only thing that happens to finished writing is that it's stuck in a folder until June, when we send the whole mass of it home, students won't invest in crafting their writing to meet and communicate their intentions, and they won't learn how to meet a reader's needs for conventional text. Because I intend that every piece of writing that students finish—that is, writing that's edited, final-copied, and proofread—goes public in some way, *is read*, I teach what finished texts should look like and why.

Adherence to conventions isn't a goal for its own sake. *Readers* need texts to be conventional in format, spelling, and usage, so they can decode them. My kids' good writing deserves to be read and respected, so I devote a lesson each year to teaching what I know about producing a final copy that's easy and inviting to read.

> "Many of you are editing your first pieces of writing of the school year, which means that by the end of the week, I'll have copyedited these and returned them to you, for you to type or handwrite as final copies. The final copy is a big step. After all the generating, thinking, crafting, and polishing of the writing process, you're finally getting your writing ready to be read.

Reproducible
Considerations for
Final Copies

Today's lesson is about what readers' eyes expect. The goal is for your writing to be read and appreciated, not cast aside because it doesn't look right or dismissed as kids' stuff.

Please take a copy of "Considerations for Final Copies," circulate the tape dispensers, and attach the list to the next clean page of your writing handbook. Then follow along with me. . . .

Every idea on this list is supported by a strong, important reason, but the bottom line is expressed in number ten. After June, I won't be around to assist you in proofreading and correcting final copies. These are habits of mind and practice you need to work hard to develop now, in anticipation of the time when you're on your own and a reader might judge you by the conventionality of the texts you produce. I know you won't want to appear arrogant—like you don't care—or ignorant, as if you don't know better.

So please take this list home tonight, read through it again, and highlight it: which of these considerations do you need to devote special attention to, to help you become a conscientious final-copier and proofreader? We'll talk about your goals tomorrow, around the circle.

Comments or questions?

Thinking on Paper: Planning Sheets

Preparation

✔ Overhead transparencies of "Anne's Entry Points" and "Anne's Planning Sheet" for her memoir

✔ Overhead transparencies of "Krystin's Draft," "Krystin's Planning Sheet," and "Krystin's Final Draft" for Krystin Benton's book review

✔ Optional: Overhead transparency of "Meg's Plan and Poem" by Meg Benton

✔ Optional: Overhead transparency of "Tyler's Planning Sheet" for Tyler Cadman's short story "Game Life," which appears in Appendix B

What I Was Thinking I didn't begin to write in a serious way until I was almost thirty and a graduate student at Bread Loaf. Writing still doesn't come easily to me; I'm pretty confident it never will. But over twenty years of practicing I've learned ways to make the time at my writing desk more productive. My own quirks of schedule (these days, if I'm writing, it's between the hours of 5:30 and 7:00 A.M.), of drafting and revising (I write longhand, double-spaced, on white, narrow-ruled pads), and of planning are what make my writing possible.

Planning is key. Every serious writer I know acknowledges the joke of the topic outline as a way of forecasting a piece of writing. Everything we've learned about writing-as-process over the past forty years tells us that writing is an act of creating meaning. Good writers consistently say that they don't know everything they'll write before they write it.

At the same time, when an idea for my writing strikes, if I don't write it down somewhere, I've lost it. And at points in a draft where I'm stuck or can't see my direction, it helps me to put the draft aside, move to a clean pad of paper, and doodle with words. I've learned how to think on paper—to use writing to plan and generate writing.

In writing conferences with "blocked" students, I teach them how they can use a planning sheet to get themselves moving as writers. Later, in mini-lessons, the writers bring their plans and drafts to the rest of the class on overhead transparencies and demonstrate the benefits of thinking and planning by writing. Beginning writers, struggling to draft and craft at the same time, are relieved to be able to break down the task, focus on one problem at a time, and generate concrete solutions and ideas.

This is a strategy I revisit. As I see students creating and using different kinds of plans for different genres of writing, I reproduce their work on transparencies and take it to the group, so students will have opportunities to consider different planning strategies, experiment with them, and internalize the notion of using writing to generate writing.

When I hear writers complain about writer's block, I want to take them aside and whisper, "Pssst. Listen. Have you ever heard of a planning sheet? It gets me unstuck every time." There's nothing more effective, when I don't know how or what to write, than to doodle with words—to use writing as an aid to get myself writing again. Let me show you what I mean.

Anne was trying to begin her first memoir of seventh grade. She decided to write about a family card game at her grandmother's house, a ritual that she felt would show what her extended family is like when they're together. By the time I dropped by her desk for a conference, Anne had been staring into space over a blank piece of paper for a good twenty minutes. I asked, "What are you doing?" and she answered, "I'm trying to think of a way to begin this memoir." She was practically paralyzed—after all, this was her *first memoir of seventh grade*. You know that feeling.

I said, "Sitting here staring into space and thinking about the perfect lead isn't a productive strategy. But thinking *on paper* about the perfect lead will give you some concrete directions and, even better, a chance to make choices from among concrete options.

"Here's what I do when I'm stuck. I'd like you to try this strategy. Make a list of all the points in your experience at your grandmother's when you could enter the action of the story. In other words, list all the possible leads. Brainstorm. Go for it.

"Then comes the fun part. You get to choose, from among the possibilities on your list, the entry point you like best, the one that would be the most fun to pursue as a writer." So, as you can see from the overhead, Anne made a list of potential entry points, then decided to begin the memoir with her grandmother trying to lure reluctant grandchildren to the card table.

Overhead
Anne's Entry Points

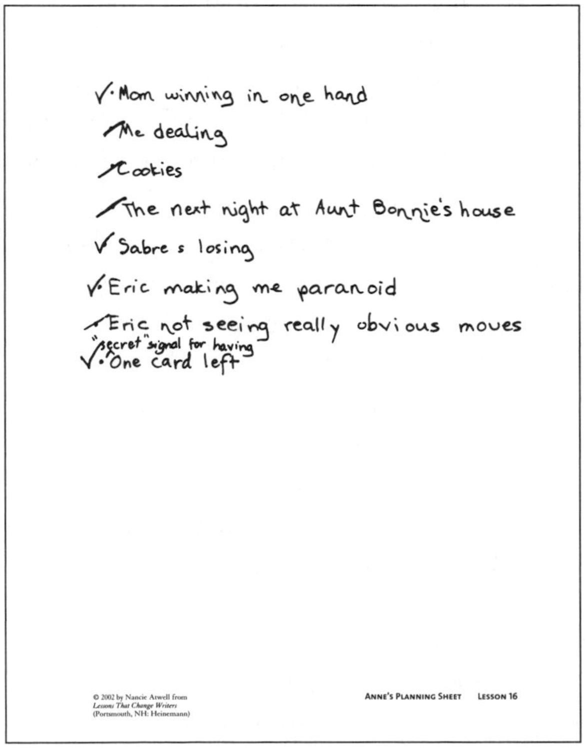

The handwritten content of the first overhead reads:

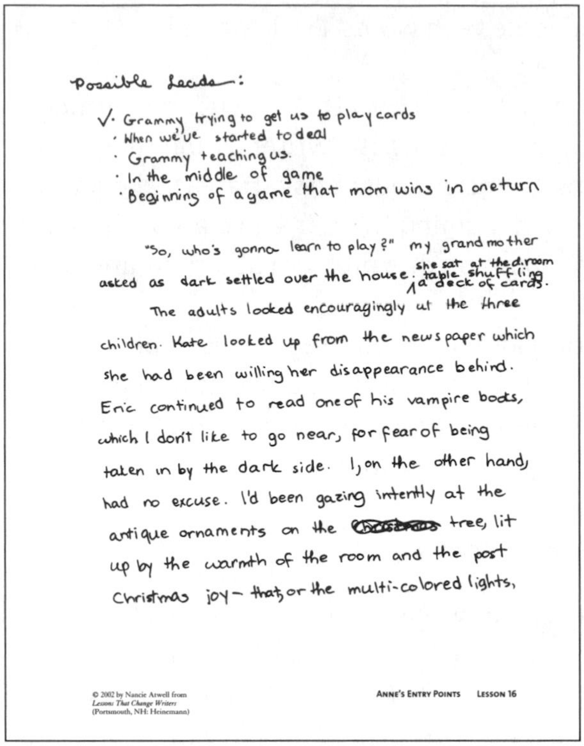

Possible Leads:

- ✓ Grammy trying to get us to play cards
- When we've started to deal
- Grammy teaching us.
- In the middle of game
- Beginning of a game that mom wins in one turn

"So, who's gonna learn to play?" my grandmother asked as dark settled over the house. she sat at the d.room table shuffling a deck of cards.
The adults looked encouragingly at the three children. Kate looked up from the newspaper which she had been willing her disappearance behind. Eric continued to read one of his vampire books, which I don't like to go near, for fear of being taken in by the dark side. I, on the other hand, had no excuse. I'd been gazing intently at the antique ornaments on the ~~Christmas~~ tree, lit up by the warmth of the room and the post Christmas joy— that, or the multi-colored lights,

© 2002 by Nancie Atwell from
Lessons That Change Writers
(Portsmouth, NH: Heinemann)
ANNE'S ENTRY POINTS LESSON 16

Overhead
Anne's Planning Sheet

The handwritten content of the second overhead reads:

- ✓ Mom winning in one hand
- ✓ Me dealing
- ✓ Cookies
- ✓ The next night at Aunt Bonnie's house
- ✓ Sabres losing
- ✓ Eric making me paranoid
- ✓ Eric not seeing really obvious moves
  "secret" signal for having
- ✓ One card left

© 2002 by Nancie Atwell from
Lessons That Change Writers
(Portsmouth, NH: Heinemann)
ANNE'S PLANNING SHEET LESSON 16

This process took her about five minutes, as opposed to twenty minutes or more of staring into space and getting nowhere. So please don't you ever sit there hoping to imagine the perfect lead. Grab a fresh sheet of paper and use it to think on paper: to generate concrete options that you can name, touch, and piggyback off in the form of new ideas.

Back to Anne. She drafted away on her memoir for three and a half pages, and then it happened: stuck again. She reached a point in the narrative where there were too many things that could happen next. When I sat next to her to confer, Anne was staring off into the distance again.

After she explained her problem—that she couldn't decide where she wanted to go next with the action of the narrative—I asked her to think on paper again: to make a list on a separate sheet of paper of all the potential incidents, then to work with the one that fit best and satisfied her most. The next overhead shows Anne's planning sheet. She ended up using it as an outline in concluding her memoir, checking off events or crossing them out as she wrote. Anne gave the final version to her grandmother as a Mother's Day present.

From then on, Anne had a strategy she could use to get unstuck: isolate a problem, use writing to generate and consider options, and work toward a solution. It can be overwhelming for young writers to draft data *and* craft data at the same time. So when you feel stuck or uncertain or overwhelmed, don't think in thin air. Instead, it's helpful and productive to think on paper: clear your desk of your manuscript, grab a fresh sheet of paper, and focus like a laser beam on the writing problem.

Here's another variation of a planning sheet. This is the first draft of Krystin's review of Stephen King's novel *Carrie*. When I was circulating for conferences that day, the doodle

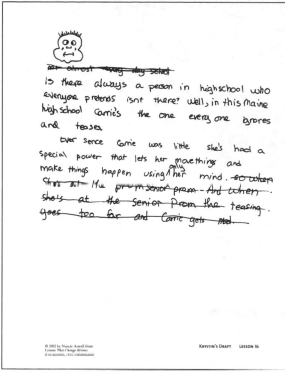

Overhead
Krystin's Draft

· EX: Ice
· she does
· she get
  the b
  girls
  and s
· when
  like I
  that t
  happe
· she's
  and
  start
· King
  a sm
· keeps
  until
  nightm
  she w

Carrie   Signet, 1975, 245 pp., $6.99
Stephen King   ISBN 0-451-15744-3

    Is there a person in every high school who the kids pretend isn't
there? Well, in this Maine high school, Carrie is the one everybody
ignores and teases.
    What they don't know is that Carrie has had a special power,
telekinesis, ever since she was born. If she keeps her anger bottled up too
long, it will explode in her mind and something will happen. For
example, when Carrie was three and got in a fight with her mother, she
made ice and rocks fall from a clear blue sky.
    While Carrie is attending her senior prom, the others tease her for
the last time, and the rest of the evening turns into one unimaginable
nightmare.
    When I read *Carrie* by Stephen King, I felt like I was right there
watching all this happen. This was King's first published novel, written
when he was a high school English teacher in small town Maine. It
shows he knows what kids can be like, and that right from the
beginning of his career he wove together great characters and horror
plots.

Krystin Benton, Grade 8
Center for Teaching and Learning, Edgecomb, Maine

Overheads
Krystin Benton's Planning
Sheet List and Final Draft

alone told me that Krystin was a stuck writer. I asked, "Let me guess. Are you trying to draft ideas for this review *and* craft them as beautiful, organized prose at the same time?"

Yep. I gave Krystin a blank sheet of paper and said, "Remember Anne's mini-lesson? You can brainstorm a plan of the things you might say about *Carrie* and King, then work from your planning sheet to help you pull together a first draft. Clear the decks, mentally and physically. Put your draft aside, and this time doodle with words."

Which she did. Now she could produce—and later she could weave the knowledge she found inside herself into a review. Krystin's final version was published in the NCTE journal *Voices from the Middle*.

Let me say it again. If you want to think productively, think on paper. Whether you call it a planning sheet, a brainstorm, an outline, you name it, it's the best way I know to get over a hurdle as a writer, not to mention work from a quantity of ideas, as opposed to the one idea that maybe might occur to you if you stared into space for long enough. And it's a great place to put new ideas into storage, until you're ready to use them.

So don't think in air. Think on paper. Throughout this year of writing workshop I want you to find ways to make the idea of this lesson work for you as a writer.

Comments? Observations? Questions?

[See the reproducible, "Tyler's Planning Sheet," for an example of a plan for a short story to share with your students when the time is right.]

16

Can a Reader See It, Hear It, Feel It?

Preparation

- ✔ Three books for reading aloud: *The Relatives Came* by Cynthia Rylant (1985), *Twilight Comes Twice* by Ralph Fletcher (1997), and *A Christmas Memory* by Truman Capote (1956)
- ✔ Overhead transparencies of Meg Benton's first and final drafts of the poem "Dragons"
- ✔ A packet for each student of photocopies of Tyler Reny's "Surprised by Blue," Colleen Connell's "At Pemaquid," Erin Witham's "Jumping in Hay," Phaelon O'Donnell's "Resting on Oak," Jed Chambers' "Navy," and Meg Benton's "Polished to Perfection"

What I Was Thinking

Many of the lessons about principles of writing perform double duty. They introduce the whole group to ways of thinking about writing that create a shared knowledge about technique, and they provide a foundation for a year's worth of writing conferences that cut to the chase. The three questions I pose in this lesson are questions I ask of writers, and they learn to ask of their own writing, throughout the school year.

The questions represent another way of asking writers for sensory detail. My straight-out requests to students to add sensory details led them to pile on minutiae and cliché. The grandmothers became gray-haired. The apples were red and juicy. The dogs wagged their tails, and the girls laughed happily.

But through wondering if a reader can see it, hear it, and feel it, writers call up their own sense memories as they slow down their writing and try to see it, hear it, and feel it again.

They move beyond cliché to get at the heart of an experience, and their memoirs and poems become richer—more conscious, perceptive, and literary.

"For the next couple of days I want us to get sensory. In the poems, memoirs, and fiction I love best, something happens inside of me as I read. The words create sensations as if *I* am seeing, hearing, and feeling the experience. It's a word picture, but more. The writing both goes inside me *and* takes me outside of myself. It's one of my favorite sensations as a reader, when I can see the writing, hear the writing, feel the writing.

Cynthia Rylant is one of my favorite authors for young adults and children. *But I'll Be Back Again*, her book about her childhood and adolescence, is a model of memoir writing—the sensory details and the *So whats?* are stunning. And many of her books for children are sensory poems—so vivid and descriptive that *I am there* when I read them. Sit back for a moment and savor one of Rylant's most sensory poems, *The Relatives Came*, as well as a gorgeous sensory poem by Ralph Fletcher titled *Twilight Comes Twice*. As I read aloud, listen for the lines you can see, hear, and feel, and then we'll talk about them. . . .

Tonight for homework I'd like you to read a small collection of poems by seventh and eighth graders. These poets used sensory details to bring their experiences to life for themselves and their readers. Your job, as you read the poems, is to underline any line you can *see*, *hear*, or *feel*. We'll talk about your annotations tomorrow.

Questions?

FOLLOW-UP LESSONS

[The next day I invite the group to discuss the student poems and the lines they marked. Then I show the overhead transparencies of Meg's first draft and fourth draft of "Dragons," and we discuss the differences in language, imagery, and sensory details.

The background story on "Dragons" is that Meg wrote it as a birthday present for her friend Erin. It's about a game they played as kindergartners, when they pretended they were dragons, flying down the steep hill behind the school. In conferences with Meg about her poem, I commented, "I can't see it or hear it, Meg. I can't feel it." These three criteria became her yardstick in measuring each draft of the poem as she moved it toward literature and a gift worthy of Erin.

Another appropriate follow-up is a read-aloud and discussion of Truman Capote's memoir *A Christmas Memory*, one of the most sensory pieces of American prose ever.

Finally, I ask students to record the three questions in their handbooks: Can a reader see it? Hear it? Feel it? I tell them, "I'll let you know when I can't see it, hear it, or feel it when I confer with you. And these are three questions you must learn to ask yourselves as you draft and revise, if you're to bring your writing to life for your readers."]

17

Overhead
Meg's Benton's First
and Final Drafts of
"Dragons"

A Movie behind Your Eyelids

Preparation

- ✔ Overhead transparency of "Make a Movie behind Your Eyelids"
- ✔ Overhead transparency of "Leah: Version 1," a scene from one of my short stories
- ✔ Photocopies of "Leah: Version 2," about the same scene
- ✔ Photocopies of Versions 1 and 2 of Siobhan Anderson's memoir "The Moon, My Mother, and I"

LESSON 18

DECEMBER

What I Was Thinking   A consistent problem in student narrative, both memoir and short fiction, is action that's described too thinly for the story and its people to come to life. Writers speed through the plot and the moments when characters and crises might become well-developed and the prose might take on the qualities of literature.

I've approached the problem of fast, thin narrative in different ways over the years, but the best solution, so far, is a lesson that asks storytellers to slow down the pace of the action by imagining it first in their mind's eye—to make a private movie of an important moment in a narrative, then to open their eyes and bring the moment to life on the page with all the rich detail they envisioned. Erin said, "It's such a simple technique, but now I use it all the time, even in poems about my experiences. It helps me concentrate and puts me *there*."

> We've already talked a lot this year about the importance of sensory writing—of prose and poetry that a reader can see, hear, feel, even smell and taste. Today I'm going to focus on sight and sound, on how writers can use descriptions of visual and auditory details to slow down their stories and bring them to life for their readers.

Overhead
Leah: Version 1

LEAH: VERSION 2

Leah brushed her bangs away from her forehead one last time and checked her watch. She was going to be late for homeroom. Where were they? She clutched her books against her sweatshirt and tapped her foot. "C'mon, guys," she muttered. When the first warning bell rang, she sighed. Were they both out sick? Crud. She looked up and down the sidewalk one last time, then headed for homeroom, disappointed that the plans she had hatched that morning wouldn't come true. School felt totally different when her friends weren't there, like a color movie shown in black and white.

Leah made it to homeroom just as the second bell—the real one—sounded. The first thing she saw as she slipped through the door were Marty and Dee, sitting next to each other in the front row. They were whispering with their heads together and didn't look up when she came in. She felt surprised, then hurt.

"Take a seat, Leah," Mrs. Orr said when the bell stopped ringing. "You're late. Well, almost late." Marty and Dee still hadn't looked her way, but Leah could see that Marty was blushing as she stumbled to an empty desk two rows behind them. She felt her own face getting hot. Were they ganging up on her about something? Great.

She leaned forward and whispered, "You guys, where were you? I was waiting. Guys? *Guys?*"

Instead of answering, they kept their heads together, Marty's red hair against Dee's blonde. "You *guys,*" she demanded, not bothering to whisper this time. "What's going on?" The back of Marty's neck glowed bright red, but still she didn't turn around.

"That's enough, Leah," Mrs. Orr warned. "It's almost time for announcements."

She sat back in a daze. Now Marty and Dee broke apart and sat rigidly, eyes facing front, as the voice of the vice-principal boomed from the intercom. They were acting as if she were invisible. She tried to remember Friday, the last time they had been together. What had she done to make them so mad at her?

"Marty," she whispered, when the intercom clicked off. "What's wrong?" The only reply was the straight line of Marty's back. Suddenly Leah realized that the boys on either side of her were watching this show with interest. She opened her math book and pretended to read. She could feel tears starting

© 2002 by Nancie Atwell from
Lessons That Change Writers
(Portsmouth, NH: Heinemann)

LEAH: VERSION 2 – PAGE 1   LESSON 18

Reproducibles
Leah: Version 2

As readers, many of you have made comments to me about the novels you're enjoying this year along the lines of "It seemed as if it was really happening," or "I felt like I was there in the story, seeing and hearing what the main character was seeing and hearing," or even "I forgot I was reading a story, it seemed so real." I think these are the moments we love best as story readers, when the prose is so thick with good, telling details that the writing disappears and we revel in the experience of a character.

This level of richness in story writing isn't accidental. The author has slowed down the important moments in a story by describing them fully—inventing or remembering the details of sights and sounds that will make the story feel real to a reader.

Every day, at the end of the status-of-the-class conference, I enjoin you to *make literature*. I think one way to make your stories literary is to work on crafting descriptions of sights and sounds. And a way to do that is to close your eyes, make a private movie of your story behind your eyelids, then use language to capture what you saw and heard in your mind's eye.

Let me show you what I mean. The overhead shows what I'd call a chunk of thin, dead description. It's from a draft of my short story about Leah, a seventh-grade girl who arrives at school one morning to discover she's been dropped by her circle of friends. This paragraph is supposed to describe the initial moments of the rejection. Follow along with me as I read it aloud, and see if it's possible to put yourself into this story, with Leah, as you do when you lose yourself in a good novel or memoir. . . .

Could anyone see or hear any of this? Do you understand what I mean by thin, dead description? Things *are* happening here: Leah gets to school and can't find her friends, they ignore her, she finds a mean note, she goes to the bathroom and cries. But none of it is visual or auditory. It just lies there, dead on the page, too fast and too thin to take on a life of its own.

Here's a paper copy of another version of Leah's moment of crisis. It's a fourth-draft attempt of the same incident. But this version depended, heavily, on the approach I'm going to teach you today. As I drafted, revised, and polished, I continuously closed my eyes, concentrated hard, and imagined the action, one frame at a time, like a movie behind my eyelids. Read along with me again and, again, try to put yourself into the story with Leah. . . .

Were you able to enter this story? Could you see and hear it in your mind's eye? . . . It covers the same plot points as the first version, but what are the differences, in terms of the writing? Please go back into the text on your own for two minutes, find and mark sentences you can see or hear, and then let's talk about them. . . .

It *is* significantly slowed down—and detailed, visual, and auditory. It's just better writing, period. I'd like you to try this technique—to make a private movie—as you compose your own memoirs and short stories.

Turn to the next clean page of your writing handbook and write this heading:

Make a Movie behind Your Eyelids

Then copy my notes from the transparency into your handbook:

This is a technique for slowing down important parts of narratives and creating images that readers can see and sounds they can hear. How to do it:

1. Close your eyes. *Concentrate.*
2. Imagine the scene you're going to write as if you're making a private movie in your mind. See and hear yourself and/or the characters in action.
3. Open your eyes and try to capture on the page exactly what happened in your mental movie—the small details of sight and sound, one frame at a time.

Overhead
Make a Movie behind
Your Eyelids

This is hard work. This level of concentration will probably make your brain hurt—I know it does mine. But the payoff is guaranteed. When *I* can see and hear the action in one of my stories, I'm more than halfway toward the goal of *my reader* being able to see and hear it, too.

This is a technique for drafting *and* revising *and* polishing. For example, I'll close my eyes and make a movie when I want to capture a first draft of the basics of what I experienced, if it's a memoir, or, if it's a short story, what my character is experiencing. Sometimes I revise by closing my eyes, then trying to see and hear more and better details and dialogue. And I always polish by closing my eyes, envisioning the action again, and checking it against the verbs in the text: does the language I used to evoke the action measure up to the images I saw in my movie?

Try this. I promise no one in the workshop will look at you funny if we notice you sitting over a draft with your eyes squeezed shut. And I promise to do everything I can to ensure that the workshop is quiet enough that you won't be distracted from making your movie.

Comments or questions?

FOLLOW-UP LESSON

[I conduct the same exercise, asking the group to contrast a *before* and an *after*, but this time with a memoir, Siobhan's "The Moon, My Mother, and I." The first version, composed badly on purpose, is a fast, thin account of an experience with her mom that doesn't begin to get at what it was like for Siobhan or why she was writing about it. The second version draws richly and effectively on the frames of the movies Siobhan created, in her memory and her imagination, over a week and a half of drafting, revising, and polishing her memoir.

Lessons 17 and 18 are essential to me in my conferences with individual writers. "I can't see or hear this. Can you make the movie?" has become my shorthand way of helping writers know when they need to slow down the pace of their narratives and provide the level of sensory detail that readers crave.]

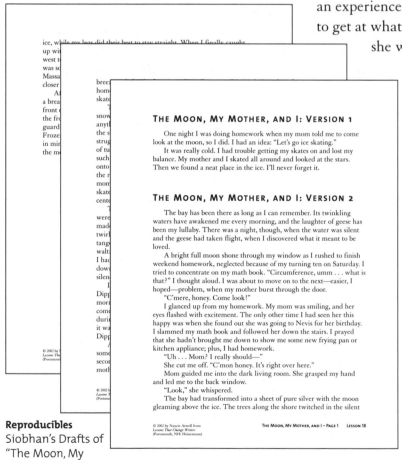

Reproducibles
Siobhan's Drafts of "The Moon, My Mother, and I"

THE MOON, MY MOTHER, AND I: VERSION 1

One night I was doing homework when my mom told me to come look at the moon, so I did. I had an idea: "Let's go ice skating."

It was really cold. I had trouble getting my skates on and lost my balance. My mother and I skated all around and looked at the stars. Then we found a neat place in the ice. I'll never forget it.

THE MOON, MY MOTHER, AND I: VERSION 2

The bay has been there as long as I can remember. Its twinkling waters have awakened me every morning, and the laughter of geese has been my lullaby. There was a night, though, when the water was silent and the geese had taken flight, when I discovered what it meant to be loved.

A bright full moon shone through my window as I rushed to finish weekend homework, neglected because of my turning ten on Saturday. I tried to concentrate on my math book. "Circumference, umm . . . what is that?" I thought aloud. I was about to move on to the next—easier, I hoped—problem, when my mother burst through the door.

"C'mere, honey. Come look!"

I glanced up from my homework. My mom was smiling, and her eyes flashed with excitement. The only other time I had seen her this happy was when she found out she was going to Nevis for her birthday. I slammed my math book and followed her down the stairs. I prayed that she hadn't brought me down to show me some new frying pan or kitchen appliance; plus, I had homework.

"Uh . . . Mom? I really should—"

She cut me off. "C'mon honey. It's right over here."

Mom guided me into the dark living room. She grasped my hand and led me to the back window.

"Look," she whispered.

The bay had transformed into a sheet of pure silver with the moon gleaming above the ice. The trees along the shore twitched in the silent

© 2002 by Nancie Atwell from *Lessons That Change Writers* (Portsmouth, NH: Heinemann)   THE MOON, MY MOTHER, AND I – PAGE 1   LESSON 18

18

72

How a Thesaurus Can Help

Preparation

✔ Overhead transparency headed "When to Use a Thesaurus . . ." for brainstorming with your students

✔ Overhead transparency of "Verbs to Beware Of"

✔ Overhead transparencies of Jimmy's thesaurus work and the lines from Annie's poem and their revisions

✔ Photocopies of Marnie Briggs's poem "The Pond"

LESSON 19

DECEMBER

What I Was Thinking For years I avoided teaching about the thesaurus as a writing reference; there was a time when I wouldn't allow one in my classroom. I was haunted by my own experience as a secondary student, at the mercy of English teachers who sent me to a thesaurus to beef up my vocabulary—to find difficult, poly-syllabic words, usually adjectives and adverbs, in an attempt to produce writing that sounded scholarly and sophisticated.

It took me a long time to understand that a polysyllabic vocabulary, not to mention the long-winded, passive sentences that were also *de rigueur* back then, served mostly as a smoke screen to hide behind in addressing topics I didn't know about or care about. After working so hard to try to unclutter my writing voice and find my intentions as a writer, I was loath to introduce a resource that might put my students' voices and intentions at risk.

But as I continued to write and to try to move my prose and poetry toward something like literature, I found myself turning to a thesaurus at specific times and places for specific kinds of assistance. And it was valuable assistance. Consulting a thesaurus inspired diction that was more vivid, sensory, and imageful. It allowed me to cut the adverbs and adjectives that clut-tered my drafts. And it helped the language of my prose and poetry become more simple, direct, and active.

My lessons about the thesaurus focus on how it can help a writer produce stronger, clearer language. But along the way, I also warn students that a thesaurus can lead a writer to language that's weak, pompous, or obscure.

The thesaurus I teach from and make available to kids, in the form of multiple, battered paperbacks, is *Roget's New Pocket Thesaurus in Dictionary Form*, edited by Norman Lewis; the most recent copyright date on any of my classroom copies is 1972. I love this thesaurus, and I patrol used bookstores and yard sales in search of additional copies. For my money it's the most complete, it offers better cross-references, and its individual entries are organized and formatted in a practical, convenient way.

"You consult a dictionary when you already know a word, but you need its spelling or definition. You consult a thesaurus when you know the definition, or at least the general idea, and you need a specific word for it.

Peter Mark Roget collected his first *Thesaurus of English Words and Phrases* in 1852. He was a medical doctor and, in his spare time, a *lexicographer*: that's a writer of dictionaries. The most famous lexicographer of American English is also the man who's credited for being the first. Who was he? . . . Right, Noah Webster. He assembled the first American dictionary, or "speller," in the 1780's.

Anyway, back to the thesaurus. How many of you have ever used one? . . . When do you use one? Brainstorm with me on the overhead. You make a record in your handbooks as I write down your ideas and my own. The heading will be

When to Use a Thesaurus . . .

Ready? . . . [See Figure 19-1 for a sample list from one of my classes.]

You may have noticed that I didn't include on our list "To find big, obscure words with lots of syllables to impress readers with my large vocabulary and obvious intelligence." I'll ask you *never* to use a thesaurus to find fancy words and *never* to use a word from the thesaurus when you're not one hundred percent clear on and comfortable with its meaning. The language of good writing is simple, direct, imageful, and active.

I'm going to ask you to focus your use of the thesaurus on verbs. E. B. White, the great prose stylist and advisor to writers, argues that it's "nouns and verbs, not their assistants, that give good writing its toughness and color." I'm convinced that almost nothing will serve your writing better than paying attention to verbs: shoot for verbs that are imageful and sensory; watch out for limp, colorless verbs; and cut adverbs whenever possible.

When to Use a Thesaurus

- To nudge my memory: when the right word is on the tip of my tongue

- To remind me of all the choices and not to settle for the first word that comes to mind

- To get rid of an ineffective repetition: to find another word for a word that shows up too often and sounds awkward

- To find out that I don't have the right word to begin with, as I compare it to its synonyms

- To discover that I don't know what I'm talking about yet: finding the right word isn't my problem; making my meaning clear is

- To take a break from drafting and creating to let another part of my brain work on the writing problem while I hunt for synonyms

- To find strong, precise verbs that a reader can see, hear, and feel—and that allow me to get rid of adverbs

- To find strong, precise nouns that cut to the chase and that a reader can see, hear, and feel

- To find adjectives that say what I mean

Figure 19-1 Nancie's Class's List of Times to Use a Thesaurus

Please write this heading on the next clean page of your handbook:

Verbs to Beware Of

There are the verbs I watch out for in my writing, both as I'm drafting and as I polish. Ready?

VERBS TO BEWARE OF

Forms of:

1. come
2. do
3. get
4. give
5. go
6. have
7. like
8. make
9. take
10. to be (is, are, was, were, etc.)

© 2002 by Nancie Atwell from
Lessons That Change Writers
(Portsmouth, NH: Heinemann)

VERBS TO BEWARE OF   LESSON 19

Overhead
Verbs to Beware Of

Forms of:

come	*like*
do	*make*
give	*take*
get	*to be* (is, are, was,
go	were, etc.)
have	

So what's wrong with these words? . . . You can't see them, feel them, hear them, taste them. They get the job done, but that's about it. They're not precise. They don't *activate* the writing.

Let me show you how a thesaurus can help you activate a sentence. Jimmy had drafted a memoir about a time in preschool when he snuck a snake into his bag and showed it off on the playground. The overhead shows his sentence, "I *had* the snake in my hands." In a conference, we agreed that a reader would have a hard time seeing this scene, so we

---

JIMMY'S THESAURUS WORK

Jimmy's Draft Sentence:
I *had* the snake in my hands.

> **HAVE**—*V.* include, accomodate, teem with (CONTAINER); possess, occupy, own (HOLD).
>
> **HOLD**—*N.* hold, control, possession, retention, occupancy, occupation, tenure, ownership, reception, maintenance; tenacity, pertinacity.
>   **grip**, grasp, purchase, clutch, clasp, clench; seizure, suspension, wring.
>   **gripping or holding device**: brace, vise, grip, clamp, grippers, clutch, cradle, net, suspensory; clasp, pin, safety pin, diaper pin, snap, hook; pincers *or* pinchers, nippers, pliers, tweezers, forceps; Stillson wrench, monkey wrench, lug wrench.
>   **handle**, hilt, hold, shaft, grip, lug, grasp, butt, stock, shank, crop, haft, helve, stele, withe, brace, snath, snead, bail, crank, ear, knob, knocker.
>   *V.* **hold**, have, possess, occupy, own, retain, hold back, withhold, contain, receive, keep, maintain, keep hold of; hold fast, hold on, cling to, cherish, nourish.
>   **grasp**, seize, grip, clutch, clasp, clench; brace, vise; wring.
>   **hug**, embrace, cuddle, cradle, clinch, grapple, wrap one's arms around, enfold.
>   *Adj.* **holding**, etc. (see *Verbs*); possessive, retentive, tenacious, pertinacious, viselike; tenable, retainable.
>   See also CONTAINER, CONTENTS, CONTROL, OWNERSHIP, RECEIVING, STINGINESS, STORE, SUPPORT, TAKING.
> *Antonyms*—See DESERTION, EXCRETION, GIVING, RELINQUISHMENT.

Jimmy's Final Sentence:
I *clutched* the snake in my tiny fists.

JIMMY'S THESAURUS WORK   LESSON 19

Overhead
Jimmy's Thesaurus Work

ANNIE'S POEM REVISIONS

Annie's Draft

> Within a few traps
> the rain was streaming from the sky,
> *meeting* harshly with our bowed heads.

Annie's Revision

> Within a few traps
> the rain was streaming from the sky,
> *lashing* harshly on our bowed heads.

Annie's Final

> Within a few traps
> the rain was streaming from the sky,
> lashing on our bowed heads.

ANNIE'S POEM REVISIONS   LESSON 19

Overhead
Annie Kass's Poem Revisions

---

consulted a thesaurus. Verbs are entered in a thesaurus alphabetically, in their present tense form, so a search for *had* wouldn't be fruitful. Instead, we looked up *have*, and here's what we found. . . .

Well, that wasn't much help, except that it did show us the next step. Of the two cross-references offered—the words in capital letters in parentheses—the closest in meaning to the *have* of Jimmy's sentence is *hold*. That's where we looked next. . . .

Jimmy hit paydirt. We scanned down the *hold* entry in search of the italicized capital *V.* in the left-hand margin that signals a list of verbs that are synonyms for *hold*. Jimmy decided the verb that best described how he'd held the snake was *clutch*. His revision read, "I clutched the snake in my tiny fists," *fists* being a more precise noun than *hands*. Now we readers have a sentence we can see, yes?

Let me show you one more quick example of thesaurus consultation. Check out this overhead. In a poem about going lobstering with her dad, Annie wrote the lines:

> Within a few traps
> the rain was streaming from the sky,
> meeting harshly with our bowed heads.

In a conference I asked Annie, "Is *meet with* the best verb? I can't see this."

She said, "I looked that one up in the thesaurus, but none of the other meanings for *meet* worked, not even the cross-references."

I suggested, "I wonder if *meet*, as a verb, is so far off from what the rain was doing to you and your dad that you need to start by looking elsewhere. Is there a more direct, obvious synonym? Try *hit* and see what you find."

Annie did. She found a great verb: *lash*. Her next revision read:

> Within a few traps
> the rain was streaming from the sky,
> lashing harshly on our bowed heads.

The final time Annie and I talked about her poem, in an editing conference, I showed her that I'd excised *harshly* and explained why. *Lash* is a strong verb. It says what Annie means all by itself; it doesn't need the assistance—or clutter—of an adverb.

If you turn to a thesaurus for help but come up empty, as Annie did, one strategy is to try another synonym. Look for a word closer in meaning to what's actually happening in your writing. If you can't think of one, ask me for help. Read along with me. . . .

Let's close the lesson with a poem by Marnie Briggs in which she sweated the diction, especially the verbs. With the assistance of a thesaurus, she worked to create word pictures of herself at her backyard pond throughout the four seasons. Read along with me. . . .

Questions, comments, observations about using a thesaurus?

19

THE POND

In winter
I trudge down to the pond.
Bundled up in my winter protection,
I carry a bag stuffed with extra mittens and socks.
I perch on the icy dock that's halfway buried in snow,
pull on my skates,
and glide onto the clean cold glass.

In spring
I skip down to the pond,
my fishing rod swung over my back.
I try to catch minnows—use leaves as bait
and daydream under the new sun.

In summer
I scamper down to the pond
with a towel wrapped around my body.
I stand at the edge of the dock
and it kills me
not knowing what lurks in the mysterious waters.
But I take a running jump into the cold glaze anyway.
It shatters, sending ripples everywhere.

In fall
I wander down to the pond.
It's barren and deserted—
no skating, no swimming.
I gaze into the still water
and watch my pure reflection
as it changes every year from younger to older,

as the murky water harbors
the seasons of my childhood.

—Marnie Briggs

THE POND   LESSON 19

Reproducible
"The Pond," by Marnie Briggs

Troubleshooting: Surefire Ways to Weaken Your Writing

20 **The Really Bad Words**

21 **Too-Long and Too-Short Paragraphs**

22 **The Missing *I***

23 **Passive Sentences**

24 **Exclamation Points**

25 **Hopefully**

26 **Stories that End "The End"**

What I Was Thinking These lessons address a collection of small sins committed by young—and old—writers. I teach about the problems as they crop up in my students' writing. Each of the lessons is one I learned late, as an adult writer; each teaches something I wish someone had pointed out to me at a tender age, before I embarrassed myself as an adult writer.

"This is going to be a continuing lesson, one I'll ask you to add to throughout the school year. So turn to the next clean page of your writing handbook and write this heading at the top:

Surefire Ways to Weaken Your Writing

Then dog-ear the next two pages, to remind yourself to leave them blank, so you have room to return to the conversation we'll start today about stylistic no-no's.

When I plan mini-lessons, I'm conscious of the ticking of the clock, of the fact that, if we're lucky, we'll have 180 days together, and maybe 170 writing lessons. That's only 170 chances for me to teach you what I hold dear about writing and what your writing shows me that you still need to know. So I'm continuously juggling my priorities as your teacher, trying to make the most of our time together.

That these lessons are showing up in mid-December should give you a sense of where they fall on my list of teaching priorities: not at the top but, still, ideas that can make a difference in your writing, that address some of the small sins writers commit that can weaken their prose and poetry.

It's easy to fall into these traps if you aren't aware of them. I know them because I fell into every one of them. Somewhere along the way a writing teacher or an editor rescued me. My concern for you is that I was old—in my thirties—to be needing rescuing as a writer. So I'll teach you a few guidelines and rules that will help your writing be strong from the start.

The Really Bad Words

Preparation

✔ Overhead transparency of "The Really Bad Words"

✔ Trimmed photocopies of "A Really Bad Paragraph" and "A Paragraph without Really Bad Words"

✔ Wall poster of first William Zinsser quotation

✔ Wall poster of second William Zinsser quotation

20 LESSON

DECEMBER

> **"Don't be kind of bold. Be bold."**
>
> *– William Zinsser*

"The first lesson comes from writing teacher Ken Macrorie and his book *The I-Search Paper* (1988). It's about what Macrorie calls "The Really Bad Words." Please write that heading on the next line in your handbook. . . .

The title of this rule is a joke, because one of Macrorie's bad words is *really*. He calls *really* an *intensifier*: a word a writer sticks in, in an attempt to make a sentence more intense—stronger, more authoritative, more powerful. The trouble is, intensifiers like *really* and *very* weaken your writing. They qualify your feelings, dilute your style, and take away your power. *Diminishers* like *sort of* and *just* do the same.

Most of these words are adverbs, which is my least favorite part of speech. Use the Really Bad Words only when necessary. Otherwise, delete them. Cross them out. Make them go away. As writing teacher William Zinsser put it in his book *On Writing Well* (1998), "Don't be kind of bold. Be bold."

Overhead
The Really Bad Words

Reproducible
A Really Bad
Paragraph

"**Good writing
is lean and
confident.**"

– William Zinsser

Please copy this list of the worst offenders from the overhead into your handbooks. These are the Really Bad Words I find most often in your prose and poems:

absolutely	just	so
all	kind of	sort of
(a) big	(a) little	totally
completely	quite	very
definitely	really	would

Let me show you some of this clutter in action. Here's an example of a Really Bad Paragraph on the overhead. Read along with me. . . .

Every night at camp, when we were totally tired out from playing the game, we would all sort of fall down in a big pile on the floor of our cabin. We would just laugh and laugh—it was really so much fun. Then, after we would calm down a little bit, we would suddenly be very, very hungry. Our counselor would be quite mad that our cabin was always awake after lights out, but hopefully we could get her to just chill out and let us eat chips and stuff we really weren't supposed to have at camp.

As a reader, you need a shovel to clear the clutter. William Zinsser says, "Good writing is lean and confident." So I tried to bring some lean confidence to this anecdote. The second paragraph tells a version without the Really Bad Words and with specific nouns, verbs, and adjectives.

At night, after we were exhausted from playing the game, we collapsed in a heap on the floor of our cabin. We lay there in a tangle of arms and legs and shook with giggles. When the laughter died out, hunger took over. We were starving. We drove our counselor crazy that summer because when the other cabins were quiet and dark, ours was alive with the sounds of eight girls shrieking, roughhousing, and rattling bags of forbidden junk food.

I rewrote every sentence as an exercise to show you the difference. I don't expect you to do the same when you polish, but I do hope you'll at least take a hard look for the Really Bad Words and see if you can cut them. Strong, meat-and-potatoes statements don't need to be intensified or diminished. Really. If someone is beautiful, she is beautiful—*really* beautiful is clutter. And if someone is very funny, couldn't he be *hysterical* or *witty* or *absurd* instead?

What about the Really Bad Words in dialogue? That's different. In capturing the way people speak in conversation—and American conversation is salted with intensifiers and diminishers—use them to bring your people to life. Absolutely.

Too-Long and Too-Short Paragraphs

Preparation

✔ Wall poster of E. B. White quotation

✔ Wall poster of first William Zinsser quotation

✔ Wall poster of second William Zinsser quotation

✔ Wall poster of Ursula K. LeGuin quotation

> "Remember that paragraphing calls for a good eye as well as a logical mind. Enormous blocks of print look formidable to a reader. He has a certain reluctance to tackle them; he can lose his way in them."
>
> – E. B. White

> "Writing is visual— it catches the eye before it has a chance to catch the brain. Shorter paragraphs put air around what you write and make it look inviting."
>
> – William Zinsser

"I have to confess that one of my criteria as a reader, when I browse in a bookstore and page through prospective volumes, is the length of their paragraphs. If the paragraphs go on for a page or more, I'm likely to put the book back on the shelf—unless it's John Updike, whose long paragraphs are worth the effort to me because his prose style is so exquisite.

I find long paragraphs hard to read. I'm not alone here. E. B. White admonished writers to "remember that paragraphing calls for a good eye as well as a logical mind. Enormous blocks of print look formidable to a reader. He has a certain reluctance to tackle them; he can lose his way in them" (1979).

William Zinsser agrees: "Writing is visual—it catches the eye before it has a chance to catch the brain. Shorter paragraphs put air around what you write and make it look inviting" (1998).

Readers need air. They need breathing space—a place to rest their eyes and minds. And they need signals from the writer. With the indentation of a new paragraph, the writer says, "Okay, reader, I'm going to shift your attention so I can develop a new direction here. Ready?"

So look at your long paragraphs. Even when it's not necessary for meaning or organization to break them into two or three shorter ones, break them anyway, as an aid to your reader. Deliver a digestible package of sense, not an enormous, formidable flock.

Can you break for new paragraphs too often? You bet. Reading prose that's broken up into many short paragraphs makes me feel as if I have the hiccups. There's so much air I'm gulping it. I feel jolted; I'm distracted; I can't relax or concentrate. As Zinsser notes, "A succession of tiny paragraphs is as annoying as a paragraph that's too long."

Is there an exception to the too-many-too-short paragraphs rule? Yes: when you write quoted dialogue, you must create a new paragraph for each speaker each time he or she takes a turn in the conversation. Here, readers need the extra air to help them make the mental shift between one speaker and the next.

So, what's the key to paragraphing? One is practice—putting sentences together into units, then reading and revising them for coherence and appearance. When you revise and edit, use the paragraph symbol at junctures where long paragraphs might sensibly be broken. If you find a too-short paragraph, use an arrow to attach it to the one above or below it, depending on where it fits and sounds best.

In other words, guess. Afterward, as your editor, I'll confirm your guesses or suggest alternatives as you get the hang of thinking and writing in paragraph units.

Let's give Ursula K. LeGuin the final word on paragraphing. She says: "It matters where you put those little indents. They show connections and separations in the flow; they are architecturally essential." I love LeGuin's language. Above all, try to think of your paragraph breaks as showing "connections and separations in the flow" of your prose.

> "A succession of tiny paragraphs is as annoying as a paragraph that's too long."
>
> – *William Zinsser*

> "It matters where you put those little indents. They show connections and separations in the flow; they are architecturally essential."
>
> – *Ursula K. LeGuin*

21

The Missing I

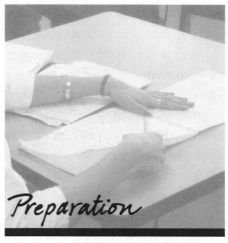

Preparation

✔ Overhead transparency of "The Missing *I*: Before and After"

22 LESSON

"There are kinds of writing where the personal pronoun *I* isn't allowed: stories in newspapers and newsmagazines, grant proposals, and business reports, for example. I understand why: the readers of these documents want objectivity—they go to sources like these for facts that are colored as lightly as possible by a writer's opinions.

But here, in writing workshop, nothing you write needs to pretend to have that kind of objectivity. Your memoirs are your impressions of your lives. Your poems are your explorations of your feelings, ideas, and experiences. Your essays are expressions of your opinions about a problem you see in the world. And your book reviews are your assessments of a book and your accounts of the experience of reading it.

So please watch out for two personal pronouns that can creep into your writing, take away your voice, and obliterate your *I*. The first is *we*.

When a writer adopts a *we* voice—this happens especially in kids' memoirs and poems—the reader has no individual to be with, to experience a moment or emotion *as*. When the actor is a *we*, readers have to trail around behind a whole clump of people. Worse, writers can't tell their own thoughts and feelings, because an *I* voice is necessary to do this—that is, unless the writer ventures into the awkward territory of "We felt scared. We were worried about the raccoon. We wondered if it could be rabid." Yuck. Can a reader feel any of this?

Overhead
The Missing *I*

Don't hide behind *we*. Tell your story; describe your actions and feelings; give your reader *you*: an individual to be with, see and feel with, and care about.

The other personal pronoun that writers sometimes hide behind is *you*. Especially in book reports and essays, students will resort to describing their own opinions under cover of what a *you* thinks about a book or a problem.

It can be daunting to put that *I* out there and take responsibility for your own feelings and ideas. So sentences like the one on the overhead turn up in kids' book reviews: "When you read Chris Crutcher's *Running Loose*, you will feel as if you are Louie, and you will cry." Or a student essayist will write, "You understand when you read teen magazines that if you want to be considered attractive, you have to lose twenty pounds, grow a longer neck and legs, and do something about your nose. You feel assaulted and demoralized."

Be confident. Take back your *I*. Use *you* only when you mean *you: the reader*, when you're speaking directly, say, giving advice or instruction.

Write, "When I read *Running Loose*, I identified so closely with Louie that I felt his feelings and, when the final tragedy struck, I cried." Write, "After I read the latest issues of the top three teen magazines, I understood that to be considered attractive, within the magazine culture, I'd have to lose twenty pounds, grow a longer neck and legs, and do something about my nose. I felt assaulted by the images. And I felt demoralized—not self-confident, not okay in my looks, not good enough."

As a reader, can you feel the difference? Can you feel the life in the *I* voice? It's interesting to me that the *you* voice, which should feel more universal and inclusive, actually involves me less as a reader, while I do relate to and empathize with that individual, idiosyncratic *I*.

Readers want to put themselves in your shoes. They want to learn what you know, to experience your ideas and emotions. So don't hold back. Be self-confident. Put your *I* out there. Your readers will thank you.

22

Passive Sentences

Preparation

✔ Wall poster of Strunk and White quotation

"Passive sentences don't have actors. Mostly they use forms of the verb *to be* to suggest that someone did something, by telling that something *was done*. Instead of putting an actor—a person—up front as the subject of a sentence, passive constructions hide the actor and weaken the writing. Here's an example of a passive sentence: "Play scripts were passed out and roles assigned." By whom? To whom? And can anyone see the action of this sentence? Let's make it active: "Pam, the drama teacher, passed out scripts to her class and assigned each student a role."

Here's an example I found in my writing: "Each English class is organized as a writing workshop." By whom? God? No, by an actor—in this case, me. My revision read, "I organize each English class in my schedule as a writing workshop." Now it's unambiguous.

An active sentence credits the actor, including the *I* persona that gets nullified in a passive construction. "I spent hours copyediting twelve of your short stories this weekend" is an active construction. "Editing twelve short stories this weekend took many hours" is timid and indirect.

In *The Elements of Style* (1979), Strunk and White say, "The habitual use of the active voice makes for forcible writing. This is true not only in narrative concerned principally with action but in writing of any kind." So in your memoirs, short stories, poems, and essays, consider your sentences: are they alive with actors?

> "The habitual use of the active voice makes for forcible writing. This is true not only in narrative concerned principally with action but in writing of any kind."
>
> – *Strunk and White*

Exclamation Points

Preparation

✔ None

"My suggestion about exclamation points is don't use them unless you have no choice. They make writing sound cute and gushy. They hit readers over the head—Be excited! Be surprised! Laugh at my joke! Notice the irony!—and rob us of the pleasure of finding excitement, wonder, humor, and irony for ourselves.

Exclamation points make me grind my teeth. They feel as if a writer is telling me how to react by giving the sentence a joke badge to wear, in the form of a tired punctuation mark at the end. Instead, I respond stubbornly: you think that's funny, huh?

Go for understatement. Remember that readers are smart. If the point you're making is funny, and if the sentence is constructed to emphasize the humor, they'll get the joke.

What about exclamation points in dialogue? That's different. For example, commands need exclamation points: "Stop!" he ordered. A quoted line like, "There's a fire in my room!" should be exclaimed. But "Hi!"? I don't think so.

Hopefully

Preparation

✔ None

"*Hopefully* is an adverb meaning "full of hope." It doesn't mean "I hope" or "we hope." For example, the literal meaning of the sentence, "Hopefully I'll graduate in June," is "When I graduate in June, I will be full of hope." The sentence, "Hopefully there will be a peace accord soon," is meaningless. *Who* is doing the hoping?

My theory is that writers and speakers hide behind *hopefully*. It takes confidence to put that personal pronoun up front—to say "*I hope* this happens." Be confident. Say, "I hope I'll graduate in June." Say, "I hope they sign a peace accord soon."

25 LESSON

JANUARY

Stories That End "The End"

Preparation

✔ None

LESSON **26**

OCTOBER

"Primary grade kids love to conclude their stories with "The End." It's a concrete way to make a piece of writing stop, and it echoes the "The End's" of the fairy tales and children's books they're reading. But by the time writers hit the upper intermediate and middle grades, "The End" at the end of a piece is no longer charming. It's unnecessary, not to mention too cute.

When there's no more writing on a page to be read, the mature reader gets it, without the assistance of a prompt. So, no more "The End's," *please*.

SECTION III:
Lessons about Genres

For me, a priority in teaching about genre is to introduce or require only genres found in the real world of literature—kinds of writing that a reader can locate in a reasonably good bookstore or library. I avoid what I call school genres, and I try not to water down too much the real-world genres that kids in school might try.

In the category of school genres I'd have to include book reports *vs.* book reviews or critical essays, personal experience narratives after fifth grade instead of memoirs, cutesy poetic formats *vs.* free verse, something called "fiction pieces" instead of short stories or children's picture books, five-paragraph essays rather than opinion pieces or letters to the editor, reports pasted together from Internet and encyclopedia research *vs.* reports, essays, feature articles, and arguments based on data a writer gathers first-hand, and a whole host of forms of writing no one ever borrowed from a library: compare-contrast themes, descriptive paragraphs, acrostic poetry, rubric writing, and steps in making a peanut butter and jelly sandwich.

When it comes to genre, the real thing is so compelling, worthwhile, and satisfying that I don't want to waste one moment of my kids' time teaching them forms that delay the pleasures of writing. I think that writing the real thing answers a crucial question for my students: "What can writing do?" The genre lessons in this section are those my students deemed useful and interesting to them as young adolescents.

Over the years I learned to collect and save examples of good writing across the genres. I sleep well at night thinking about the file cabinet in my classroom that I'm packing full of poems, memoirs, letters, essays, book reviews, gifts of writing, reports, profiles, and parodies that I love and think my students will love, too.

Whenever I teach about a genre, I begin by reading examples of it with my kids. Then we tease out and name the qualities of good—and sometimes not-so-good—pieces of this kind of writing. When students observe the features of a genre and name them, it's considerably more likely that they'll be able to strive for and attain excellence as writers of the genre.

I prepare and offer brief courses of study related to particular genres: for example, many days in early fall teaching about memoir, a couple of weeks in November focused on short stories, and two weeks in April when we get inside essay writing. Then I return to a genre periodically throughout the year to help students refresh or extend their understandings. I ask students not to tackle a genre until I've taught about it, which means they begin with memoirs in September, then add short fiction, book reviews, essays, and profiles to their repertoires as we work formally with each genre.

But I teach poetry throughout the school year, September through June, because poems offer so many possibilities, do so many different things for us as writers and readers, work in so many ways, and speak of so many facets of the human experience that it is impossible to ever teach poetry completely. Because of its generosity as a genre in terms of diversity of content, and the compactness and versatility of the form, I think poetry is the essential genre to teach in grades K–12.

Ineffective and Effective Memoirs

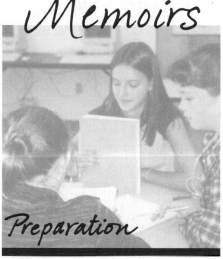

Preparation

✔ Photocopies of an ineffective memoir about an event from your life

✔ Photocopies of your best effort at an effective memoir about the same event

✔ Overhead transparencies headed "What Doesn't Work in This Ineffective Memoir?" and "Qualities of a Memoir That Works" for brainstorming with your students

✔ Wall poster of Ted Hughes quotation

✔ Wall poster of Gore Vidal quotation

✔ Wall poster of John Barth quotation

✔ Tape dispensers

LESSON 27

EARLY SEPTEMBER

What I Was Thinking Each fall, when my seventh graders draft their first memoirs of the school year, they wrestle with a host of familiar difficulties and confusions. A quick read of their initial attempts as memoirists invariably shows:

- Problems with purpose: there's no sense of why the memoirist chose this memory—of its significance to his or her life—or invitation to the reader to care about or become involved in the meaning of the memory.

- Problems with focus: the memoir is a bed-to-bed narrative that covers all the events of a day, trip, or visit, with the incident-of-interest buried in a mass of narrative.

- Problems with pace: events unfold way too fast, with little revealing detail, so it's impossible for a reader to make a movie in his or her mind.

- Problems with voice: the memoirist uses *we* so much, rather than *I*, that there's no one person for a reader to engage with throughout the events of the narrative.

- Problems with reflection: the writer doesn't tell his or her thoughts and feelings, so there's no one for a reader to empathize with.

- Problems with leads: the memoir begins with a paragraph or more of who-what-when-where-why background information that holds a reader at arm's length.

- Problems with conclusions: the memoir either stops cold or runs on, with no satisfaction or closure for a reader.

- Problems with dialogue: either people talk so much that the memoir reads like a script for a radio play and readers can't visualize the action or empathize with the memoirist, or people don't talk and aren't revealed.

- Problems with setting and character identification: readers can't tell where or when something is happening or who all these people are that the memoirist keeps referring to by their first names.

- Problems with titles: the titles are labels or descriptions of topics, not invitations to a reader.

I address most of these concerns as discrete mini-lessons: "The Rule of *So What?*," "The Missing *I*," "Thoughts and Feelings," "Narrative Leads," "A Movie behind Your Eyelids," "Good Titles." But in this, the first genre mini-lesson of the school year, I try to jump-start kids' awareness of the qualities of effective memoirs, so they'll have some criteria to shoot for, as well as some ideas of pitfalls to try to avoid, as they draft and revise their first memoirs.

My approach is to write a bad-on-purpose memoir that suffers from many of the problems I've just described, give students an opportunity to feel superior to my dismal example, and ask them to critique it: to name what's wrong.

Then I try it again—to the best of my ability, I write a version that demonstrates what I understand to be the qualities of a good memoir. This time, my students name what works.

The two lists of criteria become the foundation for a year's worth of memoir writing. As students offer critiques, I both record their ideas and elaborate on them: in context, I introduce some of the language of writers, words like *lead, pace, dialogue, sensory details, ineffective repetition,* and *So what?* or *theme.* On the lists of qualities of poor and good memoirs I've included here, as Figures 27-2 and 27-4, I italicized the phrases that I contributed as kids were volunteering their ideas. This is an ideal opportunity to start building on what my kids already know by introducing the language I'll use all year when we talk about narrative.

This is the first of many genre lessons in which students will tease out criteria; that is, name the qualities of effective writing in a genre as a preliminary step to trying to achieve them in pieces of their own. I've become a true believer in the power of naming as one way for kids to take control of their learning and writing.

I've also included an example of one of my dismal memoirs, along with its new-and-improved version [see Figures 27-1 and 27-3], to demonstrate how I created the memoirs that my students researched. Since these narratives describe one of my own experiences—since they show me trying to make personal meaning of events from my life—they're not appropriate to be reproduced for use in another teacher's mini-lesson. Rather, they're here to illustrate the nature of the writing I created as a vehicle for teaching about memoir. I hope other teachers will take the plunge and show their students how they use memoir to find meaning in moments from their lives.

It may also help teachers to know that I wrote the two memoirs at home and brought the finished work, photocopied for the class, to the mini-lessons. I seldom write during the independent writing time of the workshop: kids need me to be available to confer with them. The writing I bring to lessons or compose on overhead transparencies during lessons provides a revealing, practical demonstration of my commitment and processes as a writer.

This memoir is one of a handful of pieces I'll compose during the school year as models to teach my students from. I'll save the drafts, possibly to use again with another class. My students don't need to perceive me as prolific. They do need to observe the processes of an adult writer and see what writing does for my life and what it might do for theirs.

This lesson is cited by more than half my students, at the end of the fall trimester each November, as one that changed them as writers. As Marcia put it, "It's like I suddenly understood memoir because you took us inside yours."

"There's a memory of mine I'm itching to explore in a memoir. Other than the itch, I don't yet know *why* this experience is meaningful to me. I hope I might be able to teach myself its significance by writing about it. The itch is something that happened to me when I was five, when I lied to my mother for the first time. She'll tell you it wasn't the last time, by a long shot.

Why write a memoir? Check out this quote from the British poet Ted Hughes: "Why memoir? It means the world becomes yours. If you don't do it, it drifts away and takes a whole piece of yourself with it, like an amputation. To attack it and attack it and get it under control—it's like taking possession of your life, isn't it?"

> "Why memoir? It means the world becomes yours. If you don't do it, it drifts away and takes a whole piece of yourself with it, like an amputation. To attack it and attack it and get it under control—it's like taking possession of your life, isn't it?"
>
> – *Ted Hughes*

I don't want my kindergarten memory to drift away and take a piece of me with it. I want to attack it, get it under control, maybe take possession of a piece of my life by writing about it.

I've already taken a stab at this memoir, but I didn't do my best. Instead, I wrote a bad-on-purpose memoir. I drew on the accumulated experience of almost thirty years of reading ineffective memoirs, and I wrote a draft about my first lie that *doesn't* work as a memoir.

Your job, as writers and readers of narratives, is to read this one of mine and analyze what went wrong: to name the qualities of a good memoir that *aren't* here. Troubleshoot this piece of bad writing with me as a way to begin recognizing and naming the qualities of a good one.

Here's my bad-on-purpose memoir. Read along with me. . . .

Now, you talk and I'll write on the overhead. Don't take notes. Help me make this list as rich as possible. What's weak here? What's missing? What aren't you able to do, as readers of stories? . . . [See Figure 27-2 for my class's response to my bad memoir.]

This is a great, knowledgeable list. You guys should sign on as literary critics for the *New York Times Book Review*. I'm going to clean these notes up, type them, and give them back to you tomorrow in the form of a list to tape into your writing handbooks. Then we'll look together at another draft of this story from my life, this time written as well as I could write it.

Comments? Questions? Observations?

FOLLOW-UP LESSON

Here's yesterday's list, trimmed to fit on a page of your writing handbook. Please turn to the next clean page, circulate the tape dispensers, and tape it in. . . .

Let's review by reading the list around the circle. Please, will each of you read aloud one of these critiques, until we run out of readers? . . .

Again, this is a smart, perceptive analysis of a poor memoir. Now, let's see what you can observe in my best-on-purpose memoir about the same experience. Read along with me. . . .

Again, you talk and I'll write on transparencies. This time our topic is "Qualities of a Memoir That Works." Don't take notes—I'll give you a clean copy of our list of criteria tomorrow. You may want to refer to the notes from yesterday, to help you find language and parallels. Ready? To the extent that this memoir works, *what* works? . . . [See Figure 27-4 for kids' response to my better memoir.]

This is another smart, perceptive analysis. I'm going to add one final item to the list: *The memoirist invented details that fit with the spirit, intention, and truth of the story*.

You should know that I can't remember the exact words my mother spoke to me when I was five, or that I spoke to her. I think my dress was yellow—at least that's my impression—but I can't be sure. There might not have been a nap fairy in kindergarten—it might have been a first-grade thing. And *maybe* I started to chop vegetables for dinner, the afternoon Anne and I talked about her first lie.

My point is that memoir isn't reportage. As a memoirist, I get to craft *my impressions* of the events of my life. A great American writer—and memoirist—Gore Vidal says, "A memoir is how one remembers one's life." John Barth, another great American writer, agrees: "The story of your life is not your life. It is your story."

> "A memoir is how one remembers one's own life, while an autobiography is history, requiring research, dates, facts double-checked."
>
> – *Gore Vidal*

So don't be reluctant to invent as you craft a memoir, so long as you stay true to the essence of the experience.

I love your list. You've built a foundation here for a year of memoir writing. You've named the qualities to shoot for in your own memoirs, and naming is the first step to owning. I'm excited to read your memoirs as you work to bring these qualities to your writing, and I'm eager to begin teaching you lessons about them.

Tomorrow I'll give you a typed, organized copy of the list for your handbooks, we'll read it around the circle again, and then it will be yours: an excellent yardstick to measure your drafts against as you become excellent memoirists.

Comments? Questions? Observations?

THE FIRST TIME I EVER TOLD A LIE TO MY MOTHER

It was 1956. I was five years old, and it was the fall of my kindergarten year in Mrs. Brown's class. I'd never lied to my mother before, but on this day I told a big lie. Here's the story of what happened on that day.

It all started when we were at naptime. Earlier that day we played with clay in art, and a really good piece of clay was lying on the floor. I don't know why, but I picked it up and started rolling it around on my skirt. It made a big mess on my skirt.

When I got home, my mother asked me what was on my skirt. I didn't want to get in trouble, so I told her a boy named Glenn had put clay all over my skirt. She didn't believe me, because my brother's name was Glenn, but she didn't punish me. I never could figure that out. She just sent me outside to play. I'll never forget that day.

Figure 27-1 Nancie's Ineffective Memoir

WHAT DOESN'T WORK IN NANCIE'S INEFFECTIVE MEMOIR?

- The title is boring: *it's a label, not an interesting, inviting combination of words.*
- The beginning is weak: *it's an introductory paragraph of the facts, not a lead that brings readers into the action.*
- There's no personality: *none of the writer's thoughts, feelings, and observations.*
- It's too short: *the pace is too fast to draw readers in, involve them, help them make a movie in their minds.*

Figure 27-2 Nancie's Class's List of What Doesn't Work in Her Ineffective Memoir, continued on page 98

- A reader can't see people in action: *their movements: gestures, facial expressions.*

- A reader can't see, hear, or feel anything: *there are no sensory details.*

- People don't talk: *there's no dialogue to help show what people are like and how they feel.*

- The language isn't interesting: *there are ineffective repetitions, weak verbs, bad words (really, just, sort of, all).*

- There's no conclusion: *the memoir just stops.*

- What's the point? The reader can't tell why the writer is writing about this: *there's no* So what? *or theme.*

- The reader doesn't think or feel anything at the end.

TWO LIES

"What is that on your dress?"

I looked up into my mother's gray eyes. "What do you mean?"

"I mean the pink stuff all over the dress I spent forty-five minutes ironing," she sputtered. I looked down and took a deep breath. Could I do it? Could I tell her the lie?

That morning at naptime, curled up on my kindergarten mat, I had spied a prize on the classroom floor: an exquisite lump of pink clay. I remembered how much fun it had been to stretch, pound, and eat clay at art time. Now I considered how much fun it would be to flatten out that lump. But on what?

I looked around. There was my mat—too sticky. There was the floor—too dirty. And ooooo—there was my dress. I spread the skirt of the dress on the mat, smoothed the material, and started kneading the clay.

By the time the boy who was the nap fairy came along to tap me with the nap wand and tell me I could get up, the skirt of my yellow dress had turned pink. I was wearing the lump of clay. As I rolled up my mat, the realization of what I had just done began to dawn. My mother was going to be upset with me. No, my mother was going to be mad at me. No, my mother was going to kill me.

I grew up in a house where the refrigerator was full of damp, rolled up clothes lying in wait in plastic bags for my angry mother to shake out and use for target practice with her iron. The dresses I wore to school—back then it was a federal statute or something that girls had to wear dresses to school—were smocked, sashed, and splashed with ribbons and lace. I think they must have been a mother's nightmare. Once my mother had ironed one of those suckers, I wore it until it was soiled; then she opened the refrigerator, and Glenn, Bonnie, and I ran and hid in our bedrooms until the fit of ironing had passed.

Figure 27-2 Nancie's More Effective Memoir

On the way home from kindergarten, I stared at my reflection in the window of the bus, ignored my friends and the laughter and singing around me, and worried. What would my mother say? Worse, what would she *do*? My mother was a spanker and screamer; I could feel the spanks and hear the screams.

Suddenly I sat up. Of course—why hadn't it occurred to me before? When my mother asked about the clay on my dress, I would *lie*. Yeah, lie. I'd heard about lying; people did it all the time. I'd just make up a story. What a relief. For the rest of the ride home I invented and polished the lie.

When the bus pulled up at the end of our driveway, I jumped down the steps, skipped up to our porch, burst through the back door, and yelled, "Mommy, I'm home!" When she saw the dress, which she did immediately, and asked about it, which came next, I took a deep breath, and I lied.

"See, at naptime, this boy who was on the mat next to me found a ball of clay and he picked it up and he rolled it all over my dress."

"What?" my mother asked.

"At naptime, this boy who was on the mat next to me found a ball of clay and he picked it up and he rolled it all over my dress."

"Uh-huh. I think I'd better call Mrs. Brown and have a little talk with her about this boy—or maybe I'll call his mother and have a little talk with her. What's his name?"

I began to lose confidence. A name? A name hadn't been part of the plan. Frantically I cast around for a boy's name. A boy. A boy. Did I know any boys? I blurted out the only name I could think of.

"Glenn. It was Glenn." Glenn *was* a boy's name. Unfortunately it was also my brother's name. I could tell by the look on her face that the coincidence was proving too much for my mother. She pinched her lips together and gripped my shoulders. I cringed and felt the tears begin. Her hands rested on my shoulders. I could feel her looking at me, but I was afraid to meet her gaze. I stared at our shoes. A silence of a few seconds stretched for an eternity.

Suddenly she released me. "Change your clothes and go outside and play," she sighed.

What?

"Go on—put on your play clothes."

I stumbled into the bedroom, stepped out of the dress, and pulled on a t-shirt and pants. In half a minute I was standing in our fenced-in backyard, alone and as confused as I had ever been in my whole life. Where were the screaming and spanking? It's not that I missed them. I missed the certainty of crime and punishment, of the way things were supposed to happen at my house. Why was my mother not acting like my mother?

She didn't mention the dress when my father came home from work or at dinner or the next day—or ever. In fact, I never saw the yellow dress again. It was a mystery I couldn't solve—until the day my daughter came home from kindergarten and lied to me for the first time, a small, dumb lie that I saw right through.

Anne cried. Then we talked about why she had lied to me. "Because I was afraid of what you'd do if I told the truth," she sobbed.

Continued on page 100

My heart sank. Anne was afraid of me—me, her mother, who loved her more than anything. We talked, until she understood I wasn't angry and her tears had dried. Then she went off to play, and I began to chop the vegetables for dinner. Standing over the cutting board in the late afternoon light, I remembered my first lie and its mysterious resolution.

And I understood power. Parents have so much of it. We're the monarchs of our children's worlds. I want my child to respect my power—to let me show her how to be honest, kind, civil, and safe—but I don't want her to fear it, to fear me.

Maybe the angry queen of my childhood didn't always enjoy her power, either. Maybe on a fall day forty-five years ago she looked through her daughter's tears and in that first lie felt the fear of Mom. Maybe her heart sank, too.

QUALITIES OF A MEMOIR THAT WORKS

The title invites and fits: *it came last; it was chosen from among possibilities that the writer brainstormed*

The lead brings readers right into the action of the story

Background information that a reader needs is woven in—*the who-what-what-when-where-why context is embedded in the narrative*

There's lots of *I*: *lots of thoughts, feelings, and observations of the memoirist*

The pace is slowed down: *readers can make a movie in their minds*

A reader can see, hear, and feel the experience *because the writer provides concrete, sensory details and descriptions of people in action*

The small details show what matters to the people in the memoir

There is dialogue; the writer uses it to show what people are like and how they're feeling

The language is interesting: *verbs like* sputter, knead, spy, curl, polish, pinch, *and* grip *that a reader can see, feel, and hear*

The ending is purposeful: *it leaves a reader thinking*

There's a *So what?*: *a meaning or significance that was discovered by the memoirist during the act of writing the memoir*

There's a setting: *a time and places*

The action flashes back and forward in time and creates questions in the reader's mind about what will happen next

The memoirist invented details that fit with the spirit, intention, and truth of the story

Figure 27-4 Nancie's Class's List: What Works in Her Better Memoir

A Course of Study: Fiction

28 **What's Easy about Writing Bad Fiction?**

29 **What's Hard about Writing Good Fiction?**

30 **The Main Character Questionnaire**

31 **Considerations in Creating a Character**

32 **Short Story Structure**

33 **Ways to Develop a Character**

What I Was Thinking For a long time my advice to students who aspired to write fiction was *please don't*. Their fiction overwhelmed me. I didn't know where to begin by way of response, it was so bad: bereft of plausibility, specificity, theme, coherence, and, especially, characters even remotely convincing or motivated. Novice fiction writers defined the genre as a daydream on paper: "My new story is about a C.I.A. agent who lives in Hawaii." Their plots went wherever they took them and ended—if the writer actually got that far before he or she surrendered to frustration—with the punch line *Then he woke up and realized it was all a dream.*

Kids had no concept of pace—enough plot happened in a page and a half to fill a novel. Often I couldn't tell who the main character was. When I could, I knew her hair color, complexion, eye color, birthday, and height to the half inch, but I didn't understand one thing about the character's needs, problems, feelings, or dreams. And theme was negligible. At best the conclusion presented a crude moral: "Erik learned that might doesn't make right, but he was glad he killed the evil wizard."

This series of lessons grew from a serious desire on the part of my students to write fiction—to pretend other lives, create from a different place than experience, and write what they love to read, which is, most often, fiction. Rudyard Kipling wrote that "Fiction is truth's older sister." My adolescent students clamored to make friends with the big sister.

I ask my kids to wait to attempt fiction until November, until after a course of study about the pitfalls and challenges of the genre, as well as lessons about approaches to creating fiction that provide scaffolds for their imaginations, for the hard work of invention.

We begin with a discussion of their memories of earlier, failed attempts at writing fiction and name what can go wrong. We look at what it takes to craft good fiction. We consider the themes, problems, and premises of the fiction they've been reading in reading workshop. Individuals develop lists of problems and premises they find intriguing and select one to explore in a short story (see Lesson 5: "Problems to Explore in Fiction"). Using a questionnaire, we collaborate in the creation of a main character, then discuss what they learned from the demonstration. As individuals are ready, they use a blank copy of the questionnaire to sketch their own main characters. And all along the way I read aloud good short stories, including the student short fiction in Appendix B and the published stories listed in Appendix E, so together we can tease out and name the ways that fictional narratives are structured and characters are developed.

This course of study doesn't guarantee great short stories, but it does put kids' feet under them as writers of fiction. Before they draft the first line, they have a sense of purpose, some good ideas that intrigue them, and a character they want to be with over the long weeks it takes to craft a convincing, compelling short story.

What's Easy about Writing Bad Fiction?

Preparation

✔ Overhead transparency headed "What's Easy about Writing Bad Fiction?" for brainstorming with your students the potential pitfalls of fiction writing

"Would you raise your hand if you've ever suffered through an unsuccessful attempt at writing fiction? . . . Yikes—lots of you. I sympathize, but I'm not surprised.

Fiction is the most difficult genre to write well. Ironically, young writers often see it as the easiest: all you have to do is daydream on paper, right?

This morning I'm interested in thinking about that bad old fiction and what can be learned from your failed attempts, as a way to help you get some perspective and avoid some of the pitfalls. So, on the next clean page of your writing handbook, please write this heading:

What's Easy about Writing Bad Fiction?

Now, would each of you take the next three minutes to reflect on your earlier attempts. List what you *didn't* do, what you *didn't* pay attention to, as you went your merry way as a writer of bad fiction. I'll be making my own list, because I have started and abandoned some of the lamest short stories in the annals of American literature. . . .

Let's come back together. Talk to me about your discoveries, and I'll record them. If I or a classmate mentions a pitfall that hadn't occurred to you, add it to your list, so that at the end of the lesson, the entry in your handbook contains all the ideas I've recorded on the transparency. Ready? . . . [See Figure 28-1 for a list created by me and my students.]

WHAT'S EASY ABOUT WRITING BAD FICTION?

The events or the characters' experiences don't have to be grounded in anything: it's a daydream on paper.

The characters are like paper dolls you're moving around: the characters don't have a character.

You don't have to include dialogue; if you do, it can be pointless.

You don't have to bother with a climax or high point of the action.

You don't need a *So what?* or theme.

You can spin as much plot or action as you want.

You don't have to provide background and details.

It can be just a string of events.

You don't have to tell characters' thoughts and feelings.

The lead doesn't have to grab the reader.

You don't have to craft a resonating conclusion: it can just end.

The story doesn't have to make sense.

You don't have to convince a reader that this is a real world.

Changes can be made at your discretion.

You can write it off the top of your head.

When you don't finish it, no one will be surprised or blame you.

Figure 28-1 A Sample List from Nancie's Class of What's Easy about Writing Bad Fiction

This is a great list of pitfalls. It *is* easy to write bad short stories if you don't understand the work of a fiction writer. My job in this series of lessons is to teach you what I know about the work of a writer of good fiction.

So, toward that end, here's your homework. Turn to the next clean page in your writing handbook and write this heading:

What's Hard about Writing Good Fiction?

Under the heading, write this sentence starter:

The writer of good fiction has to:

Tonight I'd like you to spend about fifteen minutes considering and recording what you understand about the work of crafting good fiction. Lean on the sentence starter and make a bulleted list beneath it of the things that writers of good fiction need to think about, create, include, and leave out.

Comments or questions?

What's Hard about Writing Good Fiction?

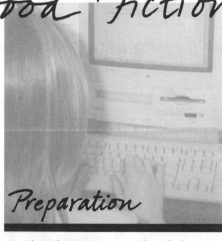

Preparation

✔ Overhead transparency headed "What's Hard about Writing Good Fiction?" for brainstorming with your students the considerations of successful writers of fiction

✔ Wall poster of Rudyard Kipling quotation

LESSON **29**

NOVEMBER

> "I'll begin by writing today's heading at the top of a transparency. Talk to me about the discoveries you made last night for homework; I'll talk to you about mine; and I'll record everything here. Then, tomorrow or the next day, I'll give the ideas back to you as a typed, organized entry for your writing handbook, one you can refer to and lean on during your attempts at short fiction. So don't bother recording additional notes. Just attend to and participate in the conversation.

Okay, I'm ready. . . . [See Figure 29-1 for an example of a list my students and I created.]

Wow. Another great list. We are brilliant.

Check out the quote from the novelist and poet Rudyard Kipling on the wall. You probably know him best as the author of *The Jungle Book*. Kipling said, "Fiction is truth's older sister."

You've been writing truth in your memoirs. As you move into fiction, you'll need to stretch as a writer—to stand on tiptoe so you can hold your own with truth's older sister. Fiction is harder to write because it's an act of invention, *vs.* truth telling, but I think the satisfactions in keeping company with the big sister more than make up for the challenges. Your list of what's hard about writing good fiction shows that you're ready for the challenges *and* the satisfactions of invention.

Questions? Comments? Observations?

> **"Fiction is truth's older sister."**
>
> *– Rudyard Kipling*

29

WHAT'S HARD ABOUT WRITING GOOD FICTION?

The writer of good fiction has to . . .

Develop a main character who:
> has convincing thoughts and feelings
> talks like a real person
> has a definite personality
> is believable and consistent
> has a problem/is facing a conflict
> a reader can be with and *wants* to be with

Create a problem or conflict for the main character

Create a working plan, so the story isn't a daydream on paper

Create a lead that draws the reader in

Create a conclusion that wraps up the plot *and* resonates for the reader and points to the *So what?* or theme

Keep a steady pace: action that's not too fast or too slow

Create a climax/high point: the event of greatest intensity in the story

Create a specific time and place

Create a new world, with sufficient background information to make it convincing

Create a *So what?* or theme

Base the plot in grounded experience: the writer's knowledge, gained firsthand, observed, or learned about through reading

Create dialogue that's relevant and moves the action forward

Keep a balance of action, dialogue, and the main character's thoughts and feelings

Keep a consistent verb tense (present or past) and narrative voice: usually first person (*I*) or third person (*he* or *she*)

Create a movie of the story behind his or her eyelids, then open his or her eyes and capture the specifics of the action on paper: invent details that make the story visual

Beware of too much plot

Leave out or delete the parts that a reader will skip

Write enough, in terms of length, to develop all of the above and invent a believable world

Create a title that fills the reader in, invites a reader, and fits the whole story

Put significant time into the piece: five–six weeks is probably the average for a grades 7–8 short story

Figure 29-1 A Sample List from Nancie's Class of What's Hard about Writing Good Fiction

The Main Character Questionnaire

Preparation

✔ Overhead transparency of "Main Character Questionnaire"

✔ Many photocopies of "Main Character Questionnaire"

✔ Wall poster of Margaret Banning quotation

✔ Wall poster of Virginia Woolf quotation

✔ Wall poster of John Irving quotation

✔ Extra-fine-point permanent marker

LESSON 30

NOVEMBER

What I Was Thinking The next several mini-lessons are described in Lesson 5, "Problems to Explore in Fiction," which helps students notice the themes or plot premises that authors of published fiction have selected, then generate and discuss problems they might be interested in exploring in their own short fiction. I do the same. Then I choose one problem or *What if?* from my list as the foundation for a main character I'll invent as a demonstration in the next mini-lesson, which is a long one.

> "The lists of problems you created for your short stories are intriguing and wonderful. Working from a plot premise that you like, one you're interested to imagine, will go a long way toward easing the challenges to come. A problem is one of two scaffolds that will help you build your short story; the other supporting scaffold is your main character.
>
> A main character questionnaire will help you develop a person you can become when you write your story and your readers can become when they read it. By nudging you, right from the start, toward details of character, toward *facts*, I'm hoping you'll meet and conquer probably the biggest challenge of writing good fiction.

MAIN CHARACTER QUESTIONNAIRE

1. What's your name?

2. How old are you?

3. What's the problem you're facing?

4. What's your family background?

5. Where do you live?

6. What do you like to do?

7. What's different about you?

8. What do you care about?

9. What do you fear?

10. What are your dreams?

11. Who are the important people in your life?

12. What are the important things in your life?

13. How will you change through confronting your problem? Possibilities:

14. What will you understand about yourself and your world at the end of the story? Possibilities:

© 2002 by Nancie Atwell from
Lessons That Change Writers
(Portsmouth, NH: Heinemann)

MAIN CHARACTER QUESTIONNAIRE   LESSON 30

30

Reproducible and Overhead
Main Character Questionnaire

Last night I narrowed down my own list of potential fictional problems to one. I'm interested in this premise: what if a boy who is passionate about art and history—in other words, a humanities nut—has a father who wants a different kind of son? The situation intrigues me because I know two boys who experienced childhoods with similar conflicts, and because I've been reading Homer Hickam, Jr.'s trilogy of Coalwood memoirs, about Sonny, who wants to be a rocket scientist and his dad, Homer, Sr., who wants Sonny to work with him in the coal mines.

So I've got some rough sense already of who my main character will be. Now I've got to flesh him out—to invent and develop the details that will bring the boy and his problem to life.

I've reproduced a blank copy of a main character questionnaire as a transparency. I'm going to think out loud as I fill it in, and I'd love to have your input. [See Figure 30-1 for an image of the questionnaire I completed during this demonstration.]

First, I've already decided that the boy's name is Ben. My setting is going to be rural, because the father will be a hunter, and the rural setting I know best is New England, so Ben seemed like a good New England name, plus one that wouldn't call too much attention to itself and take over my story, like, say, Stone or Seymour.

How old would you make Ben if he were your character? . . . Well, I appreciate that it would be fun for you to imagine the life of an eighteen-year-old, but I don't believe you can do it convincingly, folks. Let's get real. As seventh and eighth graders, what's the outside age you could credibly imagine? . . . Fifteen sounds realistic to me, too. I think Ben is going to be fourteen. No, make that thirteen and in the eighth grade. I'm beginning to like the idea of the conflict with his father manifesting itself around a decision about where Ben will go to high school next year.

What specifically is his problem? Okay: Ben isn't—he can't be—the kind of boy his father wants. The father is a hunter and maybe a high school baseball coach. No, make that football—the ultimate macho sport.

I've already said the setting is rural New England. Now I'll sketch Ben's family. Let's see . . . what if he has a younger sister who's an incredible tomboy, so there's an even greater contrast, in the father's eyes, between who Ben is and could be? Ben *could* have other siblings, but for

Main Character Questionnaire

1. What's your name?

   Ben

2. How old are you? Fourteen Thirteen – 8th gr.

3. What's the problem you're facing? I'm not — can't be — the kind of
   son my father wants. He's a hunter and a baseball coach.
                                                    football

4. Where do you live?

   Rural New England

5. What's your family background?

   Tomboy sister   Father: runs a John Deere
   Comfortably middle class   franchise
                                          Mother: prod. man. at local
6. What do you like to do?   paper BUT was a fash. illus.
                                          in Boston
   Draw   Paint   Birdwatch
   Read   Research history

7. What's different about you?

   I like things rural guys aren't "supposed" to ; I'm
   drawn to the humanities

8. What do you care about?

   Oil painting, etc...
   High school: attending a private arts h.s. w̄out team sports

9. What do you fear?

   My father & his disapproval; confronting him; having
   to go to the local h.s. (no art program)

10. What are your dreams?

    To find a community – people like me. To go to "Walnut
    Hill." To have my father's approval.

11. Who are the important people in your life?

    Father   Girl he paints with (Hannah)
    Mother   Friend in the Young Historian Club (Tom)

12. What are the important things in your life?

    Set of oil paints   Sketchbooks   Binoculars
    History & art books   Expensive Camera

13. How will you change through confronting your problem? Possibilities:
    I'll become stronger in my self-confidence ; accept myself;
    acknowledge my mom; understand I have to endure my dad

14. What will you understand about yourself and your world at the end of the story?
    Possibilities:
    This father cannot be pleased. The best to hope for :
    maybe we'll make peace when I'm a grown-up.

Figure 30-1 Main Character Questionnaire from Nancie's Demonstration

30

now at least I think I'll leave it there, because I don't want to bring characters into my story that I don't know what to do with, that I don't have a purpose for.

I think I want Ben's family to be comfortably middle-class, so if it's a private school Ben wants, money for tuition won't be an issue. What should the father do for a living? . . . Frankly, I don't think an English teacher at the school where he's the football coach will work for my story: he won't make enough money, and if he's an English teacher, I've lost the basis for his disapproval of Ben's interests. I know—I'll make him the owner of a John Deere franchise.

Okay. Now, what about the mother? . . . Great idea. She'll have had an interest in art when she was younger—it's *her* humanities gene that Ben is carrying. I think I'll give her a colorless job—production manager at the local newspaper?—but when she was in her twenties and living in Boston, she was, let me think, a fashion illustrator.

Now, you tell me what Ben likes to do. . . . Great list. In addition to drawing, reading, and painting, I'm going to add that he enjoys researching history. And what about this: he's a birdwatcher, like Tyler. So there's another reason he doesn't like hunting. . . . No, I won't add going to video arcades as something Ben likes to do. It doesn't fit with the character I'm creating; it's not consistent with *Ben*.

Question 7: What's different about you, Ben? I think we already know. You like to do things that rural, outdoorsy guys aren't "supposed" to; you're not macho in this way; you're drawn to the humanities.

Next, what does Ben care about? We know what he likes to do. This question is more about what he *wants*. I think Ben wants to go to a private boarding school like Walnut Hill in Massachusetts, one that doesn't have sports or teams and that emphasizes the arts.

What does Ben fear? . . . I agree: his father's disapproval and having to confront him. And I'll add having to attend the local high school, which doesn't offer an art program.

What's Ben's dream for his life? . . . To go to Walnut Hill, yes. Beyond that? I think he'd like to feel that his father loves him and approves of him.

Next, we already know that Ben's father is important in his life. I'm going to say his mother is, too. I think she'll be his quiet advocate. And he's going to need some people his own age to talk with about his problems, so I'll be able to use dialogue to develop his character and the plot and themes of the story. Let's see . . . I think I'll give him a girl he likes, whom he paints with—Hannah?—and a guy friend, too—maybe a bud in the Young Historians Club. His name will be Tom. . . .

Wait a minute. You're telling me there should be a subplot about how

30

Tom's family wants *him* to go away for high school, but Tom wants to stay home and play football for Ben's father? I'm afraid that as Ben's creator I'm going to have to put my foot down. First of all, that's too much coincidence. Secondly, I'm writing a short story. I only have twenty or so pages. I've got to keep my plot focused on Ben's character and his dilemma.

Next, the objects that matter to Ben? . . . Great: a set of oil paints—how about if his mother spent her own money to buy them for him for his birthday? What else? History books. Art books. Sketchbooks. Tyler, what would Ben own for birding? . . . Okay: binoculars and a good camera for photographing birds he sights.

Now come the two big questions, the ones that will help me find and develop my theme or *So what?* One hallmark of fiction is that over the arc of the narrative, the main character changes. How might Ben change? . . . Hmmm, I don't think Ben is going to gather his courage and have a fist-fight with his father. I'm trying to develop a consistent character here, and however much you might enjoy this father taking a punch, my Ben is not that kind of boy.

Let me think: what *is* realistic and consistent? I think maybe Ben is going to understand that he can't change his father, that he has to learn how to endure his dad *and* stand up for himself. And maybe he's going to accept and acknowledge his mom as his closer parent, in some conscious way that he hasn't before.

I know: what if the climax of the story is Ben watching and listening as his parents argue about where he'll go to high school? What if he and his mother sent in an application to Walnut Hill, Ben was accepted, and the father found and opened the letter of acceptance? And now Ben's mother stands up for him in a dramatic, convincing way? That sounds like it could be plausible and interesting.

Finally, what else will Ben understand? Maybe it's that his father can't be pleased, as least for now. But maybe Ben can hope that he and his dad will make peace, meet each other on their own terms, when Ben is a grown-up? Maybe his mother can help him with that realization and cushion the blow?

I am ready to write Ben's story. Can you see how this exercise prepared me? Turn your attention to these two quotes. Margaret Banning wrote that "Fiction is not a dream. Nor is it guesswork. It is imagining based on facts, and the facts must be accurate or the work of imagining will not stand up." And Virginia Woolf said, "Fiction is like a spider's web, attached ever so lightly perhaps, but still attached to life at all four corners."

Do you see how hard I've worked to imagine my facts, to construct my spider's web? I like this quote by John Irving, too: "I believe you have constructive accidents en route through a novel only because you mapped a

> "Fiction is not a dream. Nor is it guesswork. It is imagining based on facts, and the facts must be accurate or the work of imagining will not stand up."
>
> – *Margaret Banning*

> "Fiction is like a spider's web, attached ever so lightly perhaps, but still attached to life at all four corners."
>
> – *Virginia Woolf*

30

"I believe you have constructive accidents en route through a novel only because you mapped a clear way. If you have confidence that you have a clear direction to take, you always have confidence to explore other ways ... The more you know about a book, the freer you can be to fool around. The less you know, the tighter you get."

– John Irving

clear way. If you have confidence that you have a clear direction to take, you always have confidence to explore other ways . . . The more you know about a book, the freer you can be to fool around. The less you know, the tighter you get."

I'm going to require that you complete a main character questionnaire and flesh out your own main character and his or her situation before you draft one word of your short story. Gather your facts, attach your spider web to life, map your way, and build your confidence. But before anyone begins to write short fiction, I have one more assignment for you.

Tonight for homework, would you make notes about what you learned from my demonstration today? Turn to the next clean page in your writing handbook and copy this heading:

Considerations in Creating a Character

Under the heading, please list everything you noticed that a writer of fiction has to do, think about, and remember when inventing a main character. I'll do the same. Tomorrow we'll compile a group list of our discoveries.

Comments? Questions? Observations?

30

Considerations in Creating a Character

Preparation

✔ Overhead transparency headed "Considerations in Creating a Character" for brainstorming with students criteria for creating a fictional character

"Please talk to me about what you observed during yesterday's demonstration about character development and filling in a main character questionnaire. I'll gather your ideas in a rough way on transparencies, then give them back to you tomorrow as a typed, organized entry for you to tape into your writing handbook and use as a benchmark when you're ready to create a character of your own. So don't record notes during this lesson; do pay attention to the discussion and make contributions.

I'm ready. . . . [See Figure 31-1 for a list my students and I created.]

CONSIDERATIONS IN CREATING A CHARACTER

- Create a meaningful, interesting problem for the character, one that holds possibilities for you as a writer *and* one you can imagine.
- Choose a name that fits the family background and setting and doesn't take over or distract from the story.
- Choose an age you can imagine.
- Choose a family background you can imagine, plus one that will support the development of the problem.
- Choose a setting you know well enough to describe in accurate, believable detail.

Figure 28-1 Sample List of Character Considerations from Nancie's Class, continued on page 114

- Choose favorite things for the character to do that reveal what he or she is like and that fit with each other and the character.
- Choose a cast of supporting characters who will reveal the main character and his or her problem but won't distract from the main character.
- Let the plot grow from the tensions created by the character's problem.
- Make the change in the character believable and consistent with his or her personality and life.
- Make the resolution believable and consistent with who the character is *and* with the personalities of the supporting characters, especially those with whom the main character is in conflict.
- Keep the main character true to himself or herself: consider, at every step, would this person act this way?

This is another astute, useful summary of what you've learned about writing good fiction. Your understandings are a far cry from viewing fiction as an act of dressing up a paper doll character to inhabit a daydream on paper. I am so looking forward to meeting and believing in your fictional characters.

Comments or questions about our list?

31

Short Story Structure

Preparation

- ✔ Read-alouds of four short stories, presented over the course of the previous week (see Appendix B For "Don't Give Up the Fight" by Erin Witham and "Game Life" by Tyler Cadman; see Appendix E for the sources of two suggested published short stories, "The Ravine" by Graham Salisbury and "Fourth of July" by Robin Brancato)

- ✔ Trimmed photocopies of "Short Story Structure" for students to tape into their handbooks

- ✔ Tape dispensers

LESSON 32

NOVEMBER

"I've been reading aloud short stories to you for the past weeks with two purposes in mind: to marinate you in good examples of a genre you'll be writing, and to give you a sense of how short stories are structured—how the main character and plot develop and arc. I think there are some definite patterns we can talk about and you can bear in mind as you draft your own short fiction.

Please tape a copy of "Short Story Structure" onto the next clean page of your writing handbook, then follow along with me as I read it aloud. . . .

Can we look back together and try to apply this list to the stories I've been reading aloud to you?

For example, the lead of Erin Witham's short story "Don't Give Up the Fight" showed Ava *in action*: dreaming about running and trying to awaken from her nightmare.

SHORT STORY STRUCTURE

- Create a narrative lead: show the main character in action, dialogue, or reaction.

- Introduce the main character's character.

- Introduce the setting: the time and place of the main character's life.

- Introduce and develop the problem the main character is facing.

- Develop the plot and problem toward a climax, e.g., a decision, action, conversation, or confrontation that shows the problem at its height.

- Develop a change in the main character, e.g., an acknowledgement or understanding of something, a decision, a course of action, a regret.

- Develop a resolution: how does the main character come to terms—or not—with his or her problem?

© 2002 by Nancie Atwell from
Lessons That Change Writers
(Portsmouth, NH: Heinemann)
                                 SHORT STORY STRUCTURE   LESSON 32

32

Reproducible
Short Story
Structure

Then, how did Erin introduce Ava's character and the place Ava lives? . . . How did she develop the problem Ava is facing? . . . How did Erin move the plot along toward the climax? What is the climax of "Don't Give Up the Fight"? . . . Finally, how did Ava change? How did she resolve her problem? . . .

Let's apply the same structural outline to Tyler Cadman's short story "Game Life." We began with Mike, the main character, *reflecting*: is that last present under the tree for him? And is it what Mike hopes it is?

Then, how does Tyler introduce Mike's character? . . . What do we learn about the setting? . . . How does Tyler move the plot along to the climax? What *is* the climax of "Game Life"? . . . Finally, how does Mike change? What does he understand at the end of the story? . . .

Can we apply this structure to published short stories? You bet. Think back to and reflect on "The Ravine" by Graham Salisbury and "Fourth of July" by Robin Brancato, and tell me how this model of short story structure applies. . . .

From this point on, when I read aloud to you short stories I love, and I will and lots of them, this is one of the ways I'll ask you to respond. We'll talk about how the stories made you feel and think, but we'll also note how the author led off the story, introduced and developed the main character, implied or described a setting, created action that introduced and developed the problem the main character is facing, developed the plot and problem toward a climax, showed the main character changing, and resolved the problem.

And, from this point on, as you draft your own short stories, I expect you'll use this entry in your handbook to help you think about what you're doing. I expect that you'll develop your main characters, structure the plot, and resolve the problem deliberately and thoughtfully.

Questions or comments?

Ways to Develop a Character

Preparation

✔ Trimmed photocopies of "Ways to Develop a Character" for students to tape into their handbooks

✔ Tape dispensers

LESSON **33**

"We've talked about how the thoughtful introduction and development of the main character is crucial to a good short story. Today let's talk specifically about some of the ways that writers of fiction invent their people and show what they're like. How do you flesh out someone who doesn't exist?

Please turn to the next clean page in your handbook, tape in "Ways to Develop a Character," then follow along with me as I read it aloud. . . .

Think for a moment about the novel you're reading right now, the one you just finished, and the last few short stories I've read aloud to you. Did the authors use any of the techniques on the list to bring their characters to life? . . . How? . . . Any others? . . .

I'm going to argue that the opening paragraphs and pages are *the* most crucial to the success of your short story. This is your opportunity to get a character up and walking around, breathing, *living*. This is your chance to convince a reader—and, more important, to convince *yourself*—that your character lives and that readers will accompany a real person through the events of his or her story, not watch from a distance as a paper doll gets picked up and moved from point A to point B. The young adult novelist S. E. Hinton once said, "My characters always take shape first; they wander around my mind looking for something to do." Build people. Listen to how they sound. Observe how they think and behave. *Understand them.*

Do not skip this part. Don't imagine that you can come back later and scatter some thoughts and feelings, or give your character a sense of humor, a past, a daydream, an attitude, a yearning, a *personality*, after the fact. Invest right from the start in details of character: collect a person. Then, as you develop the problem and move toward the climax, the events of your story and your character's reactions to them can grow in an organic way from the seeds of personality that you planted in your opening pages.

Tonight for homework, please read through this list of ways to develop a character again, on your own, and mark it up. Write notes to yourself about which of the approaches you'd like to try in your short story, and capture any ideas that occur to you about how to make an approach work for your story and main character.

Comments? Questions? Observations?

WAYS TO DEVELOP A CHARACTER

■ **Reflection:**
Whether the narrative voice is first (*I*) or third (*he* or *she*), tell often and everywhere what your character is thinking and feeling: the best, most essential way to create a life is to start and end with an inner life.

■ **Dialogue:**
Get your character talking as a way to reveal himself or herself. ("I don't have a very clear idea of who the characters are until they start talking." —Joan Didion)

■ **Letters, Email Exchanges, or Diary Entries:**
Illustrate what's on your character's mind through pieces of his or her writing.

■ **Action:**
Get your character up and moving around, doing things both little and big that show what he or she is like.

■ **Flashback:**
Recall events from the past that show why your character is behaving as he or she does today.

■ **Reaction:**
Show how your character responds to the actions, words, and ideas of another character.

■ **Other Characters:**
Compare and contrast your character's actions, reactions, beliefs, or values with those of friends, family members, classmates, etc. How is he or she like the others? Shaped by the others? Different from the others?

■ **Quirks:**
Imagine the habits, interests, skills, hobbies, goals, fears, tastes and preferences, daydreams, and nightmares that will flesh out your character as a living, breathing person.

■ **Intimate Setting:**
Create your character's bedroom and fill it with the stuff of his or her life that reveals parts of the past and present.

■ **Beloved Object or Pet:**
Give your character something to love that reveals his or her private self or previous history. Maybe even have your character speak to the pet or comfort object.

© 2002 by Nancie Atwell from *Lessons That Change Writers* (Portsmouth, NH: Heinemann) WAYS TO DEVELOP A CHARACTER LESSON 33

Reproducible
Ways to Develop a Character

33

A Course of Study: How Free-Verse Poetry Works

34	**The Power of** *I*
35	**Beware the Participle**
36	**Leads: Begin Inside**
37	**Conclusions: End Strongly**
38	**Breaking Lines and Stanzas and Punctuating**
39	**Cut to the Bone**
40	**Use Repetition**
41	**Two Things at Once**

What I Was Thinking Among the genres that student writers can misperceive—and miss the challenges and joys of—poetry is right up there with fiction. Children's rhyming poems struggle to have something to say, as the effort of rhyming subsumes the making of meaning. And while children's free-verse poems do succeed in terms of being about something, too often they're weakened by a writer's lack of experience with the conventions of free-verse poetry.

I know this sounds like a contradiction—that a "free" genre should be constrained by rules—but most contemporary poets understand some things, implicitly or explicitly, about how free-verse poetry works. Their knowledge of technique raises their poems above the worst sins of the free-verse genre: cliché, clutter, cuteness, formlessness, voicelessness, intentional obscurity, and prose structures masquerading as poems—skinny paragraphs with arbitrary line breaks. Free-verse poets use the conventions of the genre to create voice, power, and meaning.

To learn, and to be able to teach, the conventions, I read contemporary free-verse and began to try to write my own. Both processes take me inside the genre. Multiple readings of poems help me understand how they mean, how they cue or signal readers, how they use the white space of the page, and how they denote and connote. My own attempts at writing poetry show me how hard it is to write a good poem. I learn about creating and resolving difficulty, and I wrestle with the myriad of minute choices and decisions that a poem needs to answer. I've never written fewer than five drafts of a poem.

In planning this series of lessons, I knew I wanted to convey to kids that good poetry takes time and revision, and that the techniques of free-verse poets can be observed, learned, and put into practice—that students, too, can create poems that surprise, signify, and satisfy.

These lessons occur in the context of regular readings of free-verse poetry. My writing workshops begin each day with a reading and discussion of one or two poems I love and think my kids will love, too. In a typical school year, this means we'll enjoy at least two hundred shared experiences with great poems, some by published poets, some by students in the group, some by kids from previous classes, and a few by me.

Chapter 13 in the second edition of *In the Middle* (1998), "Finding Poetry Everywhere," describes the daily poetry sessions in more detail. In Appendix E of this book I listed the poetry collections and anthologies that are, so far, the essential sources for our daily poems. And in this section and throughout *Lessons That Change Writers*, I've included interesting student poems that the poets and I invite teachers to photocopy to read and talk about with their students. I have just one caveat: these poems—any poems—should not be read aloud cold. They require a teacher's voice that students can trust, one they can ride into and through the meaning of a poem.

In September, entering seventh grader Jonathan was among a handful of kids who answered *no* to the questions "Are you an author?" and "Are you a poet?" on a survey I administer each fall, before the launch of writing workshop. But in his second trimester self-evaluation in March, when Jonathan identified this series of poetry lessons as *the* most useful to him as a writer, he wrote, "These mini-lessons were the most important to me of the whole school year. They changed me completely as a poet. I felt like an insider, and I think I wrote my first good poems. Now I can say it. I am a poet."

The Power of I

Preparation

✔ Overhead transparency of "One Definition of Free-Verse Poetry"

✔ Overhead transparencies of "Wind: 1st draft" and "Wind: 3rd Draft," Ceysa McKechnie's first poem of seventh grade

✔ Overhead transparency of "Remember the Power of I"

✔ Wall poster of Wesley McNair quotation

✔ Wall poster of Emily Dickinson quotation

LESSON **34**

OCTOBER

"I think you can already guess, based on the number of poems we've read together this fall, not to mention my embarrassing enthusiasm for all of them, how much I love poetry. More than any other genre, poetry helps me live my life. It connects me with others at the most essential level—one heart and mind touching another heart and mind—and it distances me, too—invites me to see the familiar with fresh eyes. And poetry is the language of my feelings. It expresses my needs, my hopes and dreams, my heartaches and the sources of my happiness, better than any other genre. Poetry is useful to my life. I want it to be useful to yours, too.

So I begin with a warning. Good poetry, the useful kind, is often hard to write. It's easy to string together collections of pretty words and parcel them into lines and stanzas. What I'm talking about is the hard work of the good poet—figuring out what the feeling is, finding your truth, choosing and arranging, cutting and splicing, writing a riddle that contains its own answers.

There's a myth about writing poetry, that's it's an exquisite experience that comes to a poet on the wings of a dove. Not true. Good poets work at it. They know good poetry because they read it—a lot of it—and they revise toward their sense of what a good poem does, is, and can do.

I love this quote from poet Wes McNair: "The capacity to revise determines the true writer. Suspect the finished poem. Your evil twin wants your poem to be finished." And I adore something Emily Dickinson wrote: "If I feel physically as if the top of my head were taken off, I know that is poetry." These good poets know *labor*.

So, how *do* you work at a poem to try to make it a good one? Is it different from drafting and revising a memoir? An essay? In some important ways, yes. I have a handful of suggestions—eight, to be exact—of techniques for you to keep in mind when you draft and revise your free-verse poems.

Please turn to the next clean page of your writing handbook and record this heading:

34

How Free-Verse Poetry Works

Then, would you dog-ear the corners of the next two pages? I may teach other writing mini-lessons among and in between these eight, and I want you to keep the poetry lessons together. The turned-down corners are a reminder to save these three pages for free-verse poetry techniques.

For starters, what is free-verse poetry? You already know a lot about free verse, as it's all we've been reading together each morning. What have you noticed? . . .

Let's create a formal definition, based on what you know and what I've observed about the genre. Please record it in your handbook. Here goes:

> Free verse is poetry that doesn't have a regular rhythm, line length, or rhyme scheme. It relies on the natural rhythms of speech. Today it is the form of poetry that most American poets prefer. Free-verse poetry invents and follows its own forms, patterns, and rules.

So, if free-verse poets create and follow their own forms, how can there be rules? In fact,

ONE DEFINITION OF FREE-VERSE POETRY

Free verse is poetry that doesn't have a regular rhythm, line length, or rhyme scheme. It relies on the natural rhythms of speech. Today it is the form of poetry that most American poets prefer. Free-verse poetry invents and follows its own forms, patterns, and rules.

ONE DEFINITION OF FREE-VERSE POETRY   LESSON 34

Overhead
One Definition of
Free-Verse Poetry

WIND: 1ST DRAFT (9/12)

The wind rustles the trees
like it does the long grasses of the meadow,
commands the water to move in ripples
like tiny mountains and rests in the sails
of a small boat on its way home.

Then the wind leaves to rustle other trees,
blow through other meadows,
move other tiny mountains,
and send other small boats home.

Ceysa McKechnie

WIND: 1ST DRAFT (9/12)   LESSON 34

Overhead
"Wind: 1st Draft" by Ceysa McKechnie

WIND: 3RD DRAFT (9/15)

I listen to the wind rustle through the trees
as it does the long grasses in the meadows.
I watch as it commands the water to move in ripples
like tiny mountains and rest in the sails of a small boat,
    pushing it home.

Then the wind abandons the small boat to rustle other trees,
blow through other meadows,
command other tiny mountains to move,
send other small boats home.

As I watch night begin to settle,
I wonder, will I ever find myself in the small boat,
watching the same wind fly over the green landscape,
longing for it to land in my sails and send me home?

—Ceysa McKechnie

WIND: 3RD DRAFT (9/15)   LESSON 34

Overhead
"Wind: 3rd Draft" by Ceysa McKechnie

---

they're more like *conventions*—approaches that free-verse poets and their readers have agreed, in a general way, make poems stronger. The first convention I'd like you to record in your handbook is

Remember the Power of I

Please read along with me the transparency of the first draft of "Wind," Ceysa's first poem of seventh grade. . . .

When I talked with Ceysa about it, in a writing conference, my question was, "In the world of the poem, where are you, physically?"

Ceysa answered, "I'm sitting on the shore, watching the sailboat."

"How are you feeling?"

"Like I want to be on it, but also like I'm glad I'm home."

I said, "That's an interesting tension, but it's not in the poem yet. Do me a favor. See what happens if you put yourself in the poem in the next draft. Right now, as your reader, I have nowhere to be and no one to be with. Start your next draft with the personal pronoun *I*, and see where it takes you."

Here's Ceysa's third draft of "Wind." Read along with me. Can you see, hear, and feel the difference? . . .

Don't underestimate the power of *I* to ground a poem—to capture you in relation to the world of a poem, to provide the single most important detail that a reader craves: a human intelligence, a presence, a specific someone to be with. Think about the poems you've been loving by Collins, Oliver, Frost, Nye, Hughes, Williams, Stafford, Pastan, Heaney, Neruda, Giovanni, Updike, and Bishop. They wave their *I* flag; these poets have voices.

I know that the temptation for beginning poets is to hide. You can't help but be self-conscious—to think, who am I to tell about my little feelings and experiences in a poem? But

34

34

> **REMEMBER THE POWER OF *I***
>
> First person experiences need a first person. Make sure your *I* is present and is thinking, feeling, seeing, *acting*. Give your readers someone to be with. Find your voice as a poet. Wave your *I* flag in your poetry.
>
> © 2002 by Nancie Atwell from
> *Lessons That Change Writers*
> (Portsmouth, NH: Heinemann)
>
> REMEMBER THE POWER OF *I*   LESSON 34

Overhead
Remember the
Power of *I*

you are the only one who can tell your feelings, your observations, your ideas, your stories. Embrace them. Wave your *I* flag. Find your voice as a poet. Give your readers someone to be with. Your poems will be stronger for it; your readers will love you for it. Please copy the notes about the Power of *I* from the overhead into your handbooks.

Comments? Questions? Observations?

Tomorrow's poetry lesson is about an insidious verb form, one you need to use with caution in your poems, because otherwise it'll eat your *I*.

Beware the Participle

Preparation

✔ Overhead transparency of "Beware the Participle"

✔ Photocopies of my poems "Green Thoughts with Participles" and "Green Thoughts"

LESSON **35**

"The verb form I mentioned at the end of yesterday's poetry mini-lesson, as one to watch out for, is the *participle*. Please copy this definition and warning in your writing handbook, directly under your notes about the Power of *I*:

BEWARE THE PARTICIPLE

A participle is a verb in disguise. It's actually a nonfinite verb that functions as an adjective. Participles make action indirect, even vague. Used badly, they can make the actors in a poem—the people, the *I*—disappear. You can usually spot participles by their endings, -ing or -ed, and where they come in a line: at the beginning and often as a substitute for a noun or pronoun, especially *I*.

Overhead
Beware the Participle

Beware the Participle

A participle is a verb in disguise. It's actually a nonfinite verb that functions as an adjective. Participles make action indirect, even vague. Used badly, they can make the actors in a poem—the people, the *I*— disappear. You can usually spot participles by their endings, *-ing* or *-ed*, and where they come in a line: at the beginning, and often as a substitute for a noun or pronoun, especially *I*.

As an editor of kids' poems, I took an early, active dislike to participles, but I couldn't put my finger on *why*. All I knew is that every time I encountered a string of *-ing* words in a student's poem, the poem suffered.

So I did some homework. I learned that the *-ing* words that make me grind my teeth are called participles, and that although they look like verbs, they work as adjectives, as words that describe nouns and pronouns. Stay with me here.

What I realized is that beginning poets use participles as a way to avoid using nouns and pronouns, especially that bold but essential personal

GREEN THOUGHTS WITH PARTICIPLES

Perched on a tree stump,
trying to admire
the lobster pound woods.

Looking at the gunmetal pond,
grey ashes dancing above
like skeletons rubbing shoulders.

Watching birch trees surrender their white,
snow sticking in shady spots,
and tired ancestors of ferns waving goodbye.

Hearing no birds call
except for three gulls circling the pond
and screaming at the wind.

Smelling old air,
not even smelling the balsams,
and noticing no signs of what's to come.

But, deep inside, knowing
and saying a prayer of thanks
for the gifts of imagination and memory—

the twin blessings of the human condition
that each spring survive
the dismal days of March in Maine.

—N. Atwelling

GREEN THOUGHTS WITH PARTICIPLES   LESSON 35

35

Reproducible
"Green Thoughts
with Participles"

GREEN THOUGHTS

I perch on a tree stump
and try to admire
the lobster pound woods.

But below me the pond is gunmetal.
Above me grey ashes dance
like skeletons rubbing shoulders.

Around me birch trees have surrendered their white.
Grainy snow sticks in a shady spot at my feet,
and the tired ancestors of fern fronds wave good-bye.

I hear no bird call
except for three gulls that circle the pond
and scream at the knife-edge wind.

The air smells old.
Even the balsams are subdued.
I can't find one sign of what's to come.

But some part of me *knows*.
So I say a prayer of thanks
for the gifts of imagination and memory—

the twin blessings of the human condition
that each spring carry me
through the dismal days of March in Maine.

—Nancie Atwell

GREEN THOUGHTS   LESSON 35

Reproducible
"Green Thoughts"

pronoun, *I*. So instead of writing the line, "I walked in the rain and felt its caress," a hider-behind-participles would word it as a phrase, "Walking in the rain and feeling its caress," with no *I* in sight.

The problem, of course, is that without an actor, there's no one for a reader to see or be with in a poem. Let me show you two versions of the same poem, which I hope will demonstrate the problem. First, check out "Green Thoughts with Participles." Read along with me. . . .

Can you feel the lack of *I* and *me*, the way all those participles distance us as readers from a direct experience? How there isn't, in fact, a speaker or an actor in this poem, and just barely a human presence?

Let's try it again. Here's the real "Green Thoughts." Read along with me again. . . .

What do you notice? . . . Is this better for you as readers? More active? More present? . . .

Let's add a coda to the notes in your handbook. I don't want to cripple you as writers, so you spend too much of your time and energy avoiding participles. Here's the *but*:

Wherever you can, make your lines active: peopled with nouns and pronouns, especially peopled with I.

Comments or questions about participles?

Leads: Begin Inside

Preparation

✔ Overhead transparency of "Leads: Begin Inside"

✔ Photocopies of Anne Atwell-McLeod's "Journey" and Nat Herz's "Boy's Life"

> "How should a free-verse poem begin? I think there's only one rule. Please copy it down as the next entry in your writing handbook.

Overhead
Leads: Begin Inside

Leads: Begin Inside

In the words of Horace, one of the greatest lyric poets of all time (65 B.C.–8 B.C.), begin poems "in the midst of things." Start your poems *inside* an experience, feeling, observation, or memory.

For me, one of the best things about writing poetry, *vs.* prose, is that I don't need to establish a detailed context—all the who-what-when-where-why information that readers of prose require. Poetry rides on the compactness of the form—on what's left out—so the reader of a poem can be as much of a creator as its writer.

And poems ride on their immediacy. So beware of throat-clearing, pre-ambles, and setting the stage—of starting a poem with background explanations of what happened leading up to the moment of the poem. Go right to the moment.

Let me show you a couple of student poems that begin inside, in the midst of things, as examples of what I mean. Anne's poem, "Journey," begins inside. Read along with me. . . .

Anne doesn't tell us where she's coming from as she's on her way home, or who she's with, or why she needs cheering up. She begins in the midst

36

> ### JOURNEY
>
> On the way home
> it rained.
> It rained as it can only
> in summer—
> a shower that brings mosquitoes
> and heat,
> a downpour when the sky
> doesn't darken.
>
> It rained like needles
> falling from a pine tree
> deep in the forest
> that silently—
> like a dream only
> one person has
> and only once.
>
> On the way home
> it rained like
> someone
> somewhere
> needed a rainbow,
> and maybe they were
> going to get one.
>
> And I reached home.
> And maybe the someone
> was me.
>
> —Anne Atwell-McLeod
>
> © 2002 by Nancie Atwell from
> *Lessons That Change Writers*
> (Portsmouth, NH: Heinemann)   JOURNEY   LESSON 36

Reproducible
"Journey" by Anne Atwell-McLeod

> ### BOY'S LIFE
>
> somewhere out there
> is a boy
> who can bench one-fifty without effort
> but as far as I'm concerned
> it will never be me
>
> showing no emotion
> he's the captain
> of the football team
> who won't leave the field
> until he's blinded by his own blood
>
> cheering mindlessly he's the number one fan
> of TV wrestlers
> who love to hear
> the loudest crunch
>
> one day
> he'll encounter the real world
> and realize what it means
> for a man to be
> strong
>
> —Nat Herz
>
> © 2002 by Nancie Atwell from
> *Lessons That Change Writers*
> (Portsmouth, NH: Heinemann)   BOY'S LIFE   LESSON 36

Reproducible
"Boy's Life" by Nat Herz

of the experience. Do you see what I mean about immediacy?

Now check out Nat's poem, "Boy's Life." Follow along with me as I read. . . .

Nat could have started the poem by clearing his throat for a stanza or two and explaining where he's coming from—"I'm small for my age. I'm not a pumped-up, macho-man sort of guy. And I'm surrounded by a culture where male strength is measured by what I see as empty, macho values." Instead, Nat goes right to the heart of the matter: "Somewhere out there is a boy . . . ."

This is a good technique to know for first drafts. But it's also a way of revising. After you've written a first draft of a poem and made your initial stab at getting your ideas and feelings down on the page, you may wish to go back and see if you need the first lines, maybe even the first stanza: to ask yourself, have I begun in the midst of things?

Observations? Questions?

Conclusions: End Strongly

Preparation

- ✔ Overhead transparency of "Conclude Strongly"
- ✔ Photocopies of Kyle Hirsch's "Answer," Colleen Connell's "Time Will Pass," Jed Chambers' "Fantasy World," and Jonathan Tindal's "Sarah"

LESSON 37

OCTOBER

"I think there are two places where readers find the deepest meanings in free-verse poems. I'll call the first a *turn*: a point in a poem where the poet moves in a new, surprising direction. The other place is a poem's conclusion.

Conclusions—last lines—are the parts of my poems I revise the most. I want a strong end—to leave a reader thinking, maybe even trying to finish my thought. I want words that will resonate, that will vibrate in a reader's mind. And I want to discover my own deepest meaning—to surprise myself so I can surprise my reader.

Take a look at a draft of "Answer," a poem by Kyle in which he learned to end strongly. Read along with me. . . .

Can you feel this good poem building toward something powerful and mysterious? Toward something elegant and subtle? The question I asked Kyle, and that I'll also pose to you, his readers, is, does this concluding line do it?

Kyle agreed that the last line wasn't strong and didn't fit as well as it might with the tone of the rest of the poem. So he drafted a bunch of alternative endings—final lines that asked the question in different ways—and chose the one that satisfied him and the needs of his poem. Kyle's last line became "how did you find your way home?"

ANSWER

The way you were brought into the harbor,
The load was light.
Not breaking one board,
you were ship shape.

The way you were beached.
The way you outlasted the storm
that the night brought.
Your contents were not so lucky.

The way you were forgotten for years.
The way you were taken for useless.
The way your rotten planks creaked and moaned
for someone to remember you,

for water to float in.
Until the day your hopes came true.
The way the two boys found you
lying beneath the dock.

The way they climbed over your low, rotten beams,
covered with moss and fungus.
The way their feet splashed in your murky belly
as the tide came in.
The way they tried to find the answer to your question:
what are you really doing here?

—Kyle Hirsch

ANSWER   LESSON 37

37

Reproducible
"Answer" by Kyle Hirsch

TIME WILL PASS

It is a typical summer day.
Our cottage awakens.
Bright sunlight pours through the open window
and into my pale blue room.
Light hits my eyes and for a moment
I am blinded by its everyday brilliance.

Now the sun that woke me this morning
reflects off the sea that surrounds Peaks Island.
I push my kayak paddle deep into the dense water
and glide along its silky surface.
I trail along behind my dad
thinking about yesterday,
when we went out kayaking but with other people,
so it wasn't as special.
This uncommon time together is precious.
It will last only an hour
and then, just as Cinderella lost everything at midnight,
our time together will end.
I glance at my watch,
inspect the second hand,
watch time fly.
It does.
Too soon, Dad turns
and I turn too,
continuing our swift pace, back to the kayak rental.
We drag our kayaks out of the water
and onto the hot grainy sand.

I hear a sharp blast of the ferry horn
arriving at Peaks.
We run to catch it,
run to catch the boat that will take us
far away from paradise island.

—Colleen Connell

TIME WILL PASS   LESSON 37

Reproducible
"Time Will Pass" by Colleen Connell

Please draw a line through "what are you really doing here?" and substitute Kyle's revision—"how did you find your way home?"—so your copy of the poem will read as he wants it to. Notice how in his revision he cut a bad word—*really*—and picked up on the word *way*, which he had repeated powerfully throughout the poem.

Here's another example of a poem that was improved by a more powerful conclusion, Colleen's "Time Will Pass." Again, read along with me. . . .

When I conferred with Colleen, I pointed out to her that the poem doesn't so much end as run out of material: after she and her family board the ferry and leave Peak's Island, she pretty much *has* to stop the poem because the experience is officially over.

I asked, "How do you want your reader to feel at the end of the poem? How did *you* feel, as the time you spent kayaking, just you and your dad, drew to a close?"

She said, "Really great and special—like it had been perfect."

"Well, what would happen if you cut the last stanza and ended with a bit of dialogue between you and your dad? Let us hear you say what you were feeling inside."

She did. Would you cross out the last stanza of Colleen's poem and substitute the revised, concluding stanza?

> "That was fun," Dad says.
> "That was perfect," I reply.

The final version of the poem carried a new title, too. Colleen called it "Perfection," so the title would echo the conclusion, and also convey her sense of the day with her dad. Please give "Time Will Pass" its proper title, "Perfection."

Colleen's idea to echo the title in the conclusion came from a poetry mini-lesson about

Reproducibles
"Fantasy World" by Jed Chambers and
"Sarah" by Jonathan Tindal

echo structure. One way for beginning poets to experiment with strong endings is to echo a poem's lead in its conclusion.

Let me show you an example of an echo structure. Check out Jed's poem about his computer as I read it aloud. . . . Can you feel at the end how Jed feels about his computer—his sense of mastery and satisfaction?

Now look at Jonathan's poem about his dog, Sarah. He used the echo structure as a jumping-off point: the conclusion doesn't exactly reproduce the opening lines, but it borrows its most poignant image. Read along with me. . . . Jonathan is left, as we are, with the image of Sarah's eyes and a feeling of being haunted by the memory.

Let's sum up the big ideas of this lesson with an entry in your writing handbooks. Please copy the overhead into your notes.

Overhead
Conclude Strongly

Conclude Strongly

The conclusion often conveys a poem's deepest meaning. It needs to be strong—to resonate after the reader has finished the poem. The conclusion should leave a reader with a feeling, idea, image, or question. Experiment: try different endings until you find the one that best conveys your meaning. Maybe try an echo structure: repeat significant lines from the lead, or elsewhere, in the conclusion. Give your poem the time it needs for the right conclusion.

Comments? Questions?

Breaking Lines and Stanzas and Punctuating

Preparation

✔ Overhead transparency of "Breaking Lines and Stanzas and Punctuating"

✔ Photocopies of "Rain Lullaby" by Molly Jordan, "Rain Poem—First and Second Drafts," and "Revealing Rain" by Nora Bradford, "The Meet" by David McDonald, and "The Storm" by Annie Kass

✔ Wall poster of Mary Oliver quotation

✔ Wall poster of Ron Padgett quotation

LESSON

38

OCTOBER

Beginning free-verse poets are often stymied by how to handle line breaks. Rhymed poems are obvious: lines end with words that rhyme. But in free verse, the length and content of a line are a matter of choice. So, how do you choose which words belong together as a line? How do your mind, eyes, ears—and even lungs—help you choose?

First, it's important to recognize that poetry is written to be spoken. Free-verse poetry generally breaks its lines to emphasize the pauses a reader's voice might make: line breaks signal the briefest of rests, breaths, or silences. The poet Mary Oliver, comparing a free-verse poem to a dance, says that the pause "is part of the motion of the poem, as hesitation is part of the dance."

Next, it's good to recognize that most poets end their lines on strong words: nouns, verbs, and modifiers, that is, adjectives and adverbs. If you look back through the poems we've read so far this year, you'll see that this is the case. Slicing a line at a weak word—an article, preposition, or conjunction, like *the*, *of*, or *and*—tells your reader to pause at an insignificant moment in the poem, rather than at a point of meaning. Mary Oliver isn't tentative about this: "The most important point in the line is the *end* of the line."

RAIN LULLABY

I listen to the rain
as it drizzles on our roof
and snuggle even deeper
under the warm weight of my covers.
My hands open my book,
and I begin to read.
In a moment I am lost
as the story unfolds.

Slowly, slowly, I feel
my eyelids turn to lead.
I shut my book
and turn off the light.
Already adrift
I close my eyes,
so glad to be where I am—
half asleep
in the warmth
of my bed
with the rain as my lullaby.

—Molly Jordan

RAIN LULLABY   LESSON 38

Reproducible
"Rain Lullaby"
by Molly Jordan

ABOUT LINES

"I cannot say too many
times how powerful the
techniques of line length
and line breaks are. You
cannot swing the lines
around, or fling strong-
sounding words, or scatter
soft ones, to no purpose."

– *Mary Oliver*

Read Molly's poem "Rain Lullaby" with me and notice the strong words at the ends of her lines. . . . Now imagine if Molly had broken her first line at *the*, or her second line at *on* or *our*, or the third line at the word *even*. Can you see and hear how her poem would have been weakened—how important the ends of her lines are?

Finally, free-verse poets need to be aware of how their poems look on the page. Line breaks and stanza breaks *are* a poem's form. Poetry is the only genre in which form matters as much as content—which is one of the reasons I have a hard time at poetry readings: my eyes itch to see how the poet has chosen to arrange the words I'm hearing as lines and stanzas. Read what Mary Oliver has to say about line length and breaks. . . .

Try to draft your free-verse poems in lines. You can always revise by shortening, lengthening, and moving lines, but I think it's important to enter into an act of poetry by visualizing your draft as a poem, not as prose, right from the start.

If that's difficult for you, it's okay to enter your poem as prose, then go back into the draft and divide it into lines, then revise and polish based on these breaks, which is what Nora did when she was starting out as a poet. Look with me at the first draft of her "Rain Poem," which went down on the page as a prose paragraph. . . .

In a conference I showed Nora how to insert double slash marks at the points where she might break lines—to listen for words, phrases, and sentences that seemed to belong together, to notice the junctures at which she breathed or rested as she read her poem. The second draft shows how Nora marked it up.

Then she rewrote the poem, this time skipping down and starting a new line each time she hit one of her slash marks. And from there, she revised by cutting and polishing. Here's the final version of Nora's poem, now titled "Revealing Rain." . . .

Take a look with me at David's poem about a swim meet. . . . Do you see how he made his lines short, on purpose, so the form of the poem would mimic its subject? As a swimmer, David was moving, so his poem moves, too: one long, fast stanza.

A word about punctuation: beginning free-verse poets are often

38

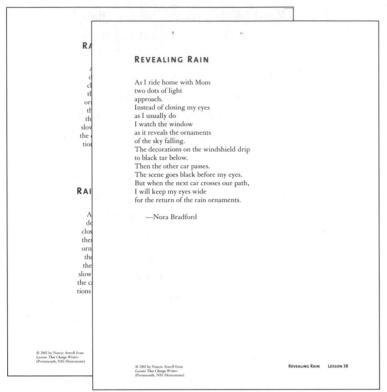

REVEALING RAIN

As I ride home with Mom
two dots of light
approach.
Instead of closing my eyes
as I usually do
I watch the window
as it reveals the ornaments
of the sky falling.
The decorations on the windshield drip
to black tar below.
Then the other car passes.
The scene goes black before my eyes.
But when the next car crosses our path,
I will keep my eyes wide
for the return of the rain ornaments.

—Nora Bradford

© 2002 by Nancie Atwell from
Lessons That Change Writers
(Portsmouth, NH: Heinemann)   REVEALING RAIN   LESSON 38

Reproducibles
"Rain Poem—First and Second Drafts" and
"Revealing Rain" by Nora Bradford

THE MEET

Step up.
Take your mark.
Go.
I burst off the starting block,
fly through the air,
slice into the water,
and glide.
I stroke,
gasp for air,
until I'm at the end of the pool,
where I flip
and push off
as hard as I can.
The screams of the crowd
fill my ears
as I take one more breath,
reach the wall,
hit it,
WIN.

—David MacDonald

© 2002 by Nancie Atwell from
Lessons That Change Writers
(Portsmouth, NH: Heinemann)   THE MEET   LESSON 38

Reproducible
"The Meet" by David MacDonald

tempted to put a comma at the end of every line—maybe as a way to enforce a breath or rest there? But since the function of the white space at the end of the line is to signal the reader to breathe or rest, the comma is redundant. Try to punctuate your free-verse poems as if they're prose sentences. That is, use commas, dashes, and periods sparingly, as if the lines of the poem came one after the other in a paragraph.

And a word about capital letters: many beginning poets, unsure about when and how to capitalize lines, play it safe by capitalizing the first word of every line. As a result, the power of a lot of good poems gets undercut. All those capital letters look pompous, as if the poet were saying, "Every line I'm writing is so profound it must be capitalized." Today most free-verse poets capitalize their poems as they would prose. That is, they capitalize the first words of sentences and the proper nouns.

Finally, what about stanza breaks? It's helpful to know that the word stanza comes from the Latin word *stantia*, which means "standing" or "stopping." The variety of Vulgar Latin that became Italian uses the word *stanza* to mean "stopping place" or "room." Ron Padgett, a poet, says it helps to think of stanzas as the rooms in the house that is your poem. He says, "The stanza-break almost always indicates a pause, however slight, just as you have to slow down to go through a door."

Look at Annie's poem "The Storm." She chose to break her stanzas at the points where the action changes in the story her poem is

THE STORM

Under gloomy gray skies hanging low
I pulled on my oilskins and climbed into the wooden skiff.
I was skeptical;
you were not.
It'll clear up, you assured me.
Off we set.

Before even the first trap was hauled,
rain began to trickle down our cheeks
and onto the orange rubber of the oilskins.
Within a few traps
it was streaming from the sky,
lashing onto our bowed heads.

Trap after trap we hauled,
and I did my jobs almost mechanically as we collected our booty:
█████████████████████
We puttered farther and farther from the dock
until it was lost behind the damp pines of the jutting shore.
The dog bounded along the seaweedy rocks, trying to keep up with us.
Water sloshed over the stern of the open boat.
I shivered beneath my hood.

Soon we pulled into the dock
with numbed faces and frozen fingers.
I met my black dog under the trees on the shore
and with stiff hands tried to unbuckle my soaked life vest
as we walked to the boat shop at the top of the hill,
as the rain poured down on the blue-gray ocean.

—Annie Kass

© 2002 by Nancie Atwell from
Lessons That Change Writers
(Portsmouth, NH: Heinemann)

THE STORM   LESSON 38

Reproducible
"The Storm"
by Annie Kass

telling, just as a writer of prose narrative would break for a new paragraph at each shift in the action. In the first stanza Annie and her dad head out to pull lobster traps, in spite of ominous skies. In the second stanza it starts to pour. In the third they haul traps in the middle of the storm. And in the final stanza they return to shore.

In free-verse poetry, stanza breaks, like line breaks, are up to the poet. As Ron Padgett puts it, you may want all the rooms in your house to be the same size, or you may want to vary the size of the rooms, depending on what they're for. He concludes: "The main thing is to make rooms that are big enough to be useful, shapely enough to be attractive, and not so empty as to be disappointing."

38

Line breaks and stanza breaks are techniques I'll help you with when we confer about your poems and when I copy edit them. My bottom-line request right now is that you experiment deliberately. Make choices, and resist settling for a poem in the form in which it first goes down on the page. I think one of the great benefits of word processing is that it's easy to experiment with line and stanza breaks—to bump words down to another line, separate lines from the lines that precede them, build white space around them, and consider how your poem reads and looks strongest.

So, let's summarize all of this as notes. Please copy the overhead into your writing handbook:

Overhead
Breaking Lines and
Stanzas and
Punctuating

Breaking Lines and Stanzas and Punctuating

Poetry is written to be spoken. Break lines to emphasize pauses or silences. Break on nouns, verbs, adjectives, and adverbs. Try to draft in lines. When you revise, insert // between words to create a new line break, and ===== between lines to indicate a new stanza break. Experiment with the size, shape, and length of lines and stanzas. In general, punctuate and capitalize poems as if they're prose.

Cut to the Bone

Preparation

- ✔ Overhead transparency of "Cut to the Bone"
- ✔ Photocopies of the poems "A Little Friendship" (Uncut) and "A Little Friendship" (Cut) by Lucas Mayer and "Music" and "Musical Emotions" by Jacob Miller
- ✔ Wall poster of Robert Wallace quotation
- ✔ Wall poster of Bobbi Katz quotation
- ✔ Wall poster of William Coles quotation

39 LESSON

OCTOBER

> **"Poetry is especially an art of compression."**
>
> – Robert Wallace

The poet Robert Wallace says, "Poetry is especially an art of compression." What do you think he means by that? . . .

The verb *compress* means to force something into less space. Some of the power of a good poem comes from the poet's ability to say or suggest a lot in a short space—to make sure that every word is loaded with meaning and necessary to the poem.

The first and last things I do when I revise a poem are cut. When I write the first draft, I know I'll say more than I need to because I'm so focused on getting my feelings and the sensory details of the experience down on the page. I try to include anything that *might* be essential. Then I let the poem sit for at least a day, come back to it, and start to tighten: get rid of obvious fluff and redundancies.

Then, as I work through subsequent revisions and drafts, I make additions, I make substitutions, and I continue to delete. Finally, when I *think* I'm done with a poem, I cut it to the bone.

A LITTLE FRIENDSHIP (UNCUT)

Of all the places
we met on a transcontinental airplane,
a 747 at that.
She was from Germany
and was going to visit
her American grandmother in the States.
I had just finished my vacation
in Germany and was going back home
to Maine with my parents.

We both spoke English and German
and we couldn't decide which of the two to speak.
At first we just visited each other.
We would listen to music
and would watch Bugs Bunny on the television
Then we would crawl under the seats,
poking other people's feet
and then scurrying away,
trying to suppress our giggling.

Near the back of the airplane, two brothers
were playing with their Batman toys.
The two of us absolutely despised Batman,
and we would chant an anti-Batman song
to the tune of "Jingle Bells."

Toward the end of the flight
we wrote down our addresses
on little slips of paper,
and we exchanged them.
We said our good-byes as we collected our luggage.
But we never saw each other again.

© 2002 by Nancie Atwell from
Lessons That Change Writers
(Portsmouth, NH: Heinemann)   A LITTLE FRIENDSHIP (UNCUT) PAGE 1   LESSON 39

Reproducible
"A Little Friendship" (Uncut) by Lucas Mayer

A LITTLE FRIENDSHIP (CUT)

We met on an airplane.
She was from Germany
and on her way to visit
her grandmother in the States.
We had finished our vacation
in Germany and were headed home to Maine.

First we exchanged visits in our airplane neighborhoods.
We listened to music
and watched Bugs Bunny videos.
Then we crawled under seats,
poked people's feet,
and scurried away,
trying to suppress our giggles.

Near the back of the plane, two brothers
played with Batman toys.
We despised Batman
and chanted an anti-Batman song
to the tune of "Jingle Bells."

We wrote our addresses
on slips of paper
and exchanged them.
We said good-bye as we collected our baggage.
But I never saw her again.

I lost my slip of paper.
I think she lost hers too.
We never wrote to each other.
So I consider her a brief friend,
one who helped pass the time on a six-hour flight
and made a memory.

—Lucas Mayer

© 2002 by Nancie Atwell from
Lessons That Change Writers
(Portsmouth, NH: Heinemann)   A LITTLE FRIENDSHIP (CUT)   LESSON 39

Reproducible
"A Little Friendship" (Cut) by Lucas Mayer

I look for clutter—unnecessary words, vagueness, flourishes, redundancies, or distractions—and I cut. I weigh every line and word: does it deserve the space it's taking up in my poem? Does a smart reader need it? Does it *do* anything? And I cut some more. In the process of seeking concision, I have cut my poems by a third or more. I live by a quote from the poet Bobbi Katz: "I know a poem is finished when I can't find another word to cut."

> "I know a poem is finished when I can't find another word to cut."
>
> – *Bobbi Katz*

39

Look with me at the first draft of "A Little Friendship," a poem by Lucas. . . . There is much here that can go: bad words like *would*; unnecessary information, like what kind of plane it is; ideas that can be compressed; redundant adverbs and adjectives like *absolutely* and *little*; and extra words. I showed Lucas how I might trim the first stanza, then told him to have a go at the rest of the poem. This was the result. Read the second draft of "A Little Friendship" along with me. . . .

Can you hear and see the difference? Lucas is learning the difference between prose narrative and the more concise language of poetry.

Consider another example, "Music," by Jacob, who learned to cut to the bone *and* cut to the chase. Read along with me. . . .

Jacob definitely used this first draft to put down everything that occurred to him. He has too much language, and much of it isn't saying anything—yet.

When we conferred, I reminded Jacob that poetry is written to be spoken. I asked him, "Can this poem be spoken? Read it to me, like

MUSICAL EMOTIONS

Music: the only power
I have over myself
to change my emotions
whenever and however I please:
from frustrating anger
to soothing calm
to enthusiastic happiness—
each new genre of music
added to my collection
equals another emotion
for me to explore.

—Jacob Miller

MUSICAL EMOTIONS   LESSON 39

Reproducibles
"Music" and "Musical
Emotions" by Jacob
Miller

CUT TO THE BONE

When the poet can't find another word to cut, a poem is
done. Weigh every line and every word: Does it do anything
for your poem? Does a smart reader need it? And, is this
poem elegant shorthand yet?

CUT TO THE BONE   LESSON 39

Overhead
Cut to the Bone

> **"Poetry is
> elegant shorthand."**
>
> *— William Coles*

this is you talking, and let's hear the sound of it."

He did. We laughed. "Jacob," I said, "it sounds like a bad translation into English from some foreign language. Could you please just talk to me for a minute and tell me what it is you're trying to say here?"

He answered, "Well, when I want to change the mood I'm in, I do it with music. And then music can give me new emotions, too."

"Can you say that in your next draft? Be short and sweet? Cut to the chase?"

"I'll try."

Read Jacob's next draft with me, now titled "Musical Emotions." . . . Did he do it? I think so. Jacob's short and sweet revision reminds me of a remark by the poet William Coles: "Poetry is elegant shorthand."

Let's put some words to the gist of this lesson. Please copy the notes from the overhead into your handbook:

Cut to the Bone

When the poet can't find another word to cut, a poem is done. Weigh every line and every word: Does it do anything for your poem? Does a smart reader need it? And, is this poem elegant shorthand yet?

Comments or questions about cutting to the bone?

39

Use Repetition

Preparation

✔ Overhead transparency of "Use Repetition"

✔ Photocopies of my poems "Out of Touch, Version 1" and "Out of Touch, Version 2"

✔ Photocopies of Rachael Miller's "Purple Shoes," Siobhan Anderson's "Tree Heartbeat," and Marcia Conley Carter's "Did You Ever?"

LESSON **40**

DECEMBER

"Today's lesson is called "Use Repetition." I realize this directive probably sounds like a contradiction, given the message of the last free-verse lesson, when I urged you to cut redundancies. But in poetry and prose, there's such a thing as effective repetition, which gives writing rhythm, movement, and feeling.

First, though, let's backtrack and deal with ineffective repetition: when the effect of repetition is wordiness that *isn't* pleasing to the ear or helpful to the poem. And let's begin by looking at an example of it. "Out of Touch, Version 1" is a draft of one of my poems, in which I used ineffective repetition on purpose. It's a poem about the dreams I had after the death of Books, my old springer spaniel. Read along with me, and you'll hear how awkward the repetition sounds. . . .

Can you hear the words and phrases that are repeated too close together, to no effect except ear-grating inelegance? Listen to the first stanza again, with its arbitrary sprinklings of *my, pet, sister, baby daughter*. . . . Or listen again for the purposeless overuse of *calm* in the second stanza. . . .

40

OUT OF TOUCH, VERSION 1

(Ineffective Repetition)

Before my baby daughter was born,
I asked my sister, whose baby was born before mine,
will my baby feel as good to pet as my dog?
My sister said, she'll feel better to pet.

But the baby felt different to pet.
The touch of baby hugs around my neck
thrilled me to my toes.
But the touch of my dog flowed through me
like a river of calm would flow.
Nothing ever felt so calm to me.
My dog felt as calm as chocolate for my hands.

Now in dreams I feel my dog's sleek brownness.
My dog feels sleek like a seal,
except she feels warm.
And for one ecstatic second upon waking up,
I live again in the country of my dog's touch.

—Nancie Atwell

© 2002 by Nancie Atwell from
Lessons That Change Writers
(Portsmouth, NH: Heinemann)

OUT OF TOUCH, VERSION 1   LESSON 40

Reproducible
"Out of Touch, Version 1"

OUT OF TOUCH, VERSION 2

(Effective Repetition and Cut to the Bone)

Before Anne was born
I asked my sister, already a mother,
will the baby feel as good to pet
as my dog?
Better, she said.

Different, in fact.
Baby hugs—
fat arms around my neck—
thrilled me to my toes.
But the dog touch
flowed through me
like a river of calm.
Nothing
nothing
ever felt so right.
She was chocolate
for my hands.

Now in dreams
I feel her sleek brownness,
like a seal
but warm beyond warm
under my fingers.
And for one ecstatic second
upon waking
I live again
in the country of touch.

—Nancie Atwell

© 2002 by Nancie Atwell from
Lessons That Change Writers
(Portsmouth, NH: Heinemann)

OUT OF TOUCH, VERSION 2   LESSON 40

Reproducible
"Out of Touch, Version 2"

So what do you do if you've used a word twice, in too close proximity, and you hear the awkwardness when you read your writing? Try to substitute a new word or phrasing for one of the repetitions, or see if you can cut one of the repeated words or phrases altogether.

Look at the real "Out of Touch." Read along with me. Then we'll put the two versions side by side. . . .

Compare the first stanzas of the two poems. How did I revise or delete the instances of ineffective repetition? . . . What about the middle stanza? . . . The concluding stanza? . . .

In order to recognize and revise ineffective repetition, first you need to hear it: to read—not skim—the words of your poem, to *say them*, in your head or softly aloud.

Effective repetition, on the other hand, can be one of a poet's best tools. Effective repetition happens when a poet chooses a word or phrase that's significant to the meaning of the poem, then uses it to deepen the meaning and move the poem.

Rachael, a beginning poet, recognized that repetition was a device she could try, when metaphor and simile still seemed beyond her. She experimented with it in a poem about a cherished childhood possession: a pair of purple shoes that were just like her friend's. Read along with me and listen for how the repetition of *purple shoes* helps give the poem rhythm and life. . . .

Siobhan knew that repetition was the device for her when she began her poem "Tree Heartbeat." She remembered how, when she was little, her dad told her that if she listened, she could hear the heartbeat of the big old tree in their yard. But then the tree, diseased, had to be cut down. Siobhan decided to describe the life of the tree and the life of her family through the four seasons and over time, so already there's a theme of cycles and repetition.

PURPLE SHOES

I remember wearing, for the first time ever,
a pair of purple shoes with a white heel
and a clear bubble on the sole.

TREE HEARTBEAT

The tree was there. It was always there,
gently *tap tap tapping* at my window
for me to come and play.
A warm breeze lingered in its branches,
a leftover from summer,

DID YOU EVER? (FOR MARY OLIVER)

Did you ever stop and think
how hard it must have been
for her to write that poem?
To think of a subject, one
to intrigue readers, one
you could write about yourself, one
you could make sense of, one
that could reach out and touch a life?
Imagine the long hours she sat writing
before dawn at her desk,
crossing out as the sun came up and revealed the dew.
Crossing out, trying it again and again,
diving for the right word
until she can't swim another stroke,
until she can't write another word,
until she has to stop or this poem will kill her.
And then finally her poem makes it to you.
You read it and nod in satisfaction.
You like the poem—some good lines—
and you put her book back on the shelf.
But did you ever wonder
what it must have taken
for her to write that poem?

—Marcia Conley Carter

© 2002 by Nancie Atwell from
Lessons That Change Writers
(Portsmouth, NH: Heinemann)

DID YOU EVER? (FOR MARY OLIVER)   LESSON 40

Reproducibles
"Purple Shoes" by Rachael Miller,
"Tree Heartbeat" by Siobhan Anderson,
and "Did You Ever" by Marcia Conley Carter

Then she brought in the idea of a heart's repeating beat. This is the result. . . .

Can you imagine Siobhan's "Tree Heartbeat" without the repetition? It makes the poem.

Finally, notice Marcia's use of repetition in a poem she dedicated to poet Mary Oliver. Here the repetition builds to drive home Marcia's argument: readers of poems should recognize how hard it is to write one. Read along with me and listen to the rhythm. . . .

Let's conclude by recording notes for this lesson. Please copy the overhead into your handbook.

Use Repetition

Beware of *ineffective repetition*: a word repeated in too-close proximity to no purpose or effect and that sounds awkward. Use *effective repetition* to stress an important word, phrase, idea, or theme; to move a poem; to build a poem's momentum. When you revise, read your poem with your ears and listen for its rhythms.

Is this clear? Can you do it?

USE REPETITION

Beware of *ineffective repetition*: a word repeated in too-close proximity to no purpose or effect and that sounds awkward. Use *effective repetition* to stress an important word, phrase, idea, or theme; to move a poem; to build a poem's momentum. When you revise, read your poem with your ears and listen for its rhythms.

Overhead
Use Repetition

Two Things at Once

Preparation

✔ Trimmed photocopies of "Figurative Language, or Two Things at Once"

✔ Photocopies of Jonathan Robinson's "Opening the Rift," Jonathan Tindal's "Convention of Seals," Jed Chambers' "Gas Pump" (without the title), and Emily Robinson's "Candle Dancer" (without the title)

✔ Wall poster of Donald Hall quotation

✔ Tape dispensers

41 LESSON

NOVEMBER

> *"The new metaphor is a miracle, like the creation of life."*
>
> – Donald Hall

"I saved this poetry lesson for last because it's a big one and, for me as a poet, a tough one. But if you can get create figurative language, if you can say two things at once, it's guaranteed to transform your poetry.

Let's begin with some straight background information. Please tape "Figurative Language, or Two Things at Once" into your writing handbook. Now, follow along with me as I talk you through these notes. . . .

The poet Donald Hall once said, "The new metaphor is a miracle, like the creation of life." As a famously literal writer, I so agree with him—when I can exercise the power of figurative language, it feels like a miracle: it's that hard for me to look at the world through the eyes of metaphor.

But I also know, as a reader of poetry, there's nothing more satisfying than the right metaphor. That feeling of surprise and delight—that moment when I'm reading along and think *of course*—makes me happy to be human and alive on this planet.

I practically swoon when I read poetry by Sylvia Plath, who was the Queen of Metaphor. A work like her poem "Metaphors," with thirteen or

FIGURATIVE LANGUAGE, OR TWO THINGS AT ONCE

Literal language is true to fact. It uses words in accordance with their actual (literal) meanings.
Example: My dog is a carnivore.

Figurative language makes comparisons between unrelated things or ideas, in order to show something about a subject.
Example: In the kitchen, my dog is a tap dancer.

Three Kinds of Figurative Language

- *Metaphor* (Greek): means, literally, *transference*. The writer transfers qualities of one thing to another thing. A metaphor has two parts: A = B: something *is* something else. The B part, the *something else*, shows how the poet feels about or sees the A part.
  Example:
  Thumb
  The odd, friendless boy raised by four aunts.
  —Philip Dacey

- *Simile* (from the Latin *similes*: similar): a kind of metaphor that uses *like* or *as* to compare two things: A is like B.
  Example: Thunder threatens
  Like a sound that rolls around and around
  In a mean dog's throat.
  —Martha Sherwood

- *Personification* (from the Greek *prósopa*, meaning "face" or "mask"): a metaphor that gives human or physical qualities to an object, animal, or idea.
  Example: "The yellow fog that rubs its back upon the window-panes"
  —T. S. Eliot

© 2002 by Nancie Atwell from
Lessons That Change Writers
(Portsmouth, NH: Heinemann)

FIGURATIVE LANGUAGE, OR TWO THINGS AT ONCE   LESSON 41

Reproducible
Figurative Language, or
Two Things at Once

OPENING THE RIFT

A rift opens to another part of my brain

the part that drifts
from person to place to purple elephants
to the worst possible nightmare
and somehow it feels normal.

A diverse world opens to me—
a world where my imagination soars,
wheels, turns upside down, spins.

I am sucked into the new existence
like entering a black hole,
a vast void in outer space.

It is the best escape route ever made.
In minutes
I'm in a different universe altogether,
away from my life
for what seems like a lifetime.

—Jonathan Robinson

© 2002 by Nancie Atwell from
Lessons That Change Writers
(Portsmouth, NH: Heinemann)

OPENING THE RIFT   LESSON 41

Reproducible
"Opening the Rift" by Jonathan Robinson

fourteen packed into nine short lines, makes me giddy with pleasure. Emily Dickinson's "There's a Certain Slant of Light," Elizabeth Bishop's "The Fish," Langston Hughes's "Harlem" and "Dreams," and Richard Wilbur's "Digging for China"—these and other poems with rich, figurative language sharpen my vision and change my perspectives on the world around me and on my own experiences, too. And they fill me with desire. I want to be able to do this.

Aristotle wrote that "the greatest thing by far is to be master of metaphor." But, he continued, "It is the one thing that cannot be learned from others."

So I can teach you what a metaphor is. I can show you some examples written by students. But I won't be able to teach you how to think metaphorically. That ability can only come from your own, unique visions and perceptions.

Take a look at Jonathan's poem "Opening the Rift," which is an extended metaphor. As I read, follow along, and ponder: What is this place? What *is* the rift? . . .

What is Jonathan writing about here? . . . "Opening the Rift" is a poem about dreaming. Read it again, to yourself, now that you know that "the best escape route ever made" is Jonathan's metaphor for his dream life.

As Jonathan's teacher, I can't take a lick of credit for his metaphors. He discovered what his mind could do. But for other students, who struggle as I do to cast ideas as metaphors, I have learned one helpful bit of advice. And that's to start with personification.

J. T., another seventh grader, was dying to write metaphorically, like his hero, the poet William Stafford. J. T.'s subject was ocean seals, but ocean seal metaphors would not come. By the time I stopped to confer with him one day in writing workshop, he was so

TWO THINGS AT ONCE

41

CONVENTION OF SEALS

The convention
of seals gathers
on a large rock

The president
barks
the loudest, trying
to get control
of the members

All is silent
except for
the president barking
out tonight's agenda

Who will
be next
to pretend to be playful and cute
for the gawking tourists?
Who's the next professional seal?

The president barks out the candidates
one by one

The members bark out their support
one by one

When all is said
and done
and the seal is
chosen

the convention is
adjourned
and the members swim
off into the night

—Jonathan Tindal

© 2002 by Nancie Atwell from
Lessons That Change Writers
(Portsmouth, NH: Heinemann)

CONVENTION OF SEALS   LESSON 41

Reproducible
"Convention of Seals" by Jonathan Tindal

Seemingly docile,
the battered creature
is motionless until summoned.
Then it raises a serpentine neck,
top-heavy with its metallic head,

and, spying an opening in the flank
of the other beast—
it charges.
Guided by a human master,
it smashes into the larger creature.

Once secure, it fills the beast's organs
with poison; the acrid odor of the liquid
shimmers in the air.
When finished, it withdraws its head
and rests.

—Jed Chambers

© 2002 by Nancie Atwell from
Lessons That Change Writers
(Portsmouth, NH: Heinemann)

GAS PUMP (WITHOUT TITLE)   LESSON 41

Reproducible
"Gas Pump" by Jed Chambers

frustrated he was banging his head on his desk. He showed me his best effort so far. It read:

> I watch
>
> as the lifeless bodies
>
> lie motionless
>
> on the rocks,
>
> the sun glimmering
>
> off their rubbery
>
> bodies.

I said, "It's sensory. I can see it, J. T."

He said, "But that's not enough. I want it to be metaphorical—for the seals to be something else, like Stafford does it. All I've got after four starts is their bodies were rubbery."

"Well, let's try another tack here. What if . . . the seals on the rocks were a bunch of people? Who would they be?" I wondered.

"What do you mean?"

I thought aloud. "Could they be a big family out there on the rocks? A bunch of old men? Women at a spa? A convention? A rock group?"

A light broke on J. T.'s face. "A convention," he said. "Like the kind my dad goes to. But a convention of seals."

Here's the final draft of his poem. Read along with me. . . .

Metaphor was possible for J. T. when he approached it as personification—when he sought to give a non-human subject human qualities.

Take a look at two more examples of personification. You'll notice I removed the titles from these poems. The subjects of both are inanimate objects. Can you figure out what they are? Read along with me. . . .

Jed's poem is titled "Gas Pump." Emily's is called "Candle Dancer." Please give the poems their proper titles. Now, read them again, to yourself, and discover how they work. What do you notice? How did Jed and Emily

41

The stationary dancer
stands tall
on the pedestal
and watches
over everything.
Longing to move
her feet,
the dancer
sways and bends,
but her legs
are stuck
in the sinking
quicksand.
She wishes
she could walk
in her blue shoes
and that her
yellow body wasn't
trapped
into flickering
forever.

—Emily Robinson

© 2002 by Nancie Atwell from
Lessons That Change Writers
(Portsmouth, NH: Heinemann)

CANDLE DANCER (WITHOUT TITLE)   LESSON 41

Reproducible
"Candle Dancer" by Emily Robinson

combine sensory details about the gas pump and the candle with comparisons? . . .

Personification may be your way into figurative language or metaphor. Or you may already hold inside you what Ortega y Gasset calls "probably the most fertile power possessed by man." Either way, I hope you'll try in your poetry this year to move from the particular and literal to the abstract and figurative—that you'll try to write a poem that does two things at once.

Observations about metaphors? Questions?

41

Troubleshooting: Some Poetic Forms

42 **Sestinas and Tritinas**

43 **Irregular Odes**

44 **Haiku**

45 **Thirteen-Ways Poems**

46 **Memoir Poems**

What I Was Thinking Why teach poetic forms at all, when my students and I generally are so satisfied with their efforts as free-verse poets? First, I want them to know what else is possible for their poems—effects beyond those of free verse. I also want them to learn other ways that form can support the meaning of their poetry, beyond line and stanza breaks. Finally, by spring they're ready to experience new challenges and satisfactions as poets.

Over the years I've introduced poetic forms that kids latched on to and loved, as well as forms that had few, or no, takers. I've dropped most of the latter from my teaching repertoire—no more villanelles ("do not go gentle into that good night" by Dylan Thomas is the best-known example), sonnets, rondels (look for "Rondel" by Frank O'Hara), pantoums (see "Pantoum" by John Ashbery), even, I'm embarrassed to admit, limericks, perhaps the tiredest form of all. I did not teach acrostic poems, which are less a form than a contagion that infects elementary school poetry.

The poetic forms that work best for my students depend on patterns of repetition (sestinas and tritinas), exalted language about common objects (irregular odes à la Pablo Neruda), compact meanings conveyed in limited numbers of short lines (haiku), imitations (poetry that's cut to the bone, inspired by William Carlos Williams, or thirteen-ways poems in the style of Wallace Stevens), and narrative structures (memoir poems).

Sestinas and Tritinas

Preparation

✔ Trimmed photocopies of "Sestinas" and "Tritinas" for students to tape into their handbooks

✔ Photocopies of "Sestina at 3 AM" by Linda Pastan

✔ Photocopies of Jay Spoon's "A Sestina for Michael Jordan," Suzanne Monaco's "The Price of Wisdom: A Sestina," and the tritinas "Early Evening Tritina" by Ruth Langton, "A Tritina for Mom" by Marcia Conley Carter, and "Summer Evenings" by Audrey Stoltz

✔ Tape dispensers

LESSON **42**

JANUARY

> "The first sestina I ever read is still the best one I ever read: Elizabeth Bishop's "Sestina." Her poem, and then the form itself, intrigued me. Here's how it works. Please tape this handout, "Sestinas," to the next clean page in your writing handbook, then follow along with me. . . .
>
> So, what does a sestina look and sound like? I love this one by Linda Pastan. It's called "Sestina at 3 AM." Pastan's six end words are *dark, sleep, wind, long, under,* and *stars*—as in all good sestinas, simple words. Follow along with me . . .
>
> Did you notice how the pattern works? The last end word in one stanza becomes the first end word of the next: between stanzas one and two, Pastan moves from "the common *stars*" to "Tonight the *stars*." The repetition gives the poem a hypnotic feeling—it's as if the poem's rhythm is lulling the speaker to sleep.

42

SESTINAS

Sestina comes from the Latin for *sixth*. A sestina is a repetitive form of poetry invented by the troubadour poet Arnaut Daniel. It consists of seven stanzas. The six lines of each of the first six stanzas end in one of six words, repeated in the order below. The seventh stanza, which has only three lines, is called the *envoy*. It includes two of the six words in each of its lines.

Stanza 1:	1	Stanza 4:	5
	2		3
	3		2
	4		6
	5		1
	6		4
Stanza 2:	6	Stanza 5:	4
	1		5
	5		1
	2		3
	4		6
	3		2
Stanza 3:	3	Stanza 6:	2
	6		4
	4		6
	1		5
	2		3
	5		1

Stanza 7:	1-2
	3-4
	5-6

© 2002 by Nancie Atwell from
Lessons That Change Writers
(Portsmouth, NH: Heinemann)

SESTINAS   LESSON 42

Reproducible
Sestinas

Here are a couple of student sestinas. Jay wrote about Michael Jordan retiring then returning, yet again, to pro basketball. His six words were *Michael, GAME, game, shoes, dunks*, and *moves. . . .*

Suzanne wrote about her family in the year before Curt, her big brother, left home for college. She gave this sestina to her parents as a gift. Suzanne worked with the six words *table, Curt, laughing, wise, talk*, and *me. . . .*

If you'd like to try a sestina, I have two warnings. First, the form is a bear. Using the same words again and again, and saying something even slightly different each time, is the kind of brainwork that will take off the top of your head, to paraphrase Emily Dickinson. So anticipate spending serious time and thought.

Secondly, in deciding on your six end words, try to select words that have a lot to offer. For example, *light* can function as a noun, a verb, an adjective, or an adverb. *Promise, sleep, talk,*

SESTINA AT 3 AM

In the imperfect dark
no hope of either love or sleep,
I listen to the wind
and water's long
bewildering dialogue, under
the common stars.

Tonight the stars
abrade the dark.
If I could under-
stand why you left, then I could sleep.
How long
until you call? No message in the wind,

not in the wind.
Braided with stars
the sky's long
awning shelters the world. And now the dark—
that first mother of sleep—
coaxes: "Go under,

let yourself go under,
let the wind
whisper you to sleep
and the stars
will go out, the dark
surf will rock you in its hammock all night long."

© 2002 by Nancie Atwell from
Lessons That Change Writers
(Portsmouth, NH: Heinemann)

SESTINA AT 3 AM – PAGE 1   LESSON 42

Reproducible
"Sestina at 3 AM" by Linda Pastan

A SESTINA FOR MICHAEL JORDAN

The NBA wasn't the same without Michael.
What was THE GAME
Became just a game.
I missed watching him in his hundred dollar shoes
Do his million dollar dunks
After pulling some of his million dollar moves.

Other people tried the same moves,
But they couldn't make them as smoothly as Michael.
They tried to copy his dunks,
To make it more of a GAME.
Some of them even wore his shoes.
But without him it was always, only, a game.

It got boring just watching a game,
Even if there were a few good moves,
And someone was wearing some really nice shoes.
In their hearts the fans knew that without Michael,
There would never be another great GAME—
Just lay-ups and shots from outside, but no great dunks.

Sure, they all tried to do powerful dunks,
But they never made it more than a game.
The thing that would make it more of a GAME
Again were the magnificent moves
Of the fabulous Michael—
With or without his hundred dollar shoes.

© 2002 by Nancie Atwell from
Lessons That Change Writers
(Portsmouth, NH: Heinemann)

A SESTINA FOR MICHAEL JORDAN – PAGE 1   LESSON 42

Reproducible
"A Sestina for Michael Jordan" by Jay Spoon

THE PRICE OF WISDOM: A SESTINA

We sit around the table,
listening to Curt
rant and rave, and laughing.
Dad tries to get a word in edgewise
but Curt continues to talk.
I hear their laughter swell about me,

and I feel its love as it surrounds me.
I glance around this familiar table
and feel the talk
begin its work as Curt
and Dad go at each other, their wise-
cracks harmless because they are laughing.

Laughing—
I remember the times with me
talking wise,
sharing what I've learned with my crowd around this table,
and learning even from what Curt
has to say. And the talk

pulls us along a winding path in which talk
is interwoven with laughing—
or a pause for sorrow. Finally we wind down and Curt,
Mom, and Dad leave me
to wonder how this table
will be next fall without Curt to wise-

THE PRICE OF WISDOM: A SESTINA — PAGE 1   LESSON 42

Reproducible
"The Price of Wisdom: A Sestina" by Suzanne Monaco

and *wonder* can be both nouns and verbs. *You, me*, and *it* are versatile pronouns. A person's name is versatile, too.

So begin by brainstorming words around your chosen topic, then narrow down to end words that might ease your way, so you're not in an agony of frustration by the fourth stanza, wondering what else in the world can be done with a tough word like *car* or *CD* or *nice*. And, while drafting, don't be afraid to use a dictionary and a thesaurus, to see what else your six words might do in your sestina.

Questions? Observations about sestinas?

FOLLOW-UP LESSON

Tritinas

I learned about tritinas from a profile I read in the *New York Times* of poet Marie Ponsot. Her tritinas are exquisite. For those of you who are scared by the stiff demands of the sestina, this

42

TRITINAS

Tritina comes from the Latin for "three." It's a repetitive form of poetry that consists of three stanzas, plus an *envoy*. The three lines of each of the three stanzas end in one of three words, repeated in the order below. The envoy is one line that contains all three of the words.

Stanza 1:   1
              2
              3

Stanza 2:   3
              1
              2

Stanza 3:   2
              3
              1

Envoy: 1 line that uses all 3 words

TRITINAS   LESSON 42

Reproducible
Tritinas

EARLY EVENING TRITINA

The sun was low in the sky. We were going to watch for deer.
It would be dark soon.
We had only a little time, but I was with you.

I climbed the ladder of your tree stand and glanced down at the pond. You
followed and said, "We might not see a deer."
I nodded. "But if we're going to, it will be soon."

Your words were magic. *Soon*
was an understatement. I gazed down at the clover-covered field. So did you.
As if on cue, out of the woods stepped two majestic deer.

They ate and left, too soon. That evening, you gave me a miracle in the shape of
the deer.

                              —Ruth Langton

EARLY EVENING TRITINA   LESSON 42

Reproducible
"Early Evening Tritina" by Ruth Langton

A TRITINA FOR MOM

You've always made time to check on me at bedtime
and to be there whenever I worry.
And I knew I could definitely count on a great dinner.

All right, so maybe I didn't always *love* the dinner.
And it's possible that you weren't there for *every* bedtime,
and there were plenty of times I made you worry.

But then, isn't it part of a mother's job to worry?
To always come through, breakfast, lunch, and dinner?
And then, at the end of a long day, to be rewarded with a hug at bedtime?

I'm sorry I made you worry and haunted your dreams at bedtime, but I love
    you (and dinner, too).

—Marica Conley Carter

© 2002 by Nancie Atwell from
Lessons That Change Writers
(Portsmouth, NH: Heinemann)

A TRITINA FOR MOM   LESSON 42

Reproducible
"A Tritina for Mom" by Marcia Conley Carter

SUMMER EVENINGS

I long for those Sunday dinners on the deck, listening to the speech of summer
and watching with tired eyes the long day vanish into evening,
where the chatter of conversation is dotted with fireflies.

For when the sun disappears behind the trees we begin to see flashes of
    fireflies:
the true trademark of summer
and a start to another perfect Sunday evening.

Mom and Dad talk through the golden sunset and late into the evening,
while my brother and I chase the impulsive lights of fireflies,
and we all take for granted the air of warm summer.

That evening in bed my dreams floated like fireflies across a summer
    landscape.

—Audrey Stoltz

© 2002 by Nancie Atwell from
Lessons That Change Writers
(Portsmouth, NH: Heinemann)

SUMMER EVENINGS   LESSON 42

Reproducible
"Summer Evenings" by Audrey Stoltz

may be the repetitive form for you. Like the sestina, the tritina depends on effective repetition; it, too, creates a hypnotic effect through the rhythm of repeated words.

Here's how a tritina works. Tape this formula into your writing handbook, then follow along with me. . . .

In a tritina, maybe even more so than a sestina, the poet tries to make every word count. Each word is a gem in "Early Evening Tritina," which Ruthie wrote as a gift for her father. Her three words were *deer, soon,* and *you.* Follow along. . . .

Marcia gave her humorous "A Tritina for Mom" as a Mother's Day present. Her words were *bedtime, worry,* and *dinner.* . . .

And Audrey chose the words *summer, evening,* and *fireflies* for "Summer Evenings," the tritina she gave to her parents on their anniversary. . . .

Can you see how the form works? . . . How many people think they might like to try a tritina? . . .

Irregular Odes

Preparation

✔ Poems from Pablo Neruda's *Odes to Common Things* (1994), for you to read aloud

✔ Trimmed photocopies of "Tips for Neruda-esque Odes" for students to tape into their handbooks

✔ Photocopies of Jimmy Morrill's "Ode to the Sausage" and Marnie Briggs's "Ode to Watermelon"

✔ Tape dispensers

LESSON 43

FEBRUARY

"The best-known practitioner of the irregular ode is Pablo Neruda, a Chilean poet. His book *Odes to Common Things* (1994) is one of the most popular in our classroom poetry collection. But I'm getting ahead of myself.

Odes were invented long ago—around 500 B.C.—by Pindar, a Greek poet. Back then odes followed a complicated pattern of stanzas. They were serious, dignified, choral songs, performed to celebrate victories, like in the Olympic games.

In the twentieth century, Pablo Neruda turned the ode upside down. He abandoned dignified topics, discarded the rules about stanzas and meter, and sang the praises of ordinary things and everyday life: a pair of socks, onions, apples, a tomato, ironing, soap, a yellow bird, a spoon, French fries, a storm, laziness.

Jimmy and Marnie loved Neruda's *Odes to Common Things*, and their lip-smacking odes—to sausage and watermelon—show Neruda's influence. Read along with me. . . .

43

> ### ODE TO THE SAUSAGE
>
> O, sausage sizzling in your succulent fat.
> You disgust humanity's vegans and vegetarians,
> yet you dissolve in spite of them
> within the depths of my mouth.
>
> Those who say you are nothing but crude fat
> in a pigskin casing are blind to your salty sweet taste,
> your crispy softness,
> your fierce fragrance.
>
> Considered impure by many,
> you are the devil's tool of temptation—
> a serpent of kielbasa.
> You are flavor incarnate.
>
> Presidents have their nations,
> a boot has its confident shine,
> a world of imperfection has you.
>
> —Jimmy Morrill
>
> © 2002 by Nancie Atwell from
> *Lessons That Change Writers*
> (Portsmouth, NH: Heinemann)   ODE TO THE SAUSAGE   LESSON 43

Reproducible
"Ode to the Sausage" by Jimmy Morrill

After marinating themselves in Neruda, Jimmy, Marnie, and their classmates came up with some guidelines for writing irregular, or modern-day, odes. Tape these into your writing handbooks, then read along with me. . . .

My best advice about trying a Neruda-esque ode is this: you almost can't be too extreme in your praise, so pick an object that you genuinely admire and wish to exalt. And, to stay true to the spirit of Neruda's odes, part of the fun lies in choosing an everyday object that we aren't accustomed to inflating with glory. An ode to the stars or a rose wouldn't have that Neruda-esque sense of humor, spirit, and surprise.

> ### ODE TO WATERMELON
>
> I bite into you
> and relish the burst of wild flavor
> I haven't tasted all winter.
> Your sweet juice
> floods my mouth—
> buries my tongue
> in fresh pinkish flesh.
> I swallow your cold fruitiness
> and my taste buds smile
> with excitement.
> Oh, watermelon,
> the scent of June wind,
> mixed with the heat of August sun,
> washes over me
> as I take another bite
> of summer.
>
> —Marnie Briggs
>
> © 2002 by Nancie Atwell from
> *Lessons That Change Writers*
> (Portsmouth, NH: Heinemann)   ODE TO WATERMELON   LESSON 43

Reproducible
"Ode to Watermelon" by Marnie Briggs

> ### TIPS FOR NERUDA-ESQUE ODES
>
> ■ Choose a subject you have strong feelings about.
>
> ■ Describe the subject inside and out.
>
> ■ Exaggerate its admirable qualities, until it seems to become central to human existence.
>
> ■ Tap all five senses.
>
> ■ Use metaphors and similes.
>
> ■ Perhaps directly address the subject of the ode.
>
> ■ Tell your feelings about the subject *and* give exalted descriptions of its qualities: a balance.
>
> ■ Keep the lines short.
>
> ■ Choose strong words: language that's packed with meaning and cut to the bone.
>
> © 2002 by Nancie Atwell from
> *Lessons That Change Writers*
> (Portsmouth, NH: Heinemann)   TIPS FOR NERUDA-ESQUE ODES   LESSON 43

Reproducible
Tips for Neruda-esque Odes

Haiku

Preparation

- ✔ Overhead transparencies of two or three haiku written by you as models for your students (*Note:* this is easy, not to mention enjoyable.)
- ✔ Photocopies of "Five Japanese Haiku"
- ✔ Trimmed photocopies of "Guidelines for Writing Haiku"
- ✔ Tape dispensers

LESSON **44**

J U N E

" The haiku is a form of poetry that originated in Japan about seven hundred years ago. Before you put your hands up, to tell me about the three lines with five syllables, seven syllables, and five syllables, I need to interject a different angle on the art of English-language haiku.

Haiku are *meditative nuggets*. They're brief descriptions or observations of nature or everyday life. Although sometimes they do consist of three lines of five–seven–five syllables, the essence of a haiku lies less in the syllabic count and form and more in its tone and the way it connects us with our senses.

The traditional Japanese haiku doesn't count syllables, but it does count sounds. Seventeen Japanese sounds—that's where the mistaken convention of five plus seven plus five comes from—take about as long to say out loud as twelve to fifteen English syllables. So most English-speaking poets of haiku write fewer than seventeen syllables. American Robert Hass, who translates the haiku of the Japanese masters Bashō, Buson, and Issa into English, hardly ever writes them as five–seven–five English syllables.

For example, here are four of Hass's translations. The fifth, an English translation of a haiku by Bashō, is the best known poem in Japan. . . .

<table>
<tr><td>

FIVE JAPANESE HAIKU

They end their flight
one by one—
  crows at dusk.
        —Buson

The crane's legs
have gotten shorter
  in the spring rain.
        —Bashō

Misty grasses,
quiet waters,
  it's evening.
        —Buson

Crescent moon—
bent to the shape
  of the cold.
        —Issa

old pond . . .
a frog leaps in
  water's sound
        —Bashō

© 2002 by Nancie Atwell from
Lessons That Change Writers
(Portsmouth, NH: Heinemann)   FIVE JAPANESE HAIKU   LESSON 44

</td></tr>
</table>

Reproducible
Five Japanese Haiku

I wrote two haiku this weekend—by the way, it's *haiku* in both the singular and the plural. I noticed two moments, in the natural world beyond my house, that seemed made for haiku:

All night the fox
patrols a bank of spring snow:
her kits sleep below.

Light
beckons the cardinal's song:
spring sunrise.

If you decide to try a haiku or two, these "Guidelines for Writing Haiku" may help you. Tape them into your handbook, then follow along with me. . . .

Comments or observations about haiku? . . . How many of you think you might try one? . . .

<table>
<tr><td>

GUIDELINES FOR WRITING HAIKU

■ Examine the literal world of the senses: what you can see, hear, taste, touch, and smell.

■ Use concrete details to ground the haiku in a specific moment.

■ Observe nature and link it to human nature.

■ Write in the present tense.

■ Make every word count: no adverbs, few adjectives, no conjunctions if you can help it.

■ Strong, simple language.

■ No rhyme.

■ No metaphors or similes.

■ A form consisting of three short lines: the first and third about the same in length, and the second one slightly longer.

© 2002 by Nancie Atwell from
Lessons That Change Writers
(Portsmouth, NH: Heinemann)   GUIDELINES FOR WRITING HAIKU   LESSON 44

</td></tr>
</table>

Reproducible
Guidelines for Writing Haiku

Thirteen-Ways Poems

Preparation

✔ Overhead transparency of "Thirteen Ways of Looking at a Blackbird" by Wallace Stevens

✔ Photocopies of "Thirteen Ways of Looking at a Blackbird" by Wallace Stevens

✔ Photocopies of student "ways" poems: "The Essence of Life" by Ruth Langton, "A Few Ways to Look at a Match" by Chris Kunitz, "Seven Ways to Look at a Marble" by Jed Chambers, and "Grandfather Plum Tree" by Noah Tucker

✔ Extra-fine-point permanent marker

LESSON 45

APRIL AND MAY

"My introduction to Wallace Stevens came through his poem "Thirteen Ways of Looking at a Blackbird." As a reader I couldn't have asked for a better way to make Stevens' acquaintance. The poem made my jaw drop, it was so rich, funny, and mysterious. It is still one of my favorite poems of all time. Read along with me. . . .

Amazing, yes? Please let's go back into the poem together, and talk about the thirteen ways. My question is, what are the "thirteen ways of looking"? I'll make notes on a transparency of the poem as we discuss it; you may want to use my annotations later, to help you with a "ways" poem of your own.

For example, how would you characterize or describe the "way of look-ing" that Stevens takes in the first stanza of his poem? . . .

[And so on. Figure 45-1, "A Gloss on 'Thirteen Ways of Looking at a Blackbird'" summarizes a discussion of the poem by a group of my

THIRTEEN WAYS OF LOOKING AT A BLACKBIRD

1
Among twenty snowy mountains
The only moving thing
Was the eye of the blackbird.

2
I was of three minds,
Like a tree
In which there are three blackbirds.

3
The blackbird whirled in the autumn
winds.
It was a small part of the pantomime.

4
A man and a woman
Are one.
A man and a woman and a blackbird
Are one.

5
I do not know which to prefer,
The beauty of inflections
Or the beauty of innuendoes.
The blackbird whistling
Or just after.

6
Icicles filled the long window
With barbaric glass.
The shadow of the blackbird
Crossed it, to and fro.
The mood
Traced in the shadow
An indecipherable cause.

7
O thin men of Haddam,
Why do you imagine golden birds?
Do you not see how the blackbird
Walks around the feet
Of the women about you?

8
I know noble accents
And lucid, inescapable rhythms;
But I know, too,
That the blackbird is involved
In what I know.

9
When the blackbird flew out of sight,
It marked the edge
Of one of many circles.

10
At the sight of blackbirds
Flying in a green light,
Even the bawds of euphony
Would cry out sharply.

11
He rode over Connecticut
In a glass coach.
Once, a fear pierced him,
In that he mistook
The shadow of his equipage
For blackbirds.

12
The river is moving.
The blackbird must be flying.

13
It was evening all afternoon.
It was snowing
And it was going to snow.
The blackbird sat
In the cedar-limbs.

—Wallace Stevens

© 2002 by Nancie Atwell from
Lessons That Change Writers
(Portsmouth, NH: Heinemann).

THIRTEEN WAYS OF LOOKING AT A BLACKBIRD   LESSON 45

Reproducible
"Thirteen Ways of Looking at a Blackbird"
by Wallace Stevens

students and me. It may be helpful as a teacher leads the group through a study of Stevens' approaches in this poem. I don't make any claims for our analysis as complete or even correct. What it did do for us was lay bare some of the literary, cultural, and historical perspectives that Stevens packed into his remarkable poem.

Attempting to name what Stevens did set the stage for students to feel confident about trying "ways" poems of their own. I told kids, "You could do this." The poems "The Essence of Life," "A Few Ways to Look at a Match," "Seven Ways to Look at a Marble," and "Grandfather Plum Tree" show four responses to the invitation that may inspire your students: Ruthie's ways of looking at a book, Chris's at a match, Jed's at a marble, and Noah's eight perspectives on the ailing plum tree in his yard, which was planted there by a soldier, home from World War I.]

A Gloss on "Thirteen Ways of Looking at a Blackbird"

Stanza 1	The blackbird is a tiny detail in a vast, still landscape
Stanza 2	A simile in which the blackbird suggests the speaker's frame of mind
Stanza 3	The world is a stage act or Punch and Judy show; the blackbird is but one of the players
Stanza 4	A metaphorical math problem
Stanza 5	A philosophical proposition or meditation
Stanza 6	A mystery story out of Poe, starring the blackbird
Stanza 7	A sermon or Bible quotation
Stanza 8	The blackbird as the salt of the earth: human intelligence and culture grounded by nature
Stanza 9	A metaphysical geometry problem
Stanza 10	A legend or myth
Stanza 11	A fairy tale
Stanza 12	A pearl of folk wisdom from the farmer's almanac
Stanza 13	Once again the blackbird is a tiny detail in a vast landscape, but this time we seem to be viewing him at something like the end of the world

Figure 45-1 A Gloss on "Thirteen Ways of Looking at a Blackbird"

THE ESSENCE OF LIFE

1.
The pages unfold.
I am drawn into a new world
of deep imagination.

2.
One book plus
one shelf equals
a library.

3
As the scribe recorded,
the world understood.

4.
"Read me the story, pleeese.
One more time, pleeese.
Just once more."

5.
She has a book in her hand.
Her mind must be traveling.

6.
The book is a link
between cultures—
the way to visit
without leaving.

A FEW WAYS TO LOOK AT A MATCH

1.
Life, fire, birth,
a new beginning.

2.
All these years in its
  box,
only to be used
    once.
    Once.

3.
The boundary between
a rollicking
fireworks display
on the fourth
day of July
and darkness

4.
I wonder,
what does it feel?
A transformation
like Cinderella's?
Strike . . .

5.
The feel
of warmth
on my fingers . . .
ghostlike.

6.
A hand.
A strike.
A fire.
A life.
A death.

—Chris Kunitz

A FEW WAYS TO LOOK AT A MATCH   LESSON 43

Reproducibles

"The Essence of Life" by Ruth Langton
and "A Few Ways to Look at a Match" by Chris Kunitz

SEVEN WAYS TO LOO

I.
A child cried
when she lost
her marbles.

II.
Could a marble
hold a galaxy?
Maybe.

III.
To the person with nothing
the marble is everything.

IV.
A child and a marble
are happiness.
Two children and a marble
are an argument.

V.
The people are falling.
The marbles must be rolling.

VI.
The marble—
glass perfection.

VII.
God dropped a marble,
and the Earth was formed.

—Jed Chambers

GRANDFATHER PLUM TREE

I
Grandfather plum tree, no!
Older than that, perhaps,
planted in the Great War
Stones rattling in a match tin, collected
outside the bloody trenches of Verdun.
II
Decay has taken hold of the plum tree,
and I wonder whether from the bud down
or the root up—
up from that very stone.
III
When farm boys who went to war didn't return,
the plum tree's branches sagged.
IV
Ode to joy! Plum tree flush with pink-white bloom,
a mantle to intoxicate hummingbirds with hope.
V
With the farmers gone,
women and children from the village
make a pilgrimage to the plum tree,
baskets heavy sweet, so sweet—yellow-jackets cling.
VI
The great oaks and rotted maples have seniority,
but the plum tree has the
wizened nobility of a poet.
VII
No hybrid, but a plum tree that casts stones
on wind and ice—in and out
of birds, to litter the ground and send up shoots—
inferior though, with small and bitter fruit.
VIII
Stout poles brace the outbound branches now,
not against the weight of fruit, but the cancer from within.
Rot of age has eaten its spine.
Life sustains the plum tree through the thin thoroughfare
beneath its bug-ridden bark.
Each April we stand a death watch.

—Noah Tucker

GRANDFATHER PLUM TREE   LESSON 45

Reproducibles

"Seven Ways to Look at a Marble" by Jed Chambers
and "Grandfather Plum Tree" by Noah Tucker

THIRTEEN-WAYS POEMS

45

Memoir Poems

Preparation

- ✔ Overhead transparency of "Memoir Poems: Anecdotes and Sagas"
- ✔ Photocopies of poems that tell anecdotes or stories: David MacDonald's "The Loon Call," Erin Witham's "Makeover," Jim Morrill's "Impressionable," Ruth Langton's "Five Days," and Audrey Stoltz's "The Perfect Cake," as well as my "Tale of Two Tails"

46 LESSON

FEBRUARY

"Poetry can do many things well, but one of my favorites is the way a poem allows me to capture and give shape to my experiences. I know there's already a prose genre—memoir—that exists specifically to serve this purpose. But there are times when my experiences don't work as memoir.

These are smaller moments, with no discernible beginning–middle–end. They're less the stuff of full-blown narrative and more *anecdotal*. A personal anecdote is a short account of a brief incident, as opposed to a memoir, which is a longer account of a significant experience. So sometimes I craft the small events of my life as poems: the experiences are important to me, but there's not enough material there to develop a full-blown memoir. I've written anecdote poems about the first time my husband kissed me, an afternoon I baked a pie with my mother, and watching my dog, Rosie, swim at our beach.

Other times my experiences seem *too* complex for a memoir: too much happens over too long a period of time to develop the events as a focused, prose narrative. It would require a ton of backing and filling: giving readers all the details of context, developing the other characters, and detailing my thoughts and feelings on several or more related occasions, plus all the

TALE OF TWO TAILS

My problem with the new spaniel was
I wanted her to be the old one.
So I shopped for small bones,
a sunbleached orange coat,
freckles and feathers,
even a rare plume of intact tail if I
    could manage it.
(I couldn't.)
I craved a gentle mouth,
parlor tricks: the name of every toy
and visitor and neighborhood dog,
a head on my knee,
the shadow out of the corner of my eye
that found peace
wherever she found me.
I wanted to be adored again with a
    sense of humor.

My problem was
I got Rose.
Rose digs catacombs in the backyard.
She runs away,
steals shoes and underwear
and bites me when I come after her
    booty,
chews sticks like they're Tootsie Rolls,
showers with me most mornings
    uninvited,
lives with a green tennis ball clamped
    in her jaws,
and to everyone she meets
presents her butt to be scratched
while our fingers itch
to touch her sweet face.

My problem is
I can't see the old dog's sweet face
    anymore.
When I close my eyes I see Rose—
the way she listens to my voice with her
    whole body,
how her eyes beg my lips to say *stick*,
the way she leaps to snag the green ball
    every time,
how she sleeps propped on a pile of
    pillows like Cleopatra's spaniel,
the way she thinks fresh water in her
    dish is a big deal,
how she wakes up ecstatic every
    morning
at her end of the bed
and wiggles up to kiss and kiss me,
the way she swims until she's so tired
    it's dangerous,
how she'll only come when I call *Bacon!*
and the summer people think it's her
    name,

and
the way I feel when she wags that
    stump of tail—
when the Rosie flag quivers with joy
as my dog catches balls, chases sticks,
sees my car, sees it's me,
when my dog sees me.

—Nancie Atwell

© 2002 by Nancie Atwell from
Lessons That Change Writers
(Portsmouth, NH: Heinemann)

TALE OF TWO TAILS   LESSON 46

Reproducibles
"The Loon Call" by David MacDonald,
"Makeover" by Erin Witham, and "Tale of Two Tails"

changes in me over time. That's when I decide to craft stories about changes that unfold over time, or about related incidents, as *saga poems*. Here I can leave out much of the who-what-when-where-why background information and focus on the different strings of moments that weave a memory of a time of my life.

Now, I know *saga* is a term given to narratives about the heroic exploits of people from legends. But today publishers use the term *saga novel* to describe fictions that chronicle people related by family or social group. So I'm going to use the term *saga poem* to describe story poems that chronicle a series of related events from our lives.

For example, I've written saga poems, instead of prose memoirs, about teaching my daughter to ride a bicycle and remembering how my mother taught me; about going ice-skating with my mother when I was ten and watching my hardworking, exhausted mom transform into a carefree girl on the ice; and about buying a puppy because she looked like my late beloved spaniel, then discovering she was her own dog, and finally growing to love her for it.

Let me show you some examples of both kinds of memoir poems. The basis for David's poem "The Loon Call" is an anecdote: he was canoeing and encountered a loon close up. It called to him and he called back. Read along with me and notice how David probably didn't have enough narrative material for a memoir but had plenty enough for a poem. . . .

Erin's anecdotal experience involved standing outside during a snowfall, her face to the sky, and letting the snow become her makeup. Read "Makeover" with me, and notice how Erin crafts an important but brief experience as a poem. . . .

Finally, Jimmy captured a memory from the time he was seven. An anecdote poem is perfect for this circumstance, when the writer has a distant, dimming memory of an experience from long ago but can't remember enough details to craft a prose memoir. One night seven-year-old Jimmy watched *Jaws* on television and scared himself silly; when it

46

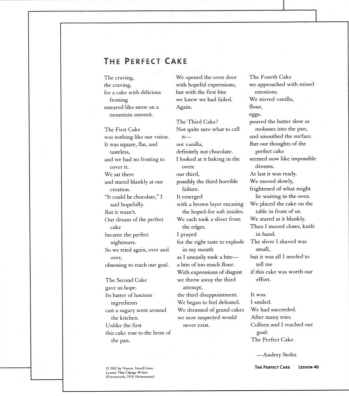

Reproducibles
"Impressionable" by Jimmy Morrill, "Five Days" by Ruth Langton, and "The Perfect Cake" by Audrey Stoltz

came time for his shower, he was haunted by the specter of the shark. Read "Impressionable" with me, and notice how Jimmy focused narrowly, on what he remembered about that night, then created the details he couldn't exactly recall. . . .

Now turn your attention from anecdote poems to saga poems: poetry in which the action unfolds over time—many or several days. In her saga poem, Ruthie compressed all of her memories of a baby varmint she found and nurtured. Read "Five Days" along with me. . . .

At first Audrey had tried to tell the story of her cake-baking experiments as a prose memoir. But after four pages of draft she lost control of the narrative—it was too many cakes over too many days. So she shifted modes and tried a saga poem. This time it worked. Read "The Perfect Cake" with me and notice how Audrey used a saga poem to relate each of the different attempts and its results. . . .

In "Tale of Two Tails," I remembered my old spaniel, Books Bagshaw, with her long, undocked tail and sweet nature, and I described various misadventures with my spaniel puppy, Rose, who resembles Books minus the tail, but otherwise isn't one bit like her. Through writing the saga of the two dogs, I discovered my *So what?*: I love Rosie for who she is. Read "Tale of Two Tails" with me. . . .

Would you turn to the next clean page of your writing handbook? I'd like you to record notes to capture this lesson:

Reproducible
Memoir Poems

Memoir Poems: Anecdotes and Sagas

When an experience feels too small for a full-blown memoir, when it's a brief but important incident, try it as an anecdote poem.

When an experience feels too complex for a memoir, when it's about changes that unfold over time or several related incidents, try it as a saga poem.

What are your comments, questions, or observations about these two approaches to memoir poems?

Gifts of Writing

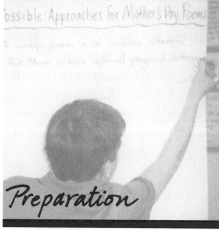

Preparation

In December

✔ Overhead transparency of "Why Gifts of Writing?"

✔ Overhead transparency headed "Possible Formats for Holiday Gifts of Writing" for brainstorming with your students

✔ Photocopies of Annie Kass's "Christmas Eve: A Tritina," Forrest Carver's "Christmas Calzones," Emily Robinson's "Delicious Memories," Ethan Rittershaus' "The Relentless Cycle of Christmas," Molly Jordan's "The Tree," Siobhan Anderson's "Walk to the Mail," Anne Atwell-McLeod's "Dinnertime Adagio," Jimmy Morrill's "To Grandma," and Hallie Herz's "A Sort of Almost Tritina for Nat"

✔ Computer paper with decorative borders and designs of holiday and other motifs

In May

✔ Overhead transparency headed "Possible Approaches for Mother's Day Poems" for brainstorming with your students

✔ Photocopies of Forrest Carver's "Five Ways of Looking at Mom in Her Garden," Chris Kunitz's "Nine Ways of Looking at You," my "Mother's Hands," Peter Wilde's "Dear Dannon," Ceysa McKechnie's "Rose," Noah Tucker's "Memories," Colby Smith's "Mom," Anne Atwell-McLeod's "As We Read," Erin Witham's "Not Yet," Jimmy Morrill's "To My Mother on Her Day," and Phaelon O'Donnell's "Knowing"

LESSON 47

DECEMBER
AND MAY

What I Was Thinking One of my jobs in the writing workshop is to look for, and direct kids toward, purposes and occasions for writing that matter to them. So during the winter holidays, on Mother's Day, and again on Father's Day if school is still in session, I invite them to craft gifts of writing for the people who matter.

Some of my students' most heartfelt poems are written as presents for mothers, fathers, grandparents, siblings, and friends. And from the perspective of their parents, I think some measure of their support for writing workshop comes from a feeling of gratitude. Adolescents aren't known for articulating love and appreciation, and some of their gifts of writing are delivered in the context of long dry spells in children's affections. So gifts of writing are important occasions for the recipients—and for the writers, too, as they uncover the *So what's?* in the relationships and rituals of their lives.

"Since my daughter Anne was six, I've written a poem for her, as a birthday gift, almost every January. I knew the bikes I bought for her would rust or become too small; I understood that as much as she cherished the new Barbies, eventually their heads would fall off and they'd end up at the Boothbay dump. But the poems I write for her—my words about her, me, and us—will last forever.

As we look forward to Hanukkah and Christmas and the season of giving, I can't think of a better present for someone you care about than the gift of a poem: words tailor-made for a person you love and appreciate. I have a fat file of poems that students wrote and gave as gifts in previous Decembers. Today we'll read a sampling of these for inspiration, and I'll ask you to name the approaches the writers chose for their gifts of writing. I hope you'll see the value in writing a poem for someone you cherish—that you'll want to give this a try.

Please turn to the next clean page in your writing handbook and record this question:

Why Gifts of Writing?

Overhead
Why Gifts of Writing?

Here are my best answers. Please add them to your notes.

They last.
They're personalized and more personal than most other gifts.
They show more thought: the writer spent a special kind of time and made a special kind of effort.
They show a writer's love better than anything.
You can make your mother, father, or granny cry.

Then, under your notes, please record this heading:

Possible Formats for Gifts of Writing

Since I'll be reading aloud the sample student poems, can I ask for a volunteer to list on the overhead the approaches we find, someone with strong, clear printing? . . . Thanks, Marcia. Don't worry—we'll tell you what to write.

The first poem, "Christmas Eve: A Tritina," was written by Annie for her parents. Read along with me. . . . It's a lovely poem about Christmas Eve rituals at Annie's house. What's the approach? . . . Right, a tritina. Marcia, please record "tritina" as number one on the master list of formats; for number two write, "family Christmas Eve ritual."

[And so on. Seven more poems are reproduced for this lesson. In "Possible Formats for Holiday Gifts of Writing" (Figure 47-1), I've listed each poem to be reproduced for this lesson, along with the approach the poet took; the right hand column shows the techniques Marcia listed on a transparency and individuals copied into their handbooks. At the end of the demonstration I pointed out the decorated printer papers available for

47

POSSIBLE FORMATS FOR HOLIDAY GIFTS OF WRITING

Poem	Approach
"Christmas Eve" Annie Kass (for her parents)	A tritina A family Christmas Eve ritual
"Christmas Calzones" Forrest Carver (for his parents)	A recipe: ingredients for a family holiday
"Delicious Memories" Emily Robinson (for her mother)	A memory A family tradition
"The Relentless Cycle of Christmas" Ethan Rittershaus (for his mother)	A Christmas morning time line
"The Tree" Molly Jordan (for her parents)	A concrete poem in a holiday shape A family ritual
"Walk to the Mail" Siobhan Anderson (for her father)	A winter memory
"Dinnertime Adagio" Anne Atwell-McLeod (for her parents)	An everyday family ritual
"To Grandma" Jimmy Morrill (for his grandmother)	An extended-family holiday tradition
"A Sort of Almost Tritina for Nat" Hallie Herz (for her brother)	A parody (of a tritina) A typical family experience

Figure 47-1 Possible Formats for Holiday Gifts of Writing

final copies. I concluded the lesson by asking students to turn to the territories section of their writing handbooks and record this heading on the next clean page:

Potential Recipients of Gifts of Writing and Potential Approaches

I said, "Please spend the next three or four minutes listing the people to whom you might give a gift of writing. Think about individuals, but about approaches, too. What forms interest you? What styles? Which rituals, traditions, memories, and messages are important? Look into your heart for the people who might love to read your words this holiday season and for the ways, as a writer, you might touch their hearts."

Not everyone will create a gift of writing. Typically about three-quarters of the group are inspired by the lesson and follow through. I can't demand that a writer produce an outpouring of affection, but I can extend my best invitation to get students' creative juices—and consciences—flowing.]

FOLLOW-UP (EARLY MAY)

"Mother's Day is just two weeks away. I know because when I strolled into the bookstore yesterday, I was bombarded by the Mother's Day clichés on the display of cards by the register:

Mom—thanks for being there.
To the world's greatest Mom.
Mother, you've always been a friend to me.
What is a mother?

See what I mean? And to me the saddest thing about messages like these is that the relationships with our mothers are among the most important of our lives. The celebration of this bond deserves better than a tired, bland, impersonal Hallmark sentiment.

Today's focus is on gifts of writing for moms that go beyond cliché, that get at the deep feelings and the *So what's?*, that explore the genuine, individual relationship between one child and one mother.

Please copy this heading onto the next clean page of your writing handbook:

Possible Approaches for Mother's Day Poems

As we did back in December, I'll read a selection of gifts of writing with you and ask you to name the approaches the writers took. Since I'll be leading the discussion, could I ask for a volunteer to record the master list on the overhead, someone with bold, clear printing? . . . Thanks, Jimmy. Here we go. . . .

[And so on. I've included eleven poems that my students and I wrote for our mothers that demonstrate a range of styles. In "Possible Approaches for Mother's Day Poems" (Figure 47-2) each poem is matched to a description of the approach the poet took. These are the techniques Jimmy listed on an overhead transparency and that his classmates recorded in their writing handbooks.]

47

POSSIBLE APPROACHES FOR MOTHER'S DAY POEMS

"Five Ways of Looking at Mom in Her Garden" Forrest Carver	A "ways" poem à la Wallace Stevens Put Mom in her special physical setting
"Nine Ways of Looking at You" Chris Kunitz	A "ways" poem Trace the history of your mother–child relationship
"Mother's Hands" Nancie Atwell	Focus on a physical attribute of your mother
"Dear Dannon" Peter Wilde	A Ted L. Nancy poem Focus on an obsession of your mother
"Rose" Ceysa McKechnie	Compare her to something appropriate and revealing
"Memories" Noah Tucker	A family saga poem (about your mother's parents, etc.)
"Mom" Colby Smith	A straightforward, specific thank-you
"As We Read" Anne Atwell-McLeod	A ritual you and your mom treasure
"Not Yet" Erin Witham	A ritual you don't treasure
"To My Mother on Her Day" Jimmy Morrill	A recipe: ingredients for a perfect Mother's Day or for Mom herself
"Knowing" Phaelon O'Donnell	An extra-special effort of your Mom's that you appreciate
"A Tritina for Mom" Marcia Conley Carter (see Lesson 42)	A tritina

Figure 47-2

Effective Book Reviews

Preparation

✔ Overhead transparency headed "Features of Good Book Reviews" for brainstorming with your students

✔ Optional: Overhead transparency of "Features of Good Book Reviews: Sample Small-Group List" to show your kids what's possible

✔ Photocopied packets of the student book reviews that appear in Appendix D

✔ Photocopies of Colleen Connell's planning sheet for a book review and her review of *To Kill a Mockingbird*

✔ Tape dispensers

What I Was Thinking   I teach about book reviews first, because I want my students to begin to write in a formal, crafted way about the literature they're reading. This is good preparation for the critical essays they'll be required to write in high school and for the book reviews I hope they'll read in the *New York Times Book Review* for all the Sundays of the rest of their lives.

But book reviews are also a highly publishable genre. Between the NCTE journal *Voices from the Middle* and the Internet site Amazon.com, every student's reviews can go public beyond the walls of our school.

This lesson, like so many of our genre studies, depends upon criteria that students tease out from successful examples of the genre. It is a full-period lesson, as it involves reading, talking, and listing in small groups, then convening in the circle to talk some more and compile a master list of criteria.

Commandeering an entire session of writing workshop this way used to give me pause, until the February I asked my students, at the end of the class, "Was this a worthwhile use of your writing time?" Their answer, unanimously, was *yes*. Why?

"It's more understandable to me than if you gave us notes about book reviews or told us to take notes on what you were saying about them."

"We get to find out for ourselves—that's always better."

"They're real criteria, not made up or from some book."

"You get to learn from what you find *and* from what the other kids and groups find."

"It's other kids' book reviews, so it's more fair and helpful than trying to learn from adults' reviews."

"The list will be helpful to me when I write—I'll use it as kind of a checklist."

"The guidelines are good because I won't have to guess at how to write a review, but I also won't feel like I'm copying the reviews we read."

"And the packet of reviews will be a good reference in the future—I can look at the things on the list in context."

"So tell me: why do you think I'm going to teach you how to write book reviews, *vs.* book reports? . . .

Your answers are right on the money. A book review is a personal account of a reading experience. It has a real audience—readers trying to decide whether to read the book—and a real purpose for writing it. It does a lot more than summarize the plot of a book, or prove to a teacher that you read it, which seem to be the chief functions of a book report. And, I would add, it's an actual genre.

After kids leave elementary or middle school, I doubt you'll ever write or read another book report. But I bet you'll read, and maybe even write, plenty of book reviews. And in high school, when you do write about books, it will be in the form of critical essays, which share many of the features of good book reviews.

So, what are the features of effective book reviews? That's your task today: to read a bunch of good ones and look for and name what the reviewers did.

I've made photocopies for you of ten reviews by seventh- and eighth-grade readers. Most of the reviews have been accepted for publication in *Voices from the Middle*, the NCTE journal for middle school teachers and their students. In a moment your job will be to gather in groups of four or five, read and mark up the reviews silently, then talk about what you found and record a group list of features of good reviews.

Let me begin by passing out the packets of reviews, then assigning you to groups. Make sure you take a pencil with you when you move out with your small group. . . .

Now, in your small groups, the person whose first letter of his or her first name comes closest to the *end* of the alphabet is the recorder today. Got that?

He or she will need a pad of paper. Here's the heading for the recorder's list and the question you'll look for answers to as you read the reviews:

What Are the Features of Good Book Reviews?

For the next ten minutes, silently read the reviews in the packet and mark them up: underline significant features and write notes to yourself, right on the reviews, about what the features are. Ready? We'll talk again in ten minutes. . . .

It's time for your small groups to go to work. Talk together and tell your recorder about the features you observed. Recorders, write fast and capture as much as you can of the conversation. To show you what I mean, I've projected a list on the overhead that was compiled by a small group of seventh and eighth graders after they read a bunch of reviews. Take no more than ten minutes to compile your group's list. . . .

It's time to come back to the circle. Recorders, bring the group lists with you. Everyone, bring your packets of reviews.

Now, you talk, and I'll record on transparencies. My heading is "Features of Good Book Reviews." Please take turns reporting out what your small groups observed in the reviews. I'll make a fast and dirty master list, which I'll give back to you tomorrow in the form of a beautiful, typed, organized version for your handbooks. I'm ready. . . . [See Figure 48-1 for one of my class's lists; note the final, italicized item and how it serves as the basis for the follow-up lesson.]

This is a tremendous list: complete, detailed, and well-observed. Was this a helpful activity to you, as potential reviewers of books? Talk with me about the benefits of the process. . . .

I'm curious about something else: how many of you found a book that you want to read, as you glossed the reviews? Which titles? . . .

Please hold on to the packets of book reviews. These are now data that you've researched. Save them in a pocket of your daily writing folders. When you compose your book review, these will come in handy, as will the final product of your research—that's the master list I'll give you tomorrow.

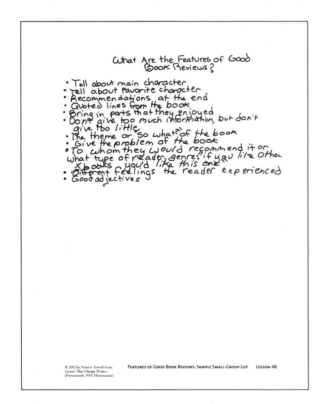

Overhead
Features of Good Book Reviews:
Sample Small-Group List

FEATURES OF GOOD BOOK REVIEWS

Inviting lead: introduce the main character or a favorite character
                ask a question of the reader
                quote from the book
                summarize the plot
                describe the theme(s) of the book

Use a first-person voice: *I*

Introduce the main character and relevant details about his or her life

Tell the main character's problem

Tell the main character's emotions

Provide a brief background into the relationships among the characters

Summarize the plot of the book

Hint at the resolution of the plot (but never reveal it)

Tell the genre

Tell if the book is a prequel, sequel, or part of a series

Tell the reviewer's opinions and reactions

Tell *how* the reviewer read the book

Tell the range of feelings the reviewer experienced

Allude to the theme(s) of the book

Recommend what kind of reader (e.g., by age, gender, genre, author preferences) would enjoy the book

Refer to the title and author by name within the review

Provide relevant biographical information about the author

Use rich, accurate adjectives to describe the writing

Make comparisons to other books or authors

Ask questions of the reader

Mention an author's choices, e.g., narrative voice and point of view, use of flashbacks and flashforwards, fast pace, realistic dialogue, visual imagery, significant conflicts, important themes, convincing character development

Conclude purposefully, often with an emphatic recommendation

Stick to a length of two–three paragraphs; a word-length range of 160–215 words

Include all the necessary garnish: title, author, publisher, copyright date, number of pages, price, ISBN number, and the reviewer's name, grade, school, town, and state

Usually begin with a planning sheet

Figure 48-1 Sample Class List of Book Review Features

Here's your list of book review criteria from yesterday. I put the items into categories where I could and created a kind of logical order, and I added a final item, which we'll talk about in today's mini-lesson.

First, circulate the tape dispensers and attach this list to the next clean page of your writing handbook. . . . Now, let's read it together around the circle, each of you taking a turn at one of the ideas on the list, until we run out. . . .

Again, it's a specific, complete, *useful* list. Thank you.

I'd like to focus in today's lesson on my final addition: the idea that good student book reviews begin with a planning sheet.

Every review you read and critiqued yesterday started with a planning sheet—with the writer thinking hard about and listing the ideas, features, characters, themes, plot twists, techniques, potential readership, you name it, that he or she brainstormed in connection with the book.

By way of example, here's the planning sheet Colleen created before—and as—she drafted a review of *To Kill a Mockingbird*. And here's the review itself. Read both along with me. . . .

You can see that not every idea from the planning sheet ended up in the review, and that the review includes ideas that aren't on the plan. Again, the planning sheet is a place to capture ideas and to doodle with words. Colleen used hers to remind herself of the characters in the novel, its themes, and some of the literary features she might mention. She spent about half an hour planning.

Then she slid her planning sheet to the corner of her desk and began drafting her review. When a new idea occurred to her, mid-draft, she jotted it on the planning sheet, so she wouldn't lose it, then continued drafting. She

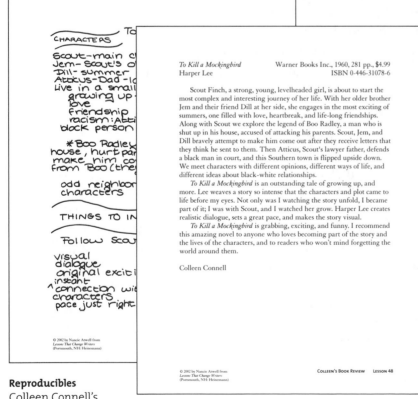

Reproducibles
Colleen Connell's Planning Sheet and Book Review

leaned on the ideas on her planning sheet as she crafted and organized her review.

I'm going to ask you to create a planning sheet before and as you draft your book reviews—to give yourself a time and place to doodle with words and ideas. I don't expect your plan to look like Colleen's or anyone else's. It should serve you as a way to think, create ideas and opinions, capture data that might otherwise be lost, and jog your memory.

Comments? Questions? Observations? Please file Colleen's planning sheet and book review in your daily writing folder, along with the packet of reviews.

Finally, please turn to the next clean page in the territories section of your writing handbooks and record this heading:

Books I Might Like to Review

Tonight for homework I'd like you to take home your independent reading record for this school year, read through it, and list at least five titles you might want to write about, when you decide the time is right for book reviewing. We'll read these around the circle tomorrow.

Questions?

A Course of Study: Essays

49 **Effective Essays: Teasing Out Criteria**

50 **How Do I Scratch the Itch?**

51 **Write with Information**

52 **Order the Information**

53 **Leads for an Essay**

54 **Experiment with Essay Conclusions**

What I Was Thinking   Writing about ideas—in other words, essay writing—is a challenging genre to sponsor in writing workshop, where it's easier and more obvious to ask students to compose the genres they read: stories, poems, parodies, plays, and reviews. As an English teacher, I had to push out into the world of ideas and pull it back into the writing workshop.

I knew the effort would be worthwhile, because the expository genres have so shaped and changed my own life. Opinions, arguments, interpretations, and persuasions are my bread and butter as a writer: my essays about the teaching of writing and reading accumulated to become *In the Middle* (1987; 1998).

So I sought ways to nurture the same potential in my kids—to support them as they used writing to act on behalf of ideas they believed in, questions they wanted to find answers to, problems they wished to solve, and itches they *had* to scratch. They, too, needed opportunities to gather their own evidence, articulate their ideas, send both out into the world, and try to have an influence there.

But in order to write essays, my students first had to read them. I began to look for and collect good essays, share them with my kids, and collaborate with them as researchers of the genre. This group knowledge became the foundation students stood upon as they figured out how essays worked and what they could do. Rather than start with a prescribed, inauthentic formula—for example, five paragraphs, each with a topic sentence—we began with real essays.

Now, every year in the early spring as I anticipate this course of study, I pore over the editorial and op-ed pages of the daily *New York Times* and *Boston Globe* with scissors in hand. I also read the *New Yorker*, the last page of *Newsweek*, the editor's column in *Rolling Stone*, and editorials and letters to the editor in local papers. All told I spend several weeks looking for well-written essays on topics that are pertinent to my kids or about which they probably have sufficient background information to be able to engage.

For example, I've clipped essays about the Electoral College, pro and con; a proposal to extend the school year by thirty days; whether sixteen-year-olds should have the vote; the phonics wars; legalizing marijuana for medical uses; a call for legislation banning captive animal performances; whether computers and the Internet are overemphasized in schools and colleges; Barbie at age forty; a mother watching her teenaged daughter become addicted to tobacco; whether oil drilling should be allowed in Alaska's Arctic National Wildlife Refuge; a resistance movement in Sturbridge, Massachusetts, to a new Wal-Mart; the banning of land mines; enforcement of air pollution rules; and an argument on behalf of Amy—not Jo—as the preferred role-model for girl readers of *Little Women*.

After students read and annotate ten or twelve essays and name the features of good ones, they engage in the topic search activity described in Lesson 7, "Itches to Scratch in Essays."

Then I draw on Donald Murray's advice, especially his book *Write to Learn* (1993), and describe a rough process for students to follow in pursuing their topics, from defining the problem to generating data for the essay to going public with it.

My students have published their essays as guest editorials in the school's weekly newsletter to parents, as contributions to our school literary magazine, as essay contest entries, and as letters to the editor and guest editorials in local weekly newspapers.

Seventh grader Jack Sherman went public with his essay about the ways that tobacco companies target kids through ads in letters to the editor of six midcoast Maine weeklies; I've included it in Appendix C. He got a ton of response, in the form of personal letters and follow-up responses in the papers, and he loved it. Jack said, "It was my first essay, and it felt cool and important to have all these people thinking about kids and smoking just because of something I wrote."

Effective Essays: Teasing Out Criteria

Preparation

✔ Photocopied packets of at least ten essays from newspapers, magazines, and other sources, written on topics pertinent and engaging to students at this grade level (see Appendix C for examples of essays by seventh and eighth graders to supplement the professionally published examples you find)

✔ Overhead transparency headed "Features of Effective Essays" for brainstorming with your students

✔ Optional: Overhead transparency of "Features of Effective Essays: Sample Small-Group List" as an example for your students of what's possible

49 LESSON

APRIL

"For the next two weeks, we're going to look at the genre that's made for writers to address their questions, concerns, and ideas about the world. This genre is the essay. How many of you would describe yourself as readers of essays? . . .

I'm not surprised, and that's okay. Unless you read a daily paper, a habit most of you are still growing into, a reader doesn't have a lot of traffic with the essay genre. So I've collected twelve essays—most by professional writers and a handful by students—that were interesting for me to read and that address topics I think you'll find interesting and accessible. As with every genre we've studied, I'll ask you to learn about essays by reading some and teasing out their features.

Please turn to the next clean page of your writing handbook and record this heading:

Features of Effective Essays

For homework, due the day after tomorrow—so you have two nights to read and think—I'd like you to choose ten of these twelve essays to read, annotate, and take notes on under that heading. What do you notice about titles, leads, conclusions, language choices, voice, length, content, and style?

Here's a packet of the twelve essays for each of you. . . .

I'm going to quickly preview the topic of each essay, to give you an overview of the subjects the essayists bit off. Follow along with me as I flip through the packet. The first essay is about . . .

As you can see, there's quite a range of topics and attitudes. From among these, you get to choose the ten you're most interested in. Read them and mark them up. Then make as complete a list as you can of what you notice about the essay form and essay writing, and we'll meet in two days to debrief.

Questions? Concerns?

49

FOLLOW-UP LESSON

[At the start of class on the day the notes on essay features are due, I walk the inside of the circle to be certain that every student has a list. Then I assign kids to form groups of four to six, appoint one student in each group as its recorder, and ask students to collaborate on small-group master lists of the features of good essays. I might show an overhead of "Features of Effective Essays: Sample Small-Group List" at this point as an example.

After ten or fifteen minutes, I reassemble the class in the mini-lesson circle, ask recorders to take turns reporting out criteria noticed by their groups, and tell kids not to take notes. I create a whole-group master list from their responses—and mine—on transparencies. See Figure 49-1, a list compiled by a group of my students and me, for a potential reference to use during the master-list process.

That evening I organize, edit, and type the criteria. Then I make a class set of photocopies,

Overhead
Features of Effective Essays:
Sample Small-Group List

trim them, and at the start of class the following day ask students to tape the clean master list of features of an effective essay onto the next page of their writing handbooks. They take turns around the circle reading aloud the criteria, pausing for discussion or elaboration. Then I pass out copies of "What Itch Needs Scratching?" and move directly into Lesson 7, which asks writers to consider and name ideas for essays of their own.]

FEATURES OF EFFECTIVE ESSAYS

Essayist has a definite opinion and wants to convince readers

Presents a balance between opinions and facts; the facts are evidence to support the opinions

Facts are embedded/woven into the essay, not listed or presented in isolation

Speaks directly to a reader in a conversational tone

No rambling: the essayist sticks to the subject

Cuts to the bone in order to punch the argument

Suggests solutions to a problem and explains why/how a solution will work

Tries to convince/inform/analyze

Provides relevant background information and history

Describes opposing arguments and critiques them

Uses statistics: hard evidence

Cites names, places, and dates to support the argument

Uses quotes to support the message

Draws on the essayist's personal experience or knowledge

Asks questions of the reader

A strong "I" voice: a particular person behind the writing

A catchy title that attracts a reader

A clear, true, inviting, and to-the-point lead

A fast pace, but not too fast

Strong diction: crafted and literary

Short, friendly paragraphs

Helpful transitional words to connect paragraphs and ideas

A logical organization that moves a reader along from one point or piece of information to the next

A powerful conclusion that resonates: leaves a reader with something to think about

Typically eight to eleven paragraphs in length

Figure 49-1 Sample Class List of Essay Features

How Do I Scratch the Itch?

Preparation

✔ Trimmed photocopies of "Essays: How Do I Scratch the Itch?" for students to tape into their handbooks

✔ Tape dispensers

LESSON **50**

APRIL

"The procedure I'll introduce for pursuing your essay topic is based on the work of Donald Murray, an essayist and writing teacher. "Essays: How Do I Scratch the Itch?" is a summary of what's involved in the process. Please tape it onto the next clean page of your writing handbook. Then follow along with me. . . .

Don't be intimidated: this is an overview of a long process. From this point on I'll break it down and teach you how to tackle each step.

Our first focus will be on focus. Please turn your attention to the initial step: *Define the problem*. Tonight for homework I'd like you to brainstorm answers to those two questions. What would *you* like to know about your issue or problem? What do *readers* need to know?

It will help you later, when you start to collect information, to act as a heat-seeking missile—to search for and pursue relevant information. So define and focus the problem now by forming the particular questions you're trying to find specific answers to.

Turn to the page in your handbook on which you wrote your essay question or statement. Tonight, in the space beneath it, brainstorm questions about what you'd like to know about the problem or issue. Then list the questions a reader might have about the problem or issue. Start your research juices flowing by taking the stance of a curious, questioning reader.

Questions for me? Observations about the essay process we'll use?

Write with Information

Preparation

✔ Trimmed photocopies of "Write with Information" for students to tape into their handbooks
✔ Tape dispensers

"Now that you've begun to focus and define your essay problem by generating questions, let's take a look at some ways of answering them through the collection of information. Please turn to the next clean page of your writing handbook and tape in a copy of "Write with Information." Then follow along with me. . . .

Again, there are many ways to collect information, and information comes in many forms. Your next task as essayists is to gather more information than you can possibly use: lots of the accurate, specific data that readers crave. I'd leave a good four or five days for this phase of the process. And I'd begin—and I'll ask you to begin—by focusing the quest.

Tonight for homework, copy your essay question or statement at the top of the "Write with Information" handout. Then read through this list of sources, methods, and forms again, on your own, and begin to make some decisions: which kinds of information are appropriate for the issue or problem you've targeted for your essay? Make a tick mark next to each kind of information that you think will feed your essay topic.

For example, if an essayist is interested in how grades affect student motivation, a survey or poll of other students would be an appropriate method for collecting. But would an opinion poll work if, for example, your essay is about the health benefits of eating red meat? . . . Why not?

WRITE WITH INFORMATION *

Donald Murray says, "The writing act begins with the collection of the raw material of writing, information that will be arranged into meaning by the act of writing." Essayists write with information—lots of specific, accurate data. And, Murray continues, "Readers read to satisfy their hunger for information—specific, accurate information that they can use."

There are many ways to collect information and many forms of information to collect:

Process: your observations of the specific actions of someone concerned with or affected by the issue

Questions: what readers will wonder

Answers: responses to the questions readers will ask

Facts: specific, accurate details from magazine and newspaper articles, books, reports, and the Internet

Statistics: numbers that reveal and illustrate the situation

Surveys and polls: statistics gathered firsthand, summarized, interpreted, and set in context

Quotations: statements by others, including authorities and person-on-the-street types

Examples: times and places that the problem turns up or the situation is encountered

Anecdotes: little stories that show people and/or the problem in action

Theories: your thoughts or the thoughts of others that explain the situation

Principles: the accepted way something is done or perceived, which may be wrong and which you can attack

Interviews: words and voices of people concerned with or affected by the issue

Solutions: steps that readers or some other party can take to solve the problem

Roadblocks: what's stopping the problem from being solved

Arguments: reasons for your point of view and your responses to the roadblocks

Personal experiences: events from your life that reveal the problem

Ideas: all the various, stray thoughts the writer wants to consider in the essay

History: a problem's past history or tradition

Implications: the future of the problem

Murray advises writers: "Collect the material to fill out such a list, and you'll stop feeling empty. In fact, you'll feel so full that you'll be eager to write to relieve yourself of the information."

* Adapted from *Write to Learn* by Donald M. Murray (1999) Fort Worth, TX: Holt, Rinehart, and Winston

WRITE WITH INFORMATION   LESSON 51

Right now, on the next clean page of your writing handbook, please write this heading:

Potential Information Sources and Forms for My Essay

Tonight, after you select and check off kinds of information, please copy from the master list the sources and forms you're considering. Add any you think of that aren't on the list. Tomorrow when we meet I'll ask you to share your ideas about forms and sources of information, and I'll help you hone your approaches as data collectors.

Questions?

FOLLOW-UP LESSON

51

[During the next two days, I either meet briefly with individuals during writing conference time about their lists of forms and sources of information, or I use mini-lessons as an occasion to troubleshoot forms and sources together: I ask each student around the circle to state the essay topic—the exact question or statement—then to read his or her list of potential sources and forms. The class and I troubleshoot these lists together, half one day and half the next, calling attention to other sources that might work and asking essayists to rethink inappropriate or irrelevant sources.]

Order the Information

Preparation

- ✔ Trimmed photocopies of "Five Ways to Organize Your Information and Plan Your Essay" for students to tape onto two pages of their handbooks
- ✔ Tape dispensers
- ✔ Large sheets of white construction paper
- ✔ Sheets of various colored construction paper
- ✔ Colored markers
- ✔ Scissors
- ✔ Glue sticks

52 LESSON

APRIL

"I know that several of you are feeling as if you've gathered enough information to embark on a draft of an essay, so I'll teach this lesson now to everyone. It's a big one. Once you've generated and collected lots of raw material, you need to figure out how to use it to make meaning as an essayist. And to do that, you'll need a plan. Please tape "Five Ways to Organize Your Information and Plan Your Essay" to the next clean page of your writing handbook.

I headed this lesson with a crucial quote, again from Donald Murray. Please read along with me: "There's no (one) way to outline.... But you should find some way of presenting what you may write.... Most of the time my drafts collapse unless I have outlines in my head or on paper."

For some of you, organizing your information and planning the essay will seem like the hardest part of the process. Hang in there. It's probably the most important part—the step that will make your essay possible and, as Murray put it, keep your draft from collapsing.

FIVE WAYS TO ORGANIZE YOUR INFORMATION AND PLAN YOUR ESSAY

"There's no (one) way to outline . . . . But you should find some way of preseeing what you may write . . . . Most of the time my drafts collapse unless I have outlines in my head or on paper."

—Donald Murray

1. **Donald Murray's favorite method:**
   - Brainstorm titles as a way to capture the direction and tone of your essay.
   - Draft ("play with") leads until you have the one you think will produce a good essay.
   - Imagine a reader, draft the questions he will ask, then put them in the order he'll ask them. Murray says, "Good writing is a conversation between an individual writer and an individual reader."
   - ▪ ▪ ▪ ▪ ▪ ▪ ▪ ▪ ▪ "a sense of destination" as a writer.
   - Start drafting the essay.

2. **Donald Graves's favorite method:**
   - Create four vertical columns on a huge sheet of white construction paper.
   - Briefly list *everything* that might be included in the essay in the far left column.
   - Head the other three columns *Beginning*, *Middle*, and *End*. Move ideas and items from the far left into the appropriate columns, based on where they seem to belong in the essay.
   - Be aware that you may not use everything in the left-hand column and that new ideas will arise and can be included there as they come to you.
   - When you're done, number the items within each of the three lists in the order you want to use them.
   - Start drafting the essay by experimenting with leads.

FIVE WAYS TO ORGANIZE YOUR INFORMATION AND PLAN YOUR ESSAY – PAGE 1
LESSON 52

3. **Colored paper**
   - Gather sheet
   - Use scissors categories: k beginning–n
   - Tape the pie construction in your essay emerge.
   - Start drafting

4. **Colored marke**
   - Gather color colors accor beginning–n
   - Start drafting focus the dat
   - Create the re highlighted i

5. **Your own forr**
   - Spread out y
   - Skim and sca What are the and end the support your
   - On a plannin outline: note
   - Start drafting

Reproducible
Five Ways to Organize Your Information and Plan Your Essay

How do you plan or outline an essay? Again, there's no one way. This is a selection of five approaches that have worked for professional writers Donald Murray and Donald Graves, student writers, and me. Please follow along as I read. . . .

How many of you already have an idea of how you'll plan your essay? . . . Tell me what you're thinking. . . .

You may have noticed that every one of these methods of planning calls for an early investment in leads. Tomorrow we'll talk about kinds of essay leads you might wish to experiment with, and I'll show you some examples.

In the meantime, I've gathered the materials and equipment you might need to organize, order, or color-code your information and ideas, from big sheets of white paper if you're going to try Don Graves's four columns, to sheets of colored paper, scissors, glue sticks, and colored markers if you want to try approach #4 or #5.

For now, what are your questions or observations about ways of planning an essay?

52

Leads for an Essay

Preparation

✔ Trimmed photocopies of "Experiment with Essay Leads" for students to tape into their handbooks

✔ Photocopies of "Examples of Essay Leads" and "Check Your Essay Lead"

✔ Tape dispensers

LESSON

APRIL

"Let's talk leads. Please tape a copy of "Experiment with Essay Leads" to the next clean page of your writing handbook.

The quote from Donald Murray that begins this lesson about leads couldn't be a stronger statement about their importance. Read along with me: "I *never* proceed without an opening that I think will produce a good piece of writing. That's the only never in my personal toolbox."

Back in the fall I saw how our discussions of different narrative leads—action, dialogue, and reflection—fueled your memoirs and short stories. So I've prepared this short list of approaches to essay leads for you to consider and experiment with, as well as some examples written by seventh- and eighth-grade students as illustrations. Please refer to the leads on the three-pager, "Examples of Essay Leads," as we read about each kind.

The first kind of lead is an anecdote: a little story that goes to the heart of an issue. Take a look at the anecdote Colby created as his lead for "How Are You Being Controlled?" Let's also look at Emily's anecdotal lead to "The Movie Theater Monopoly" and Jed's for "Beef as Health Food? You Bet." . . .

The right quotation can be effective, too. Anne used a quote to kick off "The Feminist Question": she conveys the stereotype in a nutshell by reproducing the words of an influential role model. . . .

EXPERIMENT WITH ESSAY LEADS

"I *never* proceed without an opening that I think will produce a good piece of writing. That's the only never in my personal toolbox."
—Donald Murray

Some Leads to Try

- **Anecdote:** a brief story that captures the essence of the issue or situation
- **Quotation:** a voice not your own that speaks to or exemplifies the problem or issue
- **News:** the writer gives the reader the who-what-where-when-why of a situation or issue
- **Background:** the writer gives a brief history of the issue or situation
- **Announcement:** the writer tells the reader what he or she is going to say about the issue or situation and takes an attitude

Some Leads to Avoid, Please

A dictionary definition ("*Webster's* defines *conformity* as . . . "): it's a cliché.

A question to the reader ("How did that hamburger you had for dinner last night get to the shelves of your supermarket?"): it presumes the reader cares about the answer, plus it's condescending.

A bromide or cliché ("We've all heard the expression, 'Better safe than sorry.' But is that true of today's airline security procedures?"): your reader is already snoring.

A lead that isn't focused ("Adoption programs in this country have some flaws. They aren't completely bad, but they need to be dealt with. There are a couple of things I'm concerned about, even though, overall, adoption is a good thing."): the reader is lost and confused before the writer has even started the essay.

© 2002 by Nancie Atwell from
Lessons That Change Writers
(Portsmouth, NH: Heinemann)

EXPERIMENT WITH ESSAY LEADS   LESSON 53

Reproducible
Experiment with Essay Leads

EXAMPLES OF ESSAY LEADS

ANECDOTE

How Are You Being Controlled?
by Colby Smith

You go out to buy a pair of shoes, but the Super Duper Store is the only one in town: all the smaller, family owned shops and specialty stores went out of business when the Super Duper Store moved in. Each small store couldn't get enough varieties of shoes, and customers won't pay more if they can buy something cheaper somewhere else, even though before, with all the small shops combined, consumers had a wider selection and, at certain times and places, cheaper prices.

But that's all long gone now. You go into the Super Duper Store and check out the shoe selection. You need running shoes, and you have two choices: the fifty dollar pair, or the $120 pair. Neither seems that well made, or even what you're looking for, but you don't have a choice. There's no other place to look, and you need shoes. So you buy the better pair, but not long after you've bought them, a sole falls off. Then you have to go back to the Super Duper Store and give them more money for more bad shoes you don't want. This might seem to be a worse case scenario, but it's a situation that's worsening with the growth of huge, conglomerate corporations.

The Movie Theatre Monopoly
by Emily Robinson

When I went to the movies at Hoyts Cinema in Brunswick a few weeks ago, I was shocked by the ticket prices. For an adult—which Hoyts defines as someone twelve or over—to attend an evening movie, the cost is $7.75. In other words, a motorist could buy six gallons of gasoline for as much as it costs for one person to see an hour and a half movie. Is there a way to see a movie locally, at a large movie theatre, without paying Hoyts prices? No. Hoyts is the only multiplex theater in midcoast Maine. Hoyts is a monopoly.

© 2002 by Nancie Atwell from
Lessons That Change Writers
(Portsmouth, NH: Heinemann)

EXAMPLES OF ESSAY LEADS – PAGE 1   LESSON 53

Reproducibles
Examples of Essay Leads and Check Your Essay Lead

Jack begins "Stop the Tobacco Companies from Targeting Kids" with a news-type lead: straight who-what-when-where-why factual information, starting with a statistic. . . .

Erin's lead to "Lethal Possibilities" begins with background—a brief history of the dropping of the atomic bomb—followed by an announcement: she tells us what she's going to tell us in her essay. . . . Marcia's lead to "The Right to Read" also gives background information, this time about the censorship of children's literature. . . .

Finally, check out Peter's lead to "What Is the Prize?" It's an announcement that comes through strong and clear: he's going to tell us why he's against extrinsic rewards for reading. He announces both his issue and his attitude. . . .

Now check out the addendum to "Experiment with Essay Leads," please—some entry points to try to avoid because they don't work well or at all. Read "Some Leads to Avoid, Please" along with me. . . .

Your first step as a writer of essay leads is to experiment, just as you do with narrative leads. Keep experimenting and playing until you find the way in that will produce an essay with focus and attitude. Produce alternatives. *Play.*

Questions? Observations?

FOLLOW-UP LESSON

[I distribute copies of "Check Your Essay Lead" and talk kids through the list of questions. I also use these criteria as I confer with individuals about the drafts of their leads. I suggest that writers use the criteria as they revise their leads, and I ask students to meet in pairs with copies of the checklist and confer about one another's leads.]

53

Experiment with Essay Conclusions

Preparation

✔ Trimmed photocopies of "Experiment with Essay Conclusions" for students to tape into their handbooks

✔ Photocopies of "Examples of Essay Conclusions" and "Some Transitional Words and Phrases for Essays"

✔ Photocopies of an essay checklist created by you, derived from the list of features of effective essays your class developed in Lesson 49 [see Figure 54-1 for mine]

✔ Tape dispensers

54 LESSON

APRIL

"Yesterday I conferred with several essayists who are on the verge of wrapping up their first drafts, so I knew that today we'd need to talk as a group about some approaches to concluding essays.

Please tape "Experiment with Essay Conclusions" to the next clean page of your writing handbook. . . . Next, take a copy of "Examples of Essay Conclusions." These are endings to student essays that illustrate the approaches on the master list.

You know how I feel about conclusions. They need to be strong, and they need to resonate: to leave a reader thinking, feeling, or both. For example, let's look at how Colby ended his essay about how conglomerates control our lives and how Peter concluded his argument against giving prizes for student reading. Both of them tell a concerned reader to *take action*. . . .

Reproducible

EXPERIMENT WITH ESSAY CONCLUSIONS

"The end must connect with the opening. What has been promised must have been delivered. Read the opening over to see what closing it implies."
—Donald Murray

Some Conclusions to Try

- **Admonition or instruction:** what the reader can do about the issue

- **Prediction:** an insight into how the future could be different, better, or worse

- **Strong, punched statement:** perhaps a one-sentence paragraph

- **Anecdote:** a brief story that reiterates the essence of the issue or situation

- **Pointed question:** leaves the reader thinking

- **Echo:** circles back to the lead

A Conclusion to Avoid

"Only rarely in effective writing is the closing a formal summary in which the writer repeats . . . what has already been said."
—Donald Murray

© 2002 by Nancie Atwell from *Lessons That Change Writers* (Portsmouth, NH: Heinemann)   EXPERIMENT WITH ESSAY CONCLUSIONS   LESSON 54

Reproducible
Experiment with Essay Conclusions

EXAMPLES OF ESSAY CONCLUSIONS

ADMONITION OR INSTRUCTION
Colby:
　If we succeed in leveling out the capitalistic imperfections, our whole society will be rewarded. Fight back.

Peter:
　If you are a teacher who has students who don't like to read, give them access to good books and time to read and talk about them. Don't assign books, and never give prizes for reading.

PREDICTION
Anne:
　Girls today can help achieve these important goals by taking a positive attitude toward their body image and being in control of their bodies, taking on leadership roles in the classroom and beyond, becoming active in the fight against sexism by objecting when they hear or are the subjects of sexist remarks or behavior, and setting higher education and career goals. Most importantly, girls can promote feminism by being who they want to be, not who the culture tells them they must be. Feminism is a philosophy that's not extreme, but fair. I hope that by opening a dialogue with my peers I can broaden their ways of thinking about the other half of the human race.

Erin:
　I believe to ensure that an atomic bomb will never be dropped again there is only one solution: education. Children need to be educated about the effects of nuclear and atomic weapons, and we need to be taught about what happened at Hiroshima and Nagasaki. The children of today will be the adults of tomorrow, and maybe, if we know enough about nuclear warfare and the missile treaties the U.S. needs to make and keep with other countries, we can prevent it from ever happening again.

© 2002 by Nancie Atwell from *Lessons That Change Writers* (Portsmouth, NH: Heinemann)   EXAMPLES OF ESSAY CONCLUSIONS – PAGE 1   LESSON 54

Reproducibles
Examples of Essay Conclusions

A prediction is another strong conclusion: when the writer suggests how the future might be better—or worse. Anne predicts a future for feminism, and Erin for the nuclear age. . . .

A brief, emphatic statement can also conclude an essay strongly. Look at Jack's one-paragraph sentence that ends his essay about teenagers and tobacco. . . .

Marcia ends with an anecdote—a quick story that reiterates the essence of the problem of censorship of children's literature . . .

Emily concludes by leaving her readers with a pointed question . . .

And Jed returns to his lead and echoes it by continuing the anecdote he started to tell at the beginning of the essay.

There are other kinds of essay conclusions—for example, a pertinent quotation can be a strong way to end. These examples show the range chosen by writers in one class: student essayists who experimented with different conclusions, then selected from among alternatives the best way to end their essays and leave their readers.

Please *play*. Don't be satisfied with the first way the words go down on the page. Try different ways out of your essay, just as you tried different ways into it. Then choose the one that will leave your reader thinking the hardest and feeling the strongest.

Questions? Observations? Plans?

FOLLOW-UP LESSONS

[As kids complete first drafts of their essays, I distribute and discuss copies of "Some Transitional Words and Phrases for Essays." I also give them an essay checklist (see Figure 54-1) to use as they critique their own and their peers' drafts. I base the checklist

---

on the criteria that my students and I observed back when we read and analyzed professional and student essays in Lesson 49, at the beginning of the study, so as essayists they begin and end the process with similar language, standards, and goals.

Reproducible
Some Transitional Words and Phrases for Essays

A SAMPLE ESSAY CHECKLIST

- ☐ A catchy title that attracts a reader
- ☐ A clear, true, inviting, and to-the-point lead
- ☐ A powerful conclusion that resonates: leaves a reader with something to think about
- ☐ A strong *I* voice: a particular person behind the writing, one who has a definite opinions and wants to convince readers
- ☐ Sticks to the subject: no rambling
- ☐ Cuts to the bone, in order to point to and punch the essential argument(s)
- ☐ Sufficient information to convince a reader: enough background, examples, statistics, survey results, personal experiences, quotes, etc.
- ☐ Balances opinions and facts; the facts are used as evidence to support the opinions
- ☐ Facts are embedded/woven into the essay, not listed or presented in isolation
- ☐ A fast pace, but not too fast
- ☐ Strong diction: crafted and literary
- ☐ A logical organization that moves a reader along from one point or piece of information to the next
- ☐ Short, friendly paragraphs
- ☐ Transitional words to help a reader connect paragraphs and ideas
- ☐ Eight to eleven paragraphs in length.

Figure 54-1 A Sample Essay Checklist

54

Ted L. Nancy Letters and Other Genres for Humorists

Preparation

✔ For each of the mini-genres of humor writing included in this lesson— poetry parodies, fable parodies, fairy tale parodies, Ted L. Nancy Letters, and adolescent humor—the preparation is the same: photocopy or read aloud examples of the genre, then say to kids, "You could do this. Choose your target. Choose your form. Then take aim and start playing."

LESSON **55**

MAY

What I Was Thinking Some of my favorite moments in my classroom come when I'm reading aloud a Ted L. Nancy letter or a parody news article from the latest *Onion*. I'm snorting with laughter so I can barely get the words out, while my kids roll around on the floor, collapsed in giggles. The experience is as shared, intense, and important as anything we do in our year of writing workshop.

I value the focus in writing workshop on deep feelings and ideas—on helping adolescents reflect and find meaning through writing—but I also need to acknowledge that essays, stories, and poems aren't the only genres that count. Kids are kids: they want opportunities for this other kind of self-expression, in which playfulness and craft become equal partners.

Humor writing is a time-honored tradition of American letters, from Perelman, Thurber, and Twain; to Woody Allen, Steve Martin, and Bruce McCall in the *New Yorker*; to Dave Barry's weekly column and occasional collections; to Ted L. Nancy's out-there letters to corporations and public figures, the *Onion* compilations, and the <www.theonion.com> Web site.

Perhaps the biggest lesson I've learned about humor writing is that in order to bring it successfully to a school writing program, the humor has to be relevant and timely. Kids need to get the joke with little or no explanation, which meant that Perelman, Thurber, and Twain have not proved successful models for my students, in terms of humor writers who inspire humor writing. I had to go looking.

What I found was a section in every good-sized bookstore labeled *humor* or *entertainment*. Several times each school year, but especially when I'm about to teach humor and parody, I comb the shelves in this section in search of writing that will make my kids laugh on Monday; for every fifty titles there will be one or two possibilities—books that elicit the telltale snort and bring to mind individual students who would get and love the joke.

I've included in Appendix E a list of humor titles that recently hit my kids' funny bones. But I need to add an important caveat. In five years, I can't guarantee that these sources will still be *the ones*. Recently I watched the Politically Correct Bedtime Story series lose its power; my current students think Weird Al Yankovic is just plain weird; and they have little patience these days for *Mad* magazine or Gary Larsen.

In May mini-lessons I read aloud from or distribute copies of humor and parody titles, in between and after the lessons on essay writing. The humor lessons come as a welcome counterbalance to the serious, strenuous headwork of the essays.

Humor is a wonderful way to end a year of writing workshop—to enjoy being silly together, laugh so hard we hurt, try on as writers the forms that crack us up as readers, then crack ourselves up, too.

55

Poetry Parodies:

- Kenneth Koch's "Variations on a Theme by William Carlos Williams," parodies of "This Is Just to Say" reproduced in *Knock at a Star* by X. J. and Dorothy M. Kennedy (1982)

- Jason Perry's parodies of Williams' "The Red Wheel Barrow," published in *In the Middle*, 2nd ed. (1998)

- B. J. Sherman's parody of Frost's "Nothing Gold Can Stay," also in *In the Middle*, 2nd ed.

- Parodies of Wallace Stevens' "Thirteen Ways of Looking at a Blackbird" by Nick Miller and Hallie Herz and Molly Jordan, reproduced here

- Parodies of Wallace Stevens' "Anecdote of the Jar" by Marcia Conley Carter and Nat Herz, reproduced here

- Jack Sherman's takeoff on E. E. Cummings' "Buffalo Bill's," reproduced here

Fable Parodies:

- *Squids Will Be Squids: Fresh Morals: Beastly Fables* by Jon Scieszka (1998)

- "Lemur" by Nancie Atwell, "Platypus Buys Pizza" by Colby Smith, and "Tapir and Aardvark" by Chris Kunitz, reproduced here

Fairy Tale Parodies:

- Jon Scieszka's *The Frog Prince Continued* (1991) and *The True Story of the Three Little Pigs* (1989)

- "Jack and the Bean Stock" by Forrest Carver, reproduced here

Ted L. Nancy Letters:

- Excerpts from *Letters from a Nut* (1997), *More Letters from a Nut* (1998), and *Even More Letters from a Nut* (2000) by Ted L. Nancy

- Ted L. Nancy letters written by Jimmy Morrill, Chris Kunitz and Colby Smith, and Peter Wilde, plus the response Peter received from McDonald's, reproduced here

Adolescent Humor:

- Forrest Carver's tortured paean to his computer, "~~Death~~ Life to the Computer," reproduced here

Figure 55-1 Popular Mini-Genres of Humor Writing

Test Writing as a Genre

Preparation

✔ Overhead transparency titled "Qualities We Found in Top-Rated Test Writing" for brainstorming with your students

✔ Photocopies of sample pieces of student writing at the grade level you teach that received the highest score on previous state assessments, generally a 4 or a 6, depending on the state. Obtain these in the fall by writing to the State Department of Education, Division of Testing, and asking for as many top-rated samples as they can provide. You'll need at least ten highly rated pieces, written in response to several different prompts.

✔ A list of as many sample or previously used writing prompts from state tests at your grade level as possible (again, write to obtain these from the Department of Education in the fall)

What I Was Thinking Because the Center for Teaching and Learning is a non-profit private school, certified through the New England Association of Schools and Colleges rather than the state, and is not dependent on a penny of state or federal funding, the school has been able to resist the tide of standardization and test taking that's driving instruction in U.S. classrooms. Although it's a personal nightmare every year to raise sufficient funds to keep CTL afloat, the alternative nightmare of state funds with strings attached keeps me fund-raising for all I am worth.

The teachers of CTL have rejected state standards because we believe the standards would diminish—would require an emphasis on something less than—what our students are already doing as writers, readers, and mathematicians. We've rejected state tests because the results tell us nothing we don't already know about our students as learners, because the tests waste our and our kids' precious class time, and because, in the case of writing especially, the tests don't measure or match the writing we teach or the way our kids behave as writers.

As a teacher, I know how lucky I am to be in a position where I can reject state assessments and speak so bluntly. But even if I didn't intuit my good fortune, I'd be reminded of it every time I spoke to a group of teachers or conducted a seminar about teaching writing. In any question-and-answer session, the first query is always a variation of, "In our state, students have to prove competence on a writing test that doesn't match the conditions of a writing workshop. How do I do both—teach what I know is right, and also prepare my kids so they'll do well on the state assessment?"

Although I can't answer the question from current personal experience, I can recommend a version of the test-prep process I used in the 1980's, during the years I taught at Boothbay Region Elementary School in Boothbay Harbor, Maine. In a nutshell my reply is, "Teach to the test, but treat test writing as a genre study."

We know that kids in a good writing workshop become good writers. But in order to adapt their writing abilities to the demands and conditions of a standardized writing test, they'll need help and practice—not a whole year of test prep, as some schools do, but a concentrated study during writing workshop, in the weeks prior to the test, of the genre of assessed writing.

56

> In three weeks every kid in your grade will take the state assessment in writing. I'm confident you'll do well because you're such passionate, hard-working, literary writers. Our days, weeks, and months of writing workshop have given you the best possible foundation to show what you can do as writers.
>
> Now we're going to build a nonfunctional but essential addition to that foundation and take a hard look at the genre you'll be asked to produce for the test. I want you to know it and master it as well as you have memoirs, short fiction, book reviews, poetry, and essays.
>
> The genre is called *test writing*. You'll never find it in any library or bookstore, but test companies and the State Department of Education have decreed that test writing is the best way to determine if kids in our state are good writers. So we're going to undertake an investigation of the genre, just as we went inside the genres of memoir, short fiction, poetry, book reviews, and essays and named how they worked as you began to write your own.
>
> I called the Department of Education and asked them to send me samples of the best test writing produced by kids in our state in previous years. These student pieces all received a rating of 6, the highest grade, when assessors scored the tests. The Department of Education also sent me something called a *rubric*: their list of what it takes for a piece of writing to earn a 6 from a scorer.

Well, I read the pieces rated 6, and I think the rubric falls short of capturing what's going on in these pieces—of identifying the qualities of good test writing. I know from our work as genre researchers how adept you've become at finding and naming criteria. So tonight for homework, I'd like you to take a stab at researching test writing.

Please write this heading on the next page of your writing handbook:

Qualities I Found in Top-Rated Test Writing

Then, tonight, please spend at least half an hour reading through this collection of student texts and listing everything you notice about the writing that seems to be important, any feature that might contribute to its being seen as a 6. Use the language we already know—about leads and conclusions, transitions, *So what's?*, voice, visual imagery, thoughts and feelings, spelling, capitalization, paragraphing, and so on. As always, be as specific as possible.

Comments? Questions?

FOLLOW-UP LESSON

Please gather in small groups of four with your writing handbooks. The recorder for each group is the person whose first letter of his or her first name comes closest to the *beginning* of the alphabet. Got that? The heading for your small-group notes will be: "Qualities We Found in Top-Rated Test-Writing." Your job now is to pull your individual research notes together into one document.

Once the small groups have finished compiling their criteria, I'll gather you back together, the groups will report out, and I'll create on the overhead a master list of your and my observations and insights, which I'll type up and give back to you. Ready? Off you go.

FOLLOW-UP LESSON

[In the following days, turn writing workshop into test-writing workshop. Give students at least five prompted assignments, using the sample prompts provided by the Department of Education. After each timed writing exercise, ask students to rate their own and one another's texts against the master list of criteria they created: Is this piece a 6 yet? What has to happen to make it a 6?

Circulate among students and confer about their texts, using the list of criteria as the basis for your conversations with them. Allow students multiple opportunities to practice—to learn from one test-writing experience, to apply what they've learned to the next, and to confer with one another, using the master list of criteria they developed together as a checklist.]

SECTION IV:

Lessons about Conventions

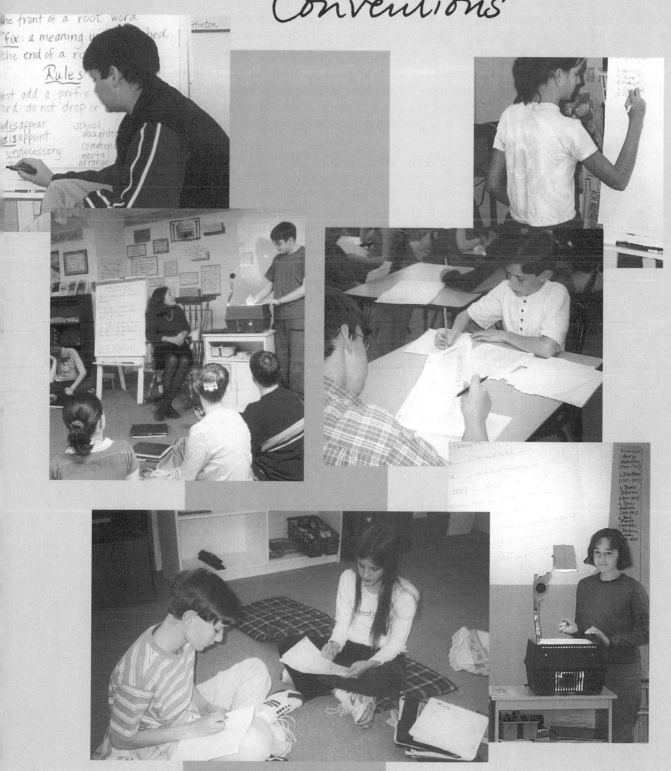

writing convention is an agreement forged over time between writers and readers about how something will be done. It's important for teachers to remember and for kids to learn that *writers* invented the conventions we use today in edited American English texts—for example, printing words left to right and top to bottom, leaving spaces between words, putting periods at the ends of sentences and capital letters at the beginnings, indenting for new paragraphs, spelling a word one way and not another.

Throughout history, writers have developed forms, rules, and standards so others could read their writing and so it would be read as a writer intended. English teachers need to approach conventions not as minutiae to be mastered but as means for helping students make their writing look and sound as they wish it to and for inviting readers to engage with texts, be *able* to engage, and take the writing seriously.

The lessons that satisfy these criteria give students accurate and relevant information, clear examples, and opportunities to practice the conventions. They are based on the errors a teacher observes as an editor of students' texts and the gaps he or she finds in kids' knowledge, like the omission of such marks as dashes, double dashes, colons, and semicolons. Conventions are taught not for their own sake but so students can take ever-increasing responsibility for editing and proofreading their writing before it goes public.

As a teacher of writing conventions, I focus in the fall on errors and omissions in the work of individual writers. During the first trimester I conduct only a handful of convention lessons and only as pressing needs arise in the writing of the whole group—for example, the difference between a hyphen and a dash as kids start word-processing their final copies.

First trimester mini-lessons are devoted to getting the group up and running as impelled, intentional crafters of writing. Then, through the winter and spring, among the lessons devoted to genres, I provide instruction about the conventions I observe, as their editor, that my kids need to know.

Most conventions lessons emerge as I edit drafts. I make notes to myself about future lessons based on the patterns I find, for example, a rash of comma splices, too many kids confusing *to/too* and *their/there/they're*, and issues around punctuating quoted dialogue. To plan a lesson I write a brief summary of the rule and create examples. I revise these as I use them in the lesson, then save everything from year to year in file folders, one folder per convention, so I don't have to spend time inventing new lessons to address what I can anticipate will be recurring problems.

I want my students to be respected as writers. I want them to be read. So I shoot straight with them about readers' needs, and I try to provide the information, examples, time, and high expectations they need to move their writing as close as they can to conventionality.

The Individual Proofreading List

Preparation

✔ Overhead transparency of "Individual Proofreading List"

✔ Three-hole-punched photocopies of "Individual Proofreading List"

✔ Overhead transparencies of Lucas Mayer's "Proofreading List" and "Editing Checksheet"

✔ Many photocopies of "Editing Checksheet" (e.g., enough for each student to edit twenty pieces of writing, September–June)

✔ Fine-point overhead marker

What I Was Thinking   Individual students will be ready to edit pieces of writing by the end of the second week of school. This lesson anticipates what every writer will need to attend to, as a self-editor and proofreader, for every piece of writing that goes to final copy for the remainder of the year. It also introduces the concept of *conventions* of writing.

In this lesson I teach about the first three entries on every student's proofreading list, and everyone records them. From this point on, each student's list will feature different conventions.

Believe me, I have tried to streamline and standardize the proofreading process. But beyond these three rules, any convention that I require be added to everyone's list, then checked for on subsequent pieces of writing, becomes a waste of someone's time. For students whose mechanics are already mature, a standardized proofreading list is an exercise in tedium. For less knowledgeable writers, it's an exercise in mystification: without the supporting context of identifiable errors in their own writing, the rules go right over their heads.

"Please attach this form, the "Individual Proofreading List," within the grommets of your daily writing folder, so it's on top and the first thing you see when you open your folder. . . .

Now, let's talk conventions.

Readers' eyes and minds are well-trained. As readers we've learned to bring specific expectations to written texts, and when a piece of writing doesn't match our expectations as readers, we're thrown.

Think back to a time when you were reading a novel and you came across a typo. I've seen kids become indignant over just one reversed-letter-order error that wasn't picked up by the publisher. You stop reading, and you focus on the error, right? Given enough typos, say, one per page, I think most of us would abandon the book.

That's because our eyes and brains have learned that texts are supposed to contain certain features and look certain ways. In fact, it's this predictable conventionality that makes reading possible.

So, what does this mean for writers? Well, if your writing is misspelled—research shows it takes as few as five or six misspellings in a three-hundred-word text—readers will say, "I can't read this." If your short story consists of one long paragraph, a reader won't *want* to attempt it—her brain will freeze up once she gets a gander at the text and realizes there are no breathing spaces, no places to rest and regroup. If your essay doesn't have sufficient periods at the ends of its sentences, a reader may start it, but without some signals about what to do with his voice as he reads, how to "chunk" the text, he'll soon abandon it. And if your free-verse poem looks like a prose paragraph, your reader will read it as a prose paragraph—so much for poetry.

Readers aren't snobs or judges. And they aren't lazy. But they do need all the help they can get, especially with written English—we'll talk on another day about why English spelling is such a bear. Readers need *conventionality*: for writers to hold up their end of the written language agreement. Readers count on writers to follow the rules and observe the forms; otherwise we can't act as readers. As writers we follow the rules and observe the forms so our writing will be read, so it will be understood as we intend, so we'll be taken seriously, and so we won't appear ignorant or arrogant.

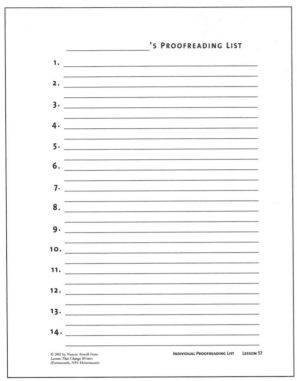

Overhead and Reproducible
Individual Proofreading List

I know that some teachers refer to spelling, punctuation, paragraphing, and capitalization as "skills," but everything you do well as a writer is a writing skill. I think it's more accurate and useful to call these "conventions."

The word *convention* comes from the Latin word for agreement. There are tons of agreements or conventions that make society possible: we drive on the right-hand side of the road, place the fork to the left of the plate, say "Hello" when we answer the phone, answer "I do" when we marry. This year, in mini-lessons and individual editing conferences, I'll teach you the conventions of writing that will help you hold up your end of the reader-writer bargain and be read, recognized, responded to, and respected as writers.

Your individual proofreading list is the place where you'll keep track of errors or omissions that show up in your writing and that you need to watch out for as you draft and edit. After today you'll make an entry on this list only after you and I have had an editing conference, that is, after I've read your writing and identified a convention you need to know, and after I've taught you about the rule or form in an editing conference.

Today we'll start the list with three common entries. Again, these are the only three conventions I'll ask all of you to focus on; after this, as I start editing your writing, your list will reflect your personal goals as an editor and proofreader.

As I record the three conventions on the overhead, please add them to your list. Ready?

Number one is

Obvious stuff

By this time in your careers as writers, you know some things about conventions. I don't want you to waste time listing every nitty-gritty convention that you've learned since first grade. What are some of the obvious things you can eyeball your writing for, as an editor and proofreader? . . . Right: capital letters at the beginnings of sentences and on people's names, your name on your writing, a title, quotation marks around words people say out loud, and so on. We'll sum these up as *obvious stuff*.

Here's the next entry. We'll talk about ways to proofread and correct spelling all year, but here's the bottom-line procedure:

Circle and look up every word I'm not 100 percent certain of

This means that at the very end, after the content of your writing is set, you'll stop reading for meaning and focus on each word and its spelling. If you're the *least* little bit unsure of a word, I expect you to circle it with your red editing pen. Then, when you've finished reading the whole piece for possible misspellings, grab a dictionary, a Spellex, or both and look up every one of the circled words. This may take a while. That's okay. Moving your writing toward mature conventionality is one of the reasons we're here.

If you're writing on the word processor, please don't run the spellcheck until after you've printed the piece and proofed it for spelling by eye-balling it yourself and seeing what you can find and correct on your own. Then you may spellcheck and ask the computer to help you, after you've helped yourself.

Item number three on your proofreading list has to do with titles. Other than correspondence, everything you write in the workshop will be titled. Here's the basic convention for handling titles:

Capitalize the first, last, and important words in a title

The unimportant words are, technically, articles, conjunctions, and prepositions—words like *the, a, and, so, but, of, in, before, with,* and *to.* The important words carry the meaning; these are nouns, pronouns, verbs, adverbs, and adjectives.

So, for example, how would you capitalize this title: *between a rock and a hard place?* What about this one: *tomorrow when the war began?* Now try *the one I've been waiting for.*

Overheads
Lucas's Proofreading List and Editing Checksheet

Great. So, from today on, every time you're ready to edit a piece of your writing, you'll copy these three conventions onto an editing checksheet—that's the cover sheet you attach to pieces of writing before submitting them to me for final editing. There's a stack of blank editing checksheets in the materials center. In red pen, you'll self-edit your piece for the three conventions you listed today, plus others I'll introduce to you individually this fall.

Next, I'll take your writing home and edit it for anything you missed. The next day in class I'll teach you one or two new conventions I think you should know about, based on the draft I edited. I'll write these down for you and me in the column on the editing checksheet headed *Teacher's Comments*. Then you'll copy these new conventions onto your individual proofreading list.

Let me demonstrate what this looks like in practice. The transparency shows Lucas's individual proofreading list as of January of his seventh-grade year, after eight pieces of writing and an editing conference about each one. Read along with me the list of conventions Lucas learned over these eight pieces. . . .

Next, here's one of Lucas's editing checksheets from December. You can see how he copied from his proofreading list the conventions he needed to focus on in the poem he was about to edit—but not *all* the conventions on his list. For example, since there are no numbers in his poem and no hyphenated phrases, Lucas doesn't need to list these rules.

This is the procedure you'll use for editing and proofreading for the rest of the school year. I'll demonstrate it again, in another mini-lesson this month, to refresh your memories and be sure you understand it. It's important to edit right, because it's important to *get things right* as a writer who has something to say and wants to use conventions to help support your meaning and clear the way for your readers.

Questions? Comments? Observations?

57

Business Letter Format and Addressing an Envelope

Preparation

✔ Three overhead transparencies ruled with $\frac{3}{8}$-inch or $\frac{1}{2}$-inch lines, one of which features your bad-on-purpose business letter, one that's relevant to the purpose of the lesson and commits the sins of students' don't-know-better attempts (see the list of sins below)

✔ The inside address for the recipient of the model letter you'll compose for the lesson

✔ A black fine-point overhead marker and a red extra-fine-point overhead marker

✔ A cup full of sharpened colored pencils in legible colors (i.e., not yellow), one for each student

✔ Trimmed photocopies of "U.S. Postal Abbreviations" and "Other Address Abbreviations" for students to tape into their handbooks

✔ A box of inexpensive No. 10 ($4\frac{1}{8}$-by-$9\frac{1}{2}$-inch) envelopes, or enough for each student, plus extras in case they mess up

✔ Overhead transparency of blank No. 10 envelope

✔ One sheet of white $8\frac{1}{2}$-by-11-inch paper for each student

✔ Tape dispensers

✔ Optional: Bailey White's collection of essays *Mama Makes Up Her Mind*, so you can read aloud "Maine," an essay about what happened when White and her first-grade class sent a pen-pal package to MA instead of ME

What I Was Thinking For years I had to look up the format of a business letter every time I wrote one. I was in my late twenties by the time I'd written enough formal correspondence to know the etiquette by heart. So while my experience tells me I can't expect kids to learn the intricacies of business letter format from one lesson, I can make sure that every student has an accurate model to work from when the time comes to direct a piece of correspondence to someone he or she doesn't know.

I teach this lesson and its follow-up—addressing an envelope—when the time is ripe—when there's a need or occasion for it, either among several members of the group or a class as a whole. For example, I've taught about business letters in the fall, when some of my students wanted to enter an essay contest that specified entries in the form of letters to authors; in the winter, when the class collaborated on a letter of complaint to an art museum, after an unpleasant encounter with security personnel during a field trip; and in the spring, the day after a parody mini-lesson about Ted L. Nancy letters (see Lesson 55), when kids wanted to get the form right in their own silly, officious letters of inquiry and complaint.

I hope other teachers will wait, too. This is a lesson topic that depends on a perceived need—on a real occasion when students want the correct format in order to be taken seriously by the adult world beyond the classroom. The etiquette of the form is so particular, arcane even, that it helps to have a compelling reason to get it right.

For the lesson I've narrated here, the occasion was the creation of a cover letter for a collection of twenty-action poems (see Lesson 6) that students wanted to mail to poet laureate Billy Collins. The day before the lesson I called the Lehman College switchboard and asked for Collins's address, ran a lined master through the photocopier to create three ruled transparencies, and, on one of them, wrote a quick, bad-on-purpose letter to Collins.

Then, during the lesson, I used another ruled transparency to write, annotate, and talk my way through a properly formatted letter. The style I demonstrated was semi-block, my preference for business correspondence. As I wrote on the overhead, students copied the model and the annotations into their handbooks, except for the address on the heading and the signature; here they substituted their own.

In my experience as an editor, the range of student errors that a teacher might commit in a bad-on-purpose business letter includes:

- Omitting the heading
- Omitting the inside address
- Omitting *dear* from the greeting
- Putting a comma, instead of a colon, after the greeting
- Indenting the greeting
- Addressing an unknown recipient by his or her first name
- Not skipping lines between the greeting and the body and the body and the closing
- Not indenting the first line of the first paragraph
- The writer telling his or her name, age, town, and state in the body of the letter

- The writer speaking inappropriately or presumptuously
- Omitting a final thank-you paragraph
- Writing an inappropriate closing
- Capitalizing the second word of a two-word closing
- Omitting the comma after the closing
- Omitting either the cursive signature or the printed/typed name beneath it

"I know you're excited to send your twenty-action poems to Billy Collins, but these can't just be stuffed in an envelope and mailed. Do you know what the letter's called that accompanies an enclosure? . . . Right, a cover letter; it covers the enclosure and explains it.

I drafted a terrible cover letter to accompany your poems, one that commits every conceivable error that the untutored writer of a business letter can make. Check out the overhead. [See Figure 58-1.]

Now, play copyeditor and tell me everything you noticed that's wrong here, in terms of what a business letter is supposed to have, do, and look like. I'll point out anything that you miss. . . .

Good job—you already know a lot about business letter format. Probably the most important awareness of all is this: serious people take business letter format seriously, meaning they expect the correspondence

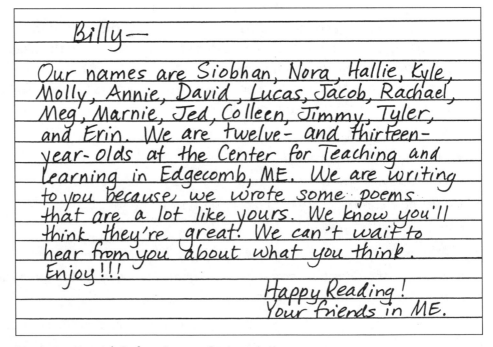

Figure 58-1 Nancie's Bad-on-Purpose Business Letter

they receive to conform to convention. When it doesn't, it's easy not to take a writer seriously.

A business letter without a heading, or a letter that addresses a stranger by his or her first name, or one that includes the writer's name in the body of the letter instead of at the end, where experienced letter readers know to find it, might as well be wearing a sign that says, "I don't know what I'm doing—I'm just a kid—you don't have to take me seriously."

I want you to be taken seriously—for your ideas to be considered and heard. So for the rest of this lesson I'm going to show you the correct way to write a business letter, using what's called the semi-block style. I'll ask you to create a model for yourself from the one I create on a transparency. I want each of you to have a personalized model, so that when the time comes, you can get business letter format right and have a fair shot at being recognized, respected, and responded to.

I'm sending around a cup of colored pencils. Choose one and pass it on. Then turn to the next clean page of your writing handbook. . . .

Each of you now has a colored pencil, along with your regular lead pencil. I have a red overhead marker and my regular black one. I'm going to draft the model business letter in black marker and label and annotate the model in red marker. You'll copy the draft in lead pencil and label and annotate it in colored pencil. The point is to create a model of what a business letter should look like *and* have notes to remind you of what you were doing. [See Figure 58-2 for the model I created during the lesson.]

So, in colored pencil, label this page in your handbook

Business Letter Format

Now switch to lead pencil, and we'll start with the heading. I'll write the school address, but you should write your home address. We'll both start writing just far enough to the left to be able to fit the entire street address on one line—by the way, with no abbreviations. I'm old-fashioned about this, so on the envelope, *yes*; in the letter, *no*.

Under the street address, and lined up with it, record your town-comma-state-no comma-ZIP. Are you with me? . . .

And under the town-state line, record today's date. You have to write it out: no numerals for months, no slashes. Don't forget the comma between the day and the year. . . .

Would you go back now, with your colored pencil, and annotate what you've done so far? Note that we started below the top line and wrote a *heading*. *Abbreviations* aren't allowed. There are *commas* between the town and state and between the date and year. Label your model as I am mine.

Now what? . . . It's time to *skip a line*, the first of many. Make a note to yourself in colored pencil to that effect. . . .

58

[And so on. I pause and circulate among kids at several points during the lesson to check that individuals are on track and to give pointers when they aren't. This is a long lesson—about thirty minutes—but worth it, I think, *vs.* the hours of conferring time it takes me to teach business letter format to one student at a time.]

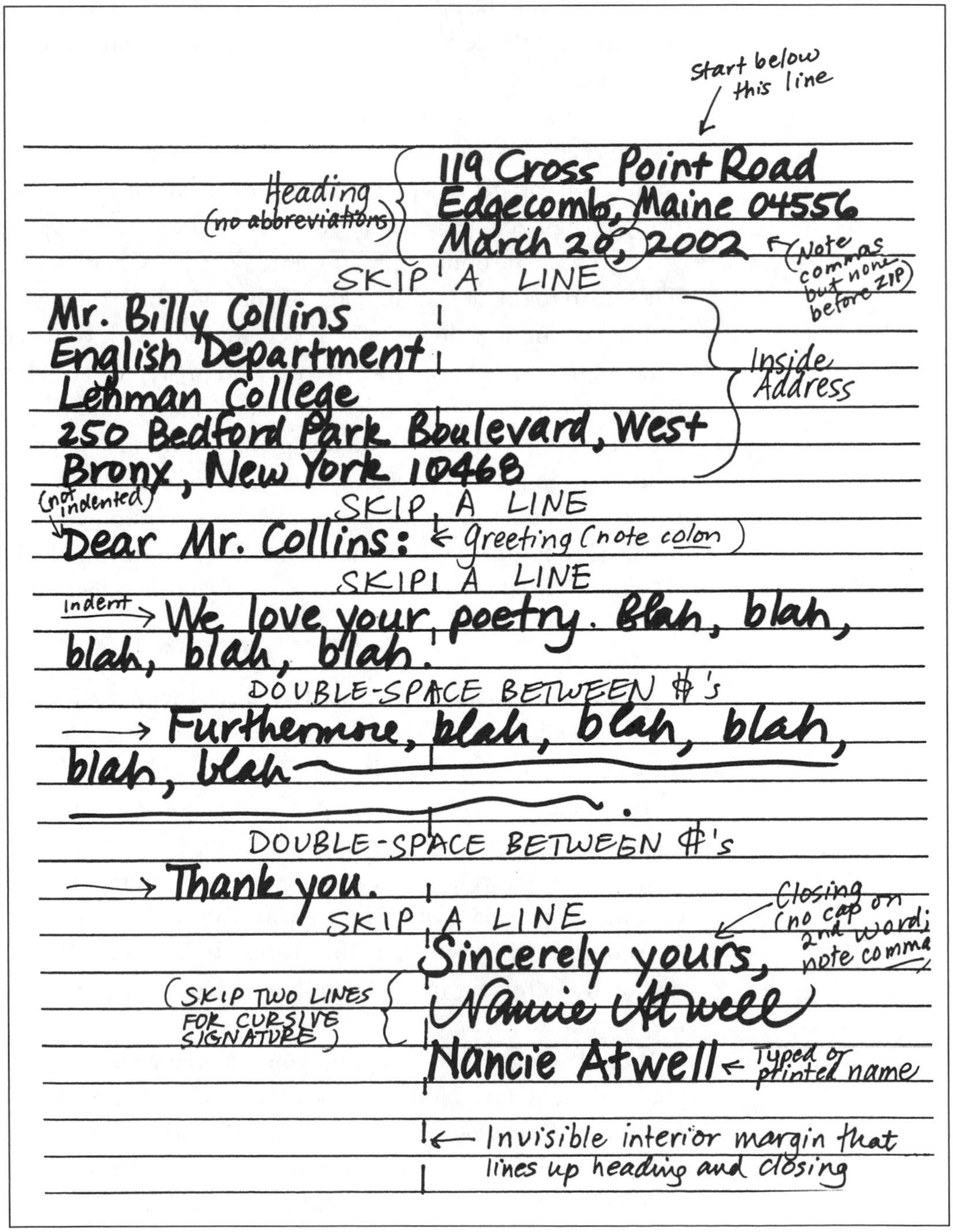

Figure 58-2 Nancie's Model Business Letter

[It doesn't hurt to write the business letter, especially if the occasion you've chosen is appropriate for a collaboration. Figure 58-3 shows the planning sheet the group created for our letter to Billy Collins. Figure 58-4 shows the cover letter we mailed along with the kids' poems. Later that spring they received a lovely—and conventional—business letter in response.]

Planning Sheet

- Think you're a great poet: accessible (?), write about particular, everyday experiences, objects, obsens. / sense of humor / images we can see and feel

- Read abt. an assignment you gave your class – the 20 actions – tried it. Here's what happened. We hope you enjoy them—

- We were also inspired to mem. poems because of your "essay "_____" : Name poems!

- Congrats on being named the p. laureate – good choice of L of Con.

- We start class ū a poem; all of us named poems by you as favorites of the trimester

- We read one of your new poems, "Litany," + looking forward already to yr. next collection

- Thank-you #: for the poems + the inspiration

Figure 58-3 Group Planning Sheet for Letter to Billy Collins

119 Cross Point Road
Edgecomb, Maine 04556
March 20, 2002

Mr. Billy Collins
English Department
Lehman College
250 Bedford Park Boulevard, West
Bronx, New York 10468

Dear Mr. Collins:

Congratulations on being named the U.S. poet laureate. We think the Library of Congress could not have made a better choice.

We love your poems. We appreciate the way you write about particular, everyday experiences and objects and turn them into art. Your images are specific and sensory, and your sense of humor knocks us out. We start class each day by reading a poem together, and all of us have named poems by you among our favorites.

We read a profile of you in *The Washington Post* and liked the assignment you gave your class so much—making the list of twenty actions that could become poems—that we tried it. The enclosed poems show what happened. We hope you enjoy them.

Your essay "The Companionship of a Poem" inspired us to choose poems that resonate for us and to memorize them. Some of us selected poems by you: "Budapest," "Morning," "Introduction to Poetry," and "Walking Across the Atlantic." They are already great companions.

This week we read one of your new poems, "Litany," and we're already looking forward to your next collection.

Thank you for the great poetry and the inspiration.

Sincerely yours,

The Seventh and Eighth Grade Class

Figure 58-4 Final Letter to Billy Collins

Addressing an Envelope and Folding a Letter

When you write and format a business letter, you're trying to satisfy the expectations of its recipient. When you address an envelope, your job is to satisfy the U.S. Postal Service. A correct address can be critical to your letter arriving on time or even at all. At the end of the lesson I'll read aloud a funny memoir by Bailey White that demonstrates the importance of getting an address right.

The address you'll write on the envelope will be exactly the same as the inside address of your letter, except that on the envelope you'll use abbreviations for states, the ones the U.S. Postal Service prefers. Here's a copy of a list of official state and possession abbreviations ("U.S. Postal Abbreviations"). And here's a list of "Some Other Address Abbreviations" to use when you address envelopes. Please tape these into your writing handbook on the next two pages. . . .

Finally, here's a standard business letter envelope, a No. 10. Don't do anything with it until I say so. We'll walk through this together. I've drawn an envelope-sized rectangle on a transparency. As I did yesterday, I'll demonstrate and you'll follow. [See Figure 58-5 for my model envelope.]

First, look at the inside address on yesterday's letter to Billy Collins. It's about to become a destination address. I'm going to start writing roughly in the center of the envelope—but because this is a five-line address, rather than the standard three-line, a bit to the left of center and slightly above it—with "Mr. Billy Collins." It's a matter of etiquette and tradition, when the addressee is an individual, rather than a company, to give him or her a title: Mr., Ms., Miss, Mrs., Dr., Rev., Sen., Gov.

Directly under the *M* in "Mr.," start the second line: "English Department." . . . Directly under the *E* in "English," begin the third line: "Lehman College." . . . The fourth line, the street address, again lines up

Nancie Atwell
119 Cross Point Rd.
Edgecomb, ME 04556

Mr. Billy Collins
English Department
Lehman College
250 Bedford Park Blvd., West
Bronx, NY 10468

Figure 58-5 Nancie's Envelope for the Letter to Billy Collins

U.S. POSTAL ABBREVIATIONS

ALABAMA	AL	MONTANA	MT
ALASKA	AK	NEBRASKA	NE
AMERICAN SAMOA	AS	NEVADA	NV
ARIZONA	AZ	NEW HAMPSHIRE	NH
ARKANSAS	AR	NEW JERSEY	NJ
CALIFORNIA	CA	NEW MEXICO	NM
COLORADO	CO	NEW YORK	NY
CONNECTICUT	CT	NORTH CAROLINA	NC
DELAWARE	DE	NORTH DAKOTA	ND
DISTRICT OF COLUMBIA	DC	NORTHERN MARIANA	
FEDERATED STATES OF		ISLANDS	MP
MICRONESIA	FM	OHIO	OH
FLORIDA	FL	OKLAHOMA	OK
GEORGIA	GA	OREGON	OR
GUAM	GU	PALAU	PW
HAWAII	HI	PENNSYLVANIA	PA
IDAHO	ID	PUERTO RICO	PR
ILLINOIS	IL	RHODE ISLAND	RI
INDIANA	IN	SOUTH CAROLINA	SC
IOWA	IA	SOUTH DAKOTA	SD
KANSAS	KS	TENNESSEE	TN
KENTUCKY	KY	TEXAS	TX
LOUISIANA	LA	UTAH	UT
MAINE	ME	VERMONT	VT
MARSHALL ISLANDS	MH	VIRGIN ISLANDS	VI
MARYLAND	MD	VIRGINIA	VA
MASSACHUSETTS	MA	WASHINGTON	WA
MICHIGAN	MI	WEST VIRGINIA	WV
MINNESOTA	MN	WISCONSIN	WI
MISSISSIPPI	MS	WYOMING	WY
MISSOURI	MO		

U.S. POSTAL ABBREVIATIONS   LESSON 58

Reproducibles
U.S. Postal Abbreviations
and Some Other Address
Abbreviations

on the left, and here we'll abbreviate *Boulevard* as "Blvd." . . . Then, on the city-state-ZIP line, we'll use the Postal Service abbreviation for New York state: "NY," with no periods.

Questions at this point? . . . Hold up your envelopes and let me eyeball what you have so far. . . .

Next, the return address should match the address of your heading. Start in the upper left corner with your first name. Then, using the appropriate abbreviations, write the street address; then bump down to the town-comma-state-no comma-ZIP line.

Okay, you're done with the envelope. The last step is to enclose your letter and here, as with everything else about business correspondence, there's a right way to do it. A letter that's folded more than twice looks amateurish.

I'm giving each of you a blank sheet of standard 8 ½-by-11-inch paper. Please sketch a rectangle in the upper right-hand corner to represent the heading—this is just to orient the paper as a mock letter.

Now, watch me and do as I do. Begin by folding up the *bottom* edge of the letter, so the paper is divided into thirds. Then fold down the *top* third. Crease the edges. Finally, place the envelope address side down, with the flap to the right, and insert the letter with its open end to the right.

Got it? . . . Try it again. Practice doing it correctly. The point is to make retrieving and reading the letter easy, predictable, and conventional—again, so you create an impression of someone who knows what he or she is doing and can be taken seriously.

Please circulate the tape dispensers and take just two pieces of tape this time. Use these to attach *one* end of your model envelope to the next clean page of your writing handbook: if you attach it all the way around, you won't have access to the letter inside, to remind yourself of how you folded it.

Label this page

Addressing an Envelope and Folding a Letter

Anytime you're ready to send a letter, consult this page and the lists of abbreviations on the previous pages, to be sure you address your envelope and fold your correspondence correctly.

Questions? Concerns? Headaches?

A Brief History of the English Language

Preparation

✔ Trimmed photocopies of "A Brief History of the English Language, or Why English Is Hard to Spell" for students to tape into their handbooks

✔ Tape dispensers

What I Was Thinking English spelling is a bear. It's only fair for kids to know this and to understand why—not so I can let them off the hook as spellers, but to help them understand how I'll teach spelling and the approach they'll take in learning it.

Because of its checkered past, English spelling, unlike the Romance languages, is only loosely rule-based, at best. There are a handful of useful generalizations, but even these have exceptions. So I teach a few spelling patterns that mostly work, and I focus our energies elsewhere: see "Troubleshooting: Spelling Essentials" for highlights of our spelling program.

This lesson sets the stage for a year's worth of spelling study as it explores English spelling and its sources, explains why English is unusually irregular, and introduces some of the hard work that lies ahead.

> "We're going to kick off a year of spelling study by looking together at the English language and understanding why spelling it can be such a headache. English is unique in the world because of its history, or rather, the history of England. You already know that English is the dominant language of North America and that it came here with English immigrants, starting back at Jamestown and Plymouth in the early 1600's. But how did the English language get to *England*?

To begin to answer that question, please circulate the tape dispensers, take *eight* pieces of tape, and affix this brief history of English to the next *two* clean pages of your writing handbook. . . .

Now, follow along with me as I read to you. We'll discuss this as we go. The source for much of the information about English is the one-volume *Columbia Encyclopedia* (1993). . . .

Are you beginning to understand why English is a bear to spell? English is actually a combination of many different languages. Contrast its development with that of Spanish, for example, and I think you'll see how history played a role in making Spanish and the other Romance languages regular and easy to spell and pronounce, while it dealt English a different hand.

From the first through the fifth centuries, Roman conquerors—soldiers and settlers—moved to Spain. These conquerors brought their language with them. What did they speak? . . . Latin, but a special kind: Vulgar Latin, the everyday language spoken by the regular people of the Roman Empire, as opposed to literary or classic Latin, which is what people today study in high school and college Latin classes.

Then, in the fifth century, the Western Roman Empire fell. Invading tribes of Huns and Visigoths took over, and the Dark Ages began in Europe. During this time the people who lived in Europe tended to stay put. They were isolated in their different regions for hundreds of years.

The Romans who were stranded in Spain continued to speak Vulgar Latin. But over the hundreds of years of isolation of the Dark Ages, they gradually developed their own dialect of Vulgar Latin, which today is called "Spanish." So except for words borrowed from Arabic, French, and Italian, today's Spanish is basically a straightforward descendent of the Vulgar Latin that was spoken by Roman settlers and soldiers, but with the addition of four letters and sounds: *ch, ll, ñ,* and *rr.*

Spanish is called a Romance language because its roots are in the language of the Romans. After the fall of the Roman Empire, other languages developed from Vulgar Latin in other former outposts of the empire. Do you know the names of any of the other Romance languages? . . .

A Brief History of the English Language, or Why English Is Hard to Spell

- English is a member of the West Germanic group of the Germanic subfamily of the Indo-European family of languages (whew).
- It's the official language of about forty-five nations and is spoken by more than 450 million people. English is one of the two working languages of the United Nations. French is the other.
- English is the mother tongue of the British Isles. English spread because of British exploration, colonization, and empire building during the seventeenth, eighteenth, and nineteenth centuries to North America, Australia, New Zealand, Africa, India, Hong Kong, the Caribbean, etc.
- The history of the English language parallels the history of the English people and the British Isles:
  1. In the middle of the fifth century, Angles, Saxons, and Jutes—tribes of Germanic invaders—brought their languages across the English Channel to the British Isles. No records exist of the preinvasion Celtic languages.
  2. In the sixth century, Christian missionaries arrived in England and brought Latin with them. Other invaders, this time from Scandinavia, established settlements in Britain and added to the complex.
  3. By the ninth century, the dialect spoken by the dominant Wessex, an Anglo-Saxon kingdom in Southern England, had become standard English. Today, one-fifth of the English words we use derive from this Anglo-Saxon English.
  4. But in the eleventh century, the Norman Conquest of Britain (1066–69) brought foreign rulers whose native language was French. French became the official language of England, eclipsing English. For more than three hundred years, French was the language of court, and English was spoken only by peasants. So another half of our English vocabulary is of French or Romance origins.
  5. In the fourteenth century, English/Wessex again became the language of the English upper class; the new standard was a London dialect, since London was now the political city. But during the three hundred years that kings of England had spoken French, the English language had changed greatly. The French spoken by the nobles had come to be more like English, and the English of the common people was now full of French words.
- There are three periods of English:
  1. *Old English* or *Anglo-Saxon* to c. 1150
  2. *Middle English* to c. 1500
  3. *Modern English* to today
  An Englishman of 1300 wouldn't have understood the English of 500; nor would he understand the English we speak today.

© 2002 by Nancie Atwell from
Lessons That Change Writers
(Portsmouth, NH: Heinemann)

A Brief History of the English Language – Page 1   Lesson 59

Reproducibles
A Brief History of the
English Language

That's right. In ancient Gaul, now France, Vulgar Latin developed into French. On the west coast of the Iberian Peninsula, Vulgar Latin evolved into Portuguese. In Rome itself, by about the tenth century, Vulgar Latin had developed into a dialect of Italian. Besides Spanish, French, Portuguese, and Italian, two other Romance languages are Catalan and Romanian.

Again, over the long period of regional isolation of the Middle Ages, Vulgar Latin differentiated into local dialects, and these became the individual Romance tongues. As a contemporary analogy, consider the way English in Maine sounds different from the English spoken in Mississippi. Now imagine no mass communication—no television, radio, newspapers, or Internet. Add to that a way of life that kept Americans isolated in Maine, Mississippi, and elsewhere. The varieties of English that would emerge over six hundred years or so would be pretty interesting.

Now think back to the history of England, to its lack of isolation, to all those invasions, and to the changes that each set of invaders brought to the language spoken in the British Isles. You can begin to appreciate why some linguists fondly refer to English as a mutt language.

So, what are the implications for English spelling? Again, let's compare English and Spanish. In Spanish writing, the letter *e* is only ever pronounced one way, like the long *a* in English. When someone wants to write the sound *a* in Spanish, he or she spells it the same way every time: it's always an *e*.

But because of all the various and sundry vocabulary sources of the English language, our letter *e* by itself can make at least five sounds and, thanks to the silent *e*, no sound at all. Worse, the sound *a* in English can be spelled almost twenty different ways, compared with one way in Español.

The bottom-line bad news for you folks is this: while most Spanish words can be spelled phonetically, only 46 percent of English words can be spelled the way they sound. A whopping 54 percent of the words in our language depend on visual memory—on our sense of what a word is supposed to look like. Is it any surprise that most good spellers of English are also good readers who read a lot?

This is one—but by no means the only or the most important—reason to read a lot. But even habitual, fluent readers need help with spelling. This is why I teach spelling. And it's why we're going to take a three-pronged approach to our study of English spelling.

First, in individualized weekly spelling studies, you'll focus on acquiring a visual memory of the correct spellings of your misspellings: a mental picture of what words are supposed to look like, just five words at a time. We've already started that work.

Next, in spelling mini-lessons, I'll focus on the handful of patterns that do hold water in English spelling. Finally, in proofreading lessons, I'll show you hints and techniques for close readings of your spellings—for using your visual memory to catch and correct errors before your writing goes public.

My purpose today was to try to set the stage for the hard but practical spelling work ahead. Did I do it? What are your questions or observations about English spelling and pronunciation, or about the history of the English language?

FOLLOW-UP LESSON

[Later in September I present a brief lesson on *etymology: the origin and development of a word, phrase, etc.; the tracing of a word as far back as possible.*

I show kids how a good dictionary, like our classroom copies of the *Random House Webster's College Dictionary*, gives spellings, syllabications, parts of speech, inflections, and definitions of words, but also, inside square brackets, each word's etymology. I make a class set of photocopies of the dictionary Abbreviation Key: the page from the preface that explains the symbols and abbreviations that appear in the etymologies. And on an overhead I show how I used a dictionary entry to trace the etymology of the word *etymology*, from ancient Greek to Middle English to Modern English.

For homework, each student chooses one word from his or her personal spelling list and consults a good home dictionary or one of the classroom college dictionaries to trace its etymology. I warn them not to choose compound words (*typewriter*) or derivatives (*recommendation* vs. *recommend*), because they won't find complete etymologies for these words.

Then, each day over the next week at the start of class, a handful of students copies the etymological backgrounds of their words onto the easel pad or overhead transparencies. The fruits of their research are fascinating and confirm much of what kids have learned about the history and development of English.]

59

212

Troubleshooting: Spelling Essentials

60 **Weekly Word Studies**

61 **Personal Survival Words**

62 **Proofreading for Spelling**

63 **The Truth about *I* before *E***

64 **Some Foreign Words Used in English Texts**

65 **Root Words and Prefixes**

66 **Suffixes: To Double or Not?**

67 **Other Suffix Rules That Mostly Work**

What I Was Thinking Spelling matters to me, and my students know it. First and foremost, correct spelling matters because it makes writing easier to read. English texts are difficult to process, so readers need all the help they can get.

Spelling also matters because misspellings can connote arrogance or, worse, ignorance. Errors create the impression that a writer either doesn't care or doesn't know better.

And spelling matters because written language represents a compact between writers and readers. Readers come to the transaction with certain expectations, and it's a writer's responsibility to try to fulfill them, so a reader's eye and mind will find what they need, and so sense can be made.

Learning how to spell takes a long time, even for good spellers. Spelling instruction at CTL begins in kindergarten and continues twice a week for the next eight years. Teachers also address spelling during writing workshop, as we provide individual instruction during editing conferences, and as we ask kids to spell as well as they can in drafts, add words they realize they don't know how to spell to their personal spelling lists, proofread to identify words they might have misspelled, look up unfamiliar spellings, correct misspellings, and add unknown words to their personal lists.

I devote most classroom spelling time to words that individual kids can't spell yet. I no longer assign the whole class to memorize high-frequency words, content area vocabulary, or grade level lists. After almost thirty years of working on and worrying about approaches to spelling, I'm convinced it's a waste of time to teach from prepared lists or tell kids to study and memorize group words. My students who are challenged as spellers *can't* learn fifteen new words a week, and those same fifteen words won't be relevant to an accurate speller. Individual spellers need to focus on the individual words they don't know how to spell yet.

Each of my kids studies just five words a week: few enough that those who study them using our procedure will learn and retain them. To quote Sandra Wilde, "It's better to spend ten minutes a week working on three words you'll remember than larger chunks of time on fifteen you'll forget." My students and I take each speller's five words directly from his or her writing.

Kids carry their spelling folders with them everywhere, every day, and copy unknown words onto their personal spelling lists as they come up. These include words I find misspelled in drafts as I edit them, along with misspellings that the math-science teacher spots in our kids' writing. Some words come from students' reading journals: each week I record the misspelled words I notice on Post-it Notes and give them to spellers when I return their journals. Also, as students are drafting, they're supposed to—and often do—note words they're unsure of on their personal lists. And I teach them not to spellcheck on the computer until the very end of a piece of writing, as part of the formal editing process, and then to record on their personal lists only true misspellings, as opposed to typographical errors.

Finally, I encourage students who are already accurate spellers to work with place names, science and math terms, foreign words, and tricky words from lists of frequently misspelled words. Identifying five appropriate, unknown words to learn each week is each student's responsibility regardless of his or her level of skill as a speller.

Individual spelling study work takes about ten minutes of class time each week. On Tuesdays at the start of class I walk the inside of the circle and quickly check each student's word study sheet, to make certain every speller listed five words and spelled them correctly. Students complete the study procedure for homework. On Thursdays at the start of writing workshop I check the completed word study sheets. Then I send students off to test each other in pairs. Materials for individual spelling study include folders with personal spelling lists attached inside, tons of blank weekly word study sheets, "Procedure for Independent Word Study" for home practice, and "Procedure for Partner Tests" for reviews with peers.

I adapted my word study procedure from the work of Rebecca Sitton (*Spelling Sourcebook*, 1996), although I don't use or recommend her word lists. The deliberateness of the procedure allows my students to enter into, live with, and come to know troublesome words, and it creates a strong visual sense in long-term memory of what a word looks like. It works better than anything I've done over three decades to help kids improve as spellers.

At the same time, I recognize that even with an individualized spelling program, some kids will have more difficulty than others in remembering correct spellings. So *proofreading* has become another focus of my spelling program: mini-lessons about how to identify potential misspellings in a piece of writing and what to do about them.

In other spelling mini-lessons during writing workshop, the group and I focus on spelling patterns, demons, mispronunciation confusions, personal survival words, helpful spelling resources, historical bases for English spelling, and the spelling rules that work often enough to be worth teaching.

I've included here the handful of lessons that students identified most often as the ones that helped them think about and take control of their spelling. As might be expected, they were among the most practical of the lessons I presented. As Jacob said after a series of discussions about suffixes and when to double final consonants, "It works. It actually works. And I even get why."

Weekly Word Studies

SEPTEMBER:
MONDAY,
TUESDAY,
THURSDAY
OF ONE WEEK

Preparation

✔ A spelling folder with grommets and pockets for each student, all in one color

✔ A personal list of five words that cause you grief as a speller

✔ Overhead transparencies of "Weekly Word Study" and "Procedure for Independent Word Study"

✔ Photocopies of "My Personal Spelling List" (hole-punched), "Procedure for Independent Word Study," and "Procedure for Partner Tests"; plus hundreds of photocopies of "Weekly Word Study"

✔ Memoir or short story to read aloud during the five pauses in Tuesday's part of the lesson

✔ Scrap paper for partner tests

✔ Fine-point overhead marker

"Over the years I tried to teach spelling so many different ways I've lost count. But since I found this approach, I've stuck with it because it *works*. The way I'm going to teach spelling to you, and you're going to learn it, will change you as a speller.

And that's because the basis of the program is you. We're not going to work from lists of somebody's idea of the words seventh and eighth graders should be able to spell. Instead, your word list will be *your word list*: the words you don't know how to spell yet, your old bad habits, your confusions, your uncertainties as a speller. Each week, five words at a time, you're going to focus like a laser on your words and learn them, I hope forever.

You'll keep the materials for your spelling program in a separate folder and carry it with you everywhere—to my classes every day and to math and science, too—as your mind becomes a magnet, in search of words you need to know how to spell.

So let's dispense with the materials. Each of you is going to receive a spelling folder and four documents: your personal spelling list, which I've three-hole-punched for you, the procedure for studying spelling words that we'll use this year, the procedure you'll use for testing each other on spelling words, and a copy of the weekly word study sheet. Please attach the personal spelling list inside the grommets of your new spelling folder. . . .

Let's begin with the "Procedure for Independent Word Study." I'll ask you to follow along carefully as I read this aloud to you, but I'm also going to demonstrate the procedure to you on the overhead with words from my own personal spelling list. Tomorrow you'll go through the procedure as a whole group again, but each of you will use your own words.

60

I'm going to be a dragon about your following this study procedure to the letter, because its effectiveness depends on your spending time—about twenty minutes each week on just five words—and on your tapping many kinds of memory: short-term, long-term, visual, auditory, and muscle. Please follow along with me as I read through the nine steps of the study procedure. . . .

Now, watch me try—and coach me through—the study process. On the overhead, I'll begin by listing in the far left column five words that confuse me as a speller and that I want to nail once and for all: *broccoli*, *vacuum*, *absence*, *presence*, and *believable*. I'll start with *broccoli*. Read to me from "Procedure for Independent Word Study" and tell me what to do next. . . .

[Students refer to the steps on the "Procedure for Independent Word Study" sheet to talk me through the process with the word *broccoli*. At step #5 I pause to let my long-term memory digest the correct spelling by

Reproducibles and Overheads
Procedure for Independent Word Study and Weekly Word Study

reading aloud a children's book or playing a track from a CD. Then I demonstrate with one more word from my own list and ask for questions and observations.

I end the lesson by assigning kids to come to class the next day with five spelling demons of their own. I instruct them to first record the five words on the personal spelling lists in their new spelling folders, then to copy the same five words into the first column of a weekly word study sheet.]

FOLLOW-UP ON TUESDAY

[I walk the inside of the circle at the start of the class on Tuesday to make sure everyone has done the homework and spelled five words correctly on the "Weekly Word Study" sheet. Then I talk everyone, all together, through the twenty-minute independent word study process with all five of their words. Each time we reach step #5, I make the whole group break by reading aloud to them chunks of a short story or memoir; afterward each tries to spell from memory the word he or she just studied.

Then we talk again: "What did you notice? What helped? Did this work for you? How do you think you'll do on a test on these words on Thursday? On a test on these words in a month?"]

FOLLOW-UP ON THURSDAY

[I walk the inside of the circle at the start of class on Thursday morning to check for correct spellings in the "Spell" or "Spell Again" column of each student's "Weekly Word Study" sheet. If a student has accepted a misspelling as correct, I pitch a minor fit—there's no way he or she could have proofread by checking letter for letter against the original spelling in the first column—and I cross the word off the sheet. It can't be tested for today; the student needs to study it again next week.

Then I distribute scrap paper, ask each kid to sit with a partner, and talk them through each step on the "Procedure for Partner Tests" sheet as a whole group.

I don't grade or collect the weekly partner tests. Instead, in a discussion after the tests, I ask the group: "Who got all five words? Who didn't? What word did you miss? Why do you think you missed it? What *part* of the word is still confusing you? Can we help you think of a

---

PROCEDURE FOR PARTNER TESTS

Tester: Say the word, use it in a sentence, and say it again.

Speller: Print the word.

Do the whole list. Then:

Tester: Spell each word out loud *slowly*, so the speller may proofread.

Speller: Proofread by touching each letter of each word with your pencil. Circle any errors: *just the part you missed*. Then, on your personal spelling list, circle any word you missed: you'll need to study it again next week. With a star or checkmark, highlight the words on your personal spelling list that you spelled correctly on the test.

Adapted from *Spelling Sourcebook I*, by Rebecca Sitton

© 2002 by Nancie Atwell from
Lessons That Change Writers
(Portsmouth, NH: Heinemann)   PROCEDURE FOR PARTNER TESTS   LESSON 60

Reproducible
Procedure for Partner Tests

mnemonic for the next time you study this word?" Then students recycle the scrap paper tests, and next week they're on their own as they study a new group of five words for homework and test each other.

Each Thursday I circulate while students give and take the partner tests, and I intervene as necessary: the tendency is for testers to rush when providing the correct spellings and not allow spellers enough time to touch each letter as they proofread.]

MONTHLY FOLLOW-UP REVIEWS THROUGHOUT THE YEAR

[About one Tuesday a month, after I check for correct spellings in the first columns of kids' "Weekly Word Study" sheets, I orchestrate a surprise review test: I want students to celebrate the spellings they've retained and identify those that still need more work.

So I instruct the group: "Please trade spelling folders with a partner. Now, independent of the speller—no helpful consulting here—please put a dot next to ten random words that your partner has highlighted on the personal spelling list as words that he or she mastered during weekly word studies. If a word is part of a homonym pair—say, *weather* and *whether*—dot both homonyms. . . . Next, number a sheet of paper one to ten. . . . Now, take turns testing your partner on his or her ten words by saying each word, using it in a sentence, and saying it again. But *do not correct* these tests. This time, as your spelling teacher, that's my job."

I check the review tests by printing the correct spelling of any error and circling or underlining the *part* of the word that's causing the student confusion. In the next day's lesson I return the tests and ask students to reflect in writing on how they did and what they need to do next as spellers: Do they need to continue using the process just as they have been, because they got 100 percent? Spend more time each week on the study? Focus on the *part* of the word that they're misspelling? Develop a mnemonic to remember a tricky spelling? Choose more realistic words to study? Students write these reflections on the test paper, then file the tests in a pocket of their spelling folders.]

60

Personal Survival Words

Preparation

✔ Overhead transparency of "Spelling: My Personal Survival List," which you have filled in with your personal information, correctly spelled

✔ Photocopies of "Spelling: My Personal Survival List"

61 LESSON

OCTOBER

"I don't think the governor of our state is unique among politicians in the weight he gives to accurate spelling. He seems constantly to be crying about how Maine students can't spell, and how, therefore, the state education system is broken and needs to be fixed by bureaucrats, starting with the governor. The proof he gives is anecdotal, and it's a version of the same anecdote I hear on the news and read in the papers, related by politicians at every level. It goes like this: a businessperson approaches the politician and complains about how inadequate the local/state/national educational system is because a potential teenage employee has misspelled some basic, obvious word on his or her job application.

Now, I don't know a teacher who doesn't want students to be good spellers—who doesn't work hard at it, provide lessons, and give and correct tests. But I also know there's a particular category of words we don't teach enough, maybe because we think these words are parents' responsibility, or maybe because we assume kids will pick them up along the way.

I'm not willing to leave the spelling of this category of words to chance. When you apply for a work permit or job—or to a summer camp, for a scholarship, or to a high school—I don't want there to be any chance that the adult who reads a form you've completed will underestimate how smart and capable you are because a spelling error got in the way. So we're going to focus this week on personal survival words: the set of specific words that comprise the data of your life.

Check out the overhead. This is my personal survival information. These are just some of the words I've had to learn how to spell about me, my history, my health, my family and acquaintances, and my community.

For example, a credit card company will ask for my mother's maiden name—her last name before she married my dad—when I apply for an account. The IRS wants to know what county I live in. My father's middle name is part of my marriage license. My passport lists the city where I was born. Every doctor I see begins any office visit by asking me to list the drugs I'm allergic to. When I check into a hotel, they want to know the make and model of the car I'm driving. When I take my dog to a vet clinic, they want to know her breed.

So I've learned the words I need to survive in the world. Being able to spell them makes me feel confident and helps convince the professional world that I'm competent. I want you to have the same opportunity to take charge of your life. So our first official spelling study will be your research into your personal data: what the data *is* and how to spell it.

Right now, take your own copy of the form "My Personal Survival List." Today I'll ask you to fill in the information you know and the words you know how to spell. Then tonight, for homework, you're to sit down with your parents and get the data and spellings you don't know. In two days I'll collect these. I'll correct them as necessary. Then I'll ask you to choose and study, five at a time, the spellings of the words you don't know yet. A few weeks down the road I'll test you on your personal survival words; the test will consist of a blank copy of this form. And a few weeks after that I'll give you the same test again. It's that important that the data of your life becomes part of your repertoire as a speller.

Questions? Comments? Observations?

Okay. Let's begin by looking together at some of the words we have in common and spelling them together. Then I'll give you a chance to fill in the individual data you already know. For example, what county do you live in? . . .

61

SPELLING: MY PERSONAL SURVIVAL LIST

My first, middle, and last names:

My mother's maiden name:

My mother's first, middle, and last names:

My father's first, middle, and last names:

My grandparents' first and last names:

My siblings' first, middle, and last names:

My street address:

My town and county:

My teachers' first and last names:

My school:

My place of birth:

The hospital of my birth:

My allergies, if any:

My physician's name:

Family cars (manufacturer and make):

© 2002 by Nancie Atwell from
Lessons That Change Writers
(Portsmouth, NH: Heinemann)

SPELLING: MY PERSONAL SURVIVAL LIST – PAGE 1   LESSON 61

Reproducible and Overhead
Spelling: My Personal Survival List

FOLLOW-UP LESSON

[Two days later, I collect the lists and check the spellings as best I can. Sometimes I have to telephone parents to verify correct spellings. Then I give the corrected lists back to kids, ask them to choose five words they aren't 100 percent sure of as the focus of the next weekly word study, and practice and learn the correct spellings.

Once everyone has studied the questionable spellings from the personal survival lists during weekly work studies, I give the review test—a blank copy of the form for them to complete—then correct these and begin the process again. I schedule one more pop-quiz-type review of the list in the winter, so I'm confident—so the kids are confident—that they know their essential words.]

61

Proofreading for Spelling

Preparation

✔ Trimmed photocopies of "Techniques for Proofreading Spelling" for students to tape into their handbooks

✔ Tape dispensers

LESSON 62

OCTOBER

"No one can spell every word, and every writer makes spelling errors.

TECHNIQUES FOR PROOFREADING SPELLING

■ Circle *each* and *every* word you're not absolutely, 100 percent certain of. Once you've proofed the whole piece, then go back and look up the spellings of the circled words. In other words, maintain your focus as a proofreader until you've finished the actual proofreading; the dictionary or spellchecker should only come into play once you've identified *every* potential misspelling.

■ As you proofread, scan each line of text backward, from right to left. Don't allow your eyes to chunk text and attend to meaning. Instead, focus on one word at a time.

■ Slow down on common homonyms (*your* and *you're*; *to*, *too*, and *two*; *its* and *it's*; *their*, *there*, and *they're*) and other homonym-type confusions (*college* and *collage*, *effect* and *affect*, *chose* and *choose*, *lead* and *led*, *than* and *then*, etc.). Check the word in question against what you know, or use a source.

■ Slow down on demons, your own and the usual suspects. You know which words you've confused in the past or continue to struggle with. Give them particular attention: *necessary, recommend, separate, a lot, all right, definitely, judgment, truly, restaurant, eighth, twelfth,* etc.

■ Slow down on words with tricky prefixes and suffixes:

■ words in which the doubling of letters becomes an issue, like *unnecessary, disappoint, disappear, granddaughter, occurred, writing, written, traveled, beginning,* and *finally*

■ words in which the dropping of letters becomes an issue, like *absolutely, ninety, forty, lonely,* and *believable*

■ Slow down on plural nouns. Ask yourself: Is that word with an *s* at the end of it a possessive noun, requiring an *apostrophe-s* (for example, "I borrowed my brother's CD")?

■ Use the available sources to help you check for correct spellings. These include a college dictionary, a Spellex speller, a good speller in the class, a master list of frequently misspelled words, the computer spellchecker, your personal spelling list, and, later on, your writing handbook, especially the lessons "Homonyms," "The Truth about *I* before *E*," "A Rule That Mostly Works: Prefixes," and "Suffix Rules That Mostly Work."

■ After you've finished proofreading and editing for spelling, ask a good speller to recheck your text for misspellings if it's handwritten, or use the computer spellchecker if the piece is word-processed.

© 2002 by Nancie Atwell from
Lessons That Change Writers
(Portsmouth, NH: Heinemann)

TECHNIQUES FOR PROOFREADING SPELLING   LESSON 62

Reproducible Techniques for Proofreading Spelling

What separates writers who create texts that contain misspellings from those who produce accurate, readable writing is the activity called *proofreading*.

In the context of spelling, I'm going to define proofreading as a writer's ability *and willingness* to slow down the process of reading over one's own writing, focus at the single-word level, and ask of each word, "Am I absolutely certain that this is the correct spelling?"

Proofreading for correct spelling is hard work. It's time-consuming and boring. But proofreading is necessary and worthwhile, because conventional texts invite readers and keep their attention.

Proofreading spelling is part of the editing process. I'd like you to view it and do it as a separate stage during editing. Either before you focus on the other conventions you've listed on the editing checksheet, or after, concentrate specifically on spelling, on making sure that each word is the right one and is spelled correctly.

Proofreading for spelling is 99 percent a visual act. It depends on your eyes telling you something's wrong—or that something *could be* wrong. So if your eyes aren't 100 percent comfortable and certain, that's a word you need to circle and look up.

Please take a copy of "Techniques for Proofreading Spelling" and tape it to the next clean page of your writing handbook. . . .

Now, follow along with me. This is the process I'll ask you to use all year in writing workshop and that I hope you'll use forever after, too . . . .

Questions? Comments? Observations about proofreading for spelling?

62

The Truth about I before E

Preparation

✔ Trimmed photocopies of "The Truth about *I* before *E*" for students to tape into their handbooks

✔ Tape dispensers

LESSON **63**

"How many of you memorized the spelling rhyme for remembering to put "*i* before *e* except after *c*"? How many of you felt betrayed by the *e* before *i* in words like *heir*, *neither*, *their*, and *weird*, where there's not a *c* in sight and nothing "sounds like an *a* as in *neighbor* and *weigh*"?

The truth about *i* before *e* is that it's less a hard-and-fast spelling rule than a generalization. I want you to learn the general principle—that in English spelling, we usually write *ie*, but after a *c* that sounds like an *s*, it'll be *ei*, not *ie*. So please tape a copy of "The Truth about *I* before *E*" to the next clean page of your writing handbook....

Please follow along with me as I read the generalization: In general, write *i* before *e*, except after a soft *c* that sounds like an *s*. Examples of *ei* after a soft *c* include . . .

Then there are the exceptions, some words that put *e* before *i* without a *c* in sight. I've listed as many as I could think of, find, or remember correcting when I edited your drafts. Read through these with me, please....

You may want to choose appropriate words from these two lists—the *ei* after *c* words, and the *ei* without a *c* words—to be among the five you'll study in a given week. But I expect that everyone will refer to this list when you're not certain if a word is spelled *ie* or *ei*. I've given you a specific, handy reference. Please use it.

Questions? Observations?

Reproducible
The Truth about *I* before *E*

Some Foreign Words Used in English Texts

Preparation

✔ Trimmed photocopies of "Some Foreign Words Used in English Texts" for students to tape into their handbooks

✔ Tape dispensers

64 LESSON

MARCH

SOME FOREIGN WORDS USED IN ENGLISH TEXTS

1. etc. (Latin: and others; and so forth; and the rest: *et cetera*)

2. i.e. (Latin: that is: *id est*)

3. e.g. (Latin: for example; such as: *exempli gratia*)

4. vice versa (Latin: in reverse)

5. via (Latin: by means of)

6. ad infinitum (Latin: to infinity; endlessly; forever)

7. ad nauseam (Latin: to nausea; to a sickening extreme)

8. cliché (French: an expression used so often that it's trite—no longer fresh)

9. naïve (French: unsophisticated; showing natural simplicity)

10. résumé (French: literally, summing up)

11. déjà vu (French: already seen)

SOME FOREIGN WORDS USED IN ENGLISH TEXTS   LESSON 64

"Having just edited the misspelling of the abbreviation for *et cetera* for what seems like the twentieth time in a week—it's *etc.*, folks, not *ect.*—I planned to teach you the correct spelling today. Then I got on a roll and came up with some other foreign terms that English spellers often need, Latin and French words and abbreviations that show up a lot in English writing. So please tape this list of "Some Foreign Words Used in English Texts" to the next clean page of your writing handbook, then follow along with me as I talk you through it. . . .

What are your observations about individual words, terms, or abbreviations? What didn't you get before that you get now? What are your questions for me? Are there any words here that you need to add to your personal spelling list? Please do so.

Reproducible
Some Foreign Words Used in English Texts

Root Words and Prefixes

Preparation

✔ Overhead transparencies of "Some Definitions" and "A Rule That Mostly Works: Prefixes"

✔ Fine-point overhead markers in colors

"Something I've noticed, as I've looked for patterns in your spelling errors, is how you often mess up around prefixes and suffixes—how it's easy to be confused about whether letters should be doubled when you stick on a prefix at the beginning of a word or add a suffix to the end.

I've decided to approach this error pattern as a course of study. Over the next two or three weeks, I hope to give you the essential information of the big picture. I'll begin with some basic definitions. Please copy "Some Definitions"—the information on the overhead—into your writing handbook, as I talk you through it. . . .

Now, take a look at the next overhead: "A Rule That Mostly Works: Prefixes." You'll be happy to know that as far as I can discover, there's only one significant prefix rule. Please copy it into your handbook. . . .

So, for example, how do I add the prefix *dis-* to the root word *appear* to create *disappear*? Can I ask for a volunteer to come up to the overhead and attack the first word on the list of examples? . . . That's correct: there's just one *s* in *disappear*, as the prefix *dis-* is added to the root *appear*.

What about *disappoint*? Who'll volunteer to come up to the overhead and convert *appoint*? . . .

[And so on. The words I ask kids to create by adding specific prefixes are listed below; I chose these for the lesson because they're so often misspelled in student writing. At the end of the lesson, I ask kids to copy onto their personal spelling lists any words on the overhead transparency that they aren't 100 percent certain of, to work on in weekly word studies.]

disappear	reenlist
disappoint	semicolon
unnecessary	deactivate
reapply	disgust
preschool	illegal
granddaughter	illiterate
recommend	irregular
immortal	redo
rearrange	subcontract
antiestablishment	transcribe
inactive	unable
demoralize	

65

SOME DEFIN

Root word: the
fore or aft

Prefix: a meani

Suffix: a meani

A RULE THAT MOSTLY WORKS: PREFIXES

To add a prefix to a root word, just attach it: don't drop or double any letters.

EX:

appear	enlist
appoint	colon
necessary	activate
apply	gust
school	legal
daughter	literate
commend	regular
mortal	do
arrange	contract
establishment	scribe
active	able
moralize	

© 2002 by Nancie Atwell from
Lessons That Change Writers
(Portsmouth, NH: Heinemann)

© 2002 by Nancie Atwell from
Lessons That Change Writers
(Portsmouth, NH: Heinemann)

A RULE THAT MOSTLY WORKS: PREFIXES   LESSON 65

Overheads
Some Definitions and A Rule That
Mostly Works: Prefixes

Suffixes: To Double or Not?

Preparation

✔ Overhead transparencies of "What's the Pattern?," "Suffix Rules That Mostly Work, Part One," and "Adding Suffixes to Words That End Single Vowel-Consonant"

✔ Photocopies of "Adding Suffixes to Words That End Single Vowel-Consonant"

✔ Fine-point overhead markers in colors

LESSON 66

MAY

"Adding suffixes is a lot more complicated than adding prefixes, when it comes to correct spelling. The basic reason is this: letters added at the ends of words often change the sounds of vowels in the words, from long to short or from short to long.

What is a long vowel sound or a short one? Let's do a little vowel review. Take a look at the overhead and the list of eight word pairs that I headed with the question "What's the Pattern?" Please copy the question and the sixteen words below it onto the next clean page of your writing handbook. . . .

Now, would you please get together with two or three others for a few minutes and puzzle out some generalizations? In your small group, try to formulate rules that tell why this word is pronounced *hop* with a short *o* and this word is *hope* with a long *o*; why we know to pronounce *fed* with a short *e* sound and *feed* with a long *e*; why we say *got* here, but say *goat* when we add that *a*. Please draft a version of the generalizations your group comes up with right in your handbooks, below the list of word pairs. . . .

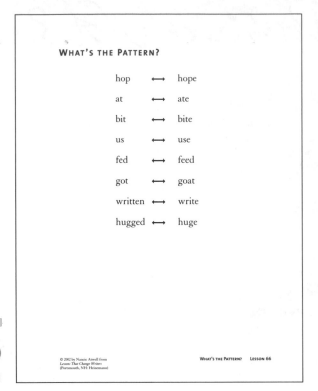

Overhead
What's the Pattern?

66

[I circulate among the small groups and coach and prompt them. Then I bring everyone back to the circle, talk about what the small groups discovered, and record a whole-group generalization along the lines of, "Silent *e*'s at the ends of words and double vowels within words create long vowel sounds. Double consonants make short vowel sounds."

I tell kids: "Keep this principle in mind this week as we look at suffixes and try to decide whether or not to double final letters of root words when we add suffixes. Often it will depend on how the pronunciation of a vowel sound will be altered. For example, *drŏp* becomes *drōped* if you don't double the *p* when you add the suffix *-ed*. You'll see what I mean tomorrow."]

FOLLOW-UP LESSON

[On the following days students and I work through the two generalizations described in "Suffix Rules That Mostly Work, Part One." I ask them to copy the generalizations about words that end single vowel-consonant into their writing handbooks, along with the examples of base words I listed with each rule. Then volunteers come up to the overhead projector and try to use the suffix generalizations to spell the new words I ask for, which I've listed in Figure 66-1.

At the end of the second lesson I pass out copies of "Adding Suffixes to Words That End Single Vowel-Consonant" and assign it as a homework exercise. We review and correct it together the next day in class on an overhead transparency.

And the following day I give everyone a test of the words listed in "To Double or Not to Double." [See Figure 66-2.] These I collect, correct, and comment on in terms of how individuals did or didn't apply the generalizations. Students who misspell words add them to their personal spelling lists, to take on as weekly study words.]

SUFFIX RULES THAT MOSTLY WORK, PART ONE

Suffix Rule #1. On one-syllable words that end with a single vowel and a consonant: double the final consonant before adding a suffix that starts with a vowel.

Some suffixes that start with vowels:

-al   -ing   -ed   -able   -ible   -er   -en   -ee   -est

Base Word

hug	→	hugged
sad	→	saddest
swim	→	swimming
skip	→	skipping

Suffix Rule #2. On words of more than one syllable that end with a single vowel and a consonant and are accented on the last syllable, double the final consonant before adding a suffix that starts with a vowel.

Base Word			**Base Word**		
refér	→	referred	góssip	→	gossiper
occúr	→	ocurred	forbíd	→	forbidden
omít	→	omitted	confér	→	conferred
contról	→	controlling	trável	→	traveled
regrét	→	regrettable	permít	→	permitting
depósit	→	deposited	fínal	→	finalist

EXCEPTION: transferred

Figure 66-1 Suffix Rules That Mostly Work, Part One

TO DOUBLE OR NOT TO DOUBLE? (A REVIEW TEST)

1. hoping	11. forbidden	21. pitted
2. conferred	12. shopping	22. picnicked
3. dotted	13. trapped	23. reformed
4. grinned	14. traveling	24. stopped
5. preferred	15. starred	25. finalist
6. beginning	16. forgetting	26. galloped
7. grabbed	17. hopping	27. transferred
8. blurred	18. happening	28. banqueted
9. medalist	19. wrapped	29. popped
10. occurred	20. blanketed	30. clipping

Figure 66-2 To Double or Not to Double? (A Review Test)

Other Suffix Rules That Mostly Work

Preparation

✔ Overhead transparency of "Suffix Rules That Mostly Work, Part Two"

✔ Fine-point overhead markers in colors

[I don't teach these lessons consecutively—it's too much information about spelling for kids to take in and keep straight—but I do conduct them within a period of two or three weeks, so my students can maintain a frame of reference for talking about and working with suffixes. In each case the structure of the lesson is the same: I teach the generalization and its notable exceptions, students copy these into their handbooks from an overhead transparency, and then I ask individuals to come up to the overhead projector or easel pad and apply the rule in the creation of new variations on the base words. Figure 67-1 shows the words I ask kids to create by adding suffixes to base words during these lessons.

I don't give review tests on the lessons, as I did with the first two suffix rules, because these are more straightforward: the complexities of syllable counting and of hearing stressed syllables don't enter into the other suffix generalizations.]

SUFFIX RULES THAT MOSTLY WORK, PART TWO

Suffix Rule #3. Adjectives that end in *l* add *-ly*:

Base Word			Base Word		
cool	→	coolly	personal	→	personally
casual	→	casually	final	→	finally
accidental	→	accidentally	usual	→	usually
occasional	→	occasionally	brutal	→	brutally

Suffix Rule #4. Words ending in *n* add *-ness*.

Base Word		
plain	→	plainness
sudden	→	suddenness
mean	→	meanness

Suffix Rule #5. Words that end in silent *e* usually drop the *e* before suffixes that start with vowels:

Base Word			Base Word		
have	→	having	arrive	→	arrival
argue	→	arguing	change	→	changing
come	→	coming	mistake	→	mistaken
force	→	forcible	guide	→	guidance
write	→	writing	combine	→	combination
manage	→	managing	fame	→	famous
love	→	lovable	believe	→	believable

EXCEPTION: words that end in soft *ce* or *ge* keep the *e* before *-able* and *-ous*: changeable, pronounceable, courageous, outrageous, noticeable, manageable, peaceable, etc.
EXCEPTION #2: Keep the final *e* in *dyeing*, *eyeing*, and *singeing*.

Suffix Rule #6. Words that end in silent *e* usually keep the *e* before suffixes that start with consonants:

Base Word			Base Word		
late	→	lately	grate	→	grateful
encourage	→	encouragement	extreme	→	extremely
lone	→	lonely	definite	→	definitely
grave	→	gravely	pave	→	pavement
nine	→	ninety	absolute	→	absolutely
use	→	useful	hope	→	hopeful

EXCEPTION: acknowledgement, argument, awful, duly, judgment, truly.

Suffix Rule #7. Verbs that end in *ie* change to *y* before adding *-ing*:

Base Word			Base Word		
die	→	dying	tie	→	tying
lie	→	lying	vie	→	vying

Figure 67-1 Suffix Rules That Mostly Work, Part Two

A Brief History of Some Common Punctuation Marks

Preparation

✔ Overhead transparency and trimmed photocopies of "Fascinating and True Facts about Punctuation"

✔ Overhead transparency of "Two Kinds of Punctuation"

✔ Tape dispensers

What I Was Thinking To kick off a refresher course on punctuation with middle school writers, I sought an entry point that did more than regurgitate rules they'd been hearing forever. So I researched punctuation and found the roots of five frequently used marks. I wanted students to perceive punctuation as a device that's useful to writers, not an arcane system for torturing schoolkids, and to understand that the punctuation they use today is the result of a process of evolution— that it was writers who invented and changed the marks.

"Where did punctuation begin? Tell me your theories. . . .

I spent most of Saturday researching this very question, and I'm here to tell you that thus far my best answer is *Aristophanes of Byzantium*.

Now, there's another, better known, ancient Greek named Aristophanes. The famous Aristophanes lived a couple of hundred years before our guy, and he wrote plays. Most scholars agree he was the greatest ancient writer of satire, or comedy.

234

Our Aristophanes was an ancient Greek scholar. He was the librarian at Alexandria and, supposedly, the inventor of the Greek diacritical marks, which are the ancestors of our punctuation.

I was excited to be able to trace the roots of some of the marks we use today back to ancient Greece and Rome. You'll have to excuse the high emotion, but I *am* an English teacher, and I love this stuff. Tape a copy of "Fascinating and True Facts about Punctuation" onto the next clean page of your writing handbook. And please don't color in the letters or pictures until after the lesson. I want your attention as I talk you through this. . . .

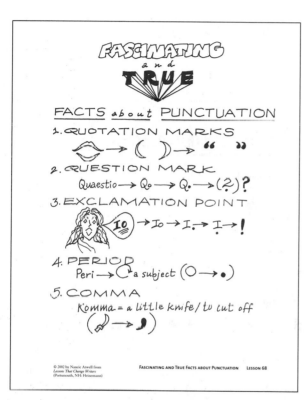

Reproducible and Overhead
Fascinating and True
Facts about Punctuation

Ready? Take a look at number one: quotation marks. Did you know they began in ancient texts as lips, but turned on their sides? Early writers wanted a way to show when the words they were writing had been spoken by someone else, so they used two curved marks, which represented the lips of a speaker. One lip was put at the beginning, as a signal to the reader: *These words aren't mine; I'm telling you what someone else said.* Then the writer inserted a second lip at the end of the quote as a way to indicate *Now I've finished telling you the other person's words.* Over time the big lips evolved into the tiny set of double lips we use today—although in British texts you'll see sets of single marks around quotes: even more liplike, I think.

What about the question mark? It started out in ancient Roman texts as the Latin word *quaestio,* which means "question." Writers inserted the word *quaestio* when they asked a question in their texts. Over time *quaestio* was shortened to *Qo,* then *Q.* Then, to save on parchment I guess, writers relocated the period to underneath the *Q.* Well, the Roman letter for *Q* looks like our Arabic numeral *2.* So the word *quaestio* evolved into the question mark we use today.

I love the history of the exclamation point. *Io* was an ancient Greek word expressing excitement—an early equivalent of our *wow.* Greek writers inserted the word *io* into their texts at points where they were excited. Over time, scholars changed the *o* to a dot. And over more time, the dot came to rest under the *I.* The result was our exclamation point: ! *Io!*

The word *period* comes from the ancient Greek word *peri,* which means "round." Writers inserted a small circle at the end of each sentence to show that they'd gone all around a subject, that the idea they expressed was now complete and well rounded. Again, writers eventually tired of drawing a circle, or maybe they wanted to save on parchment, so the *o* became the dot we use today.

Finally, the word *comma* comes from the Greek word *komma*, which means "a little knife" or "to cut off." Writers inserted the little curved blade of a knife—that is, a comma—whenever they wanted to show a clause or phrase: a group of words cut from the body of a sentence.

Can you understand why I was psyched by my discoveries? I love it that the marks were so concrete from the start, so practical. And I think it's fascinating how they evolved. My research got me thinking.

If ancient writers and scholars invented marks to show their readers how to read texts, isn't it time for some new ones? Your homework

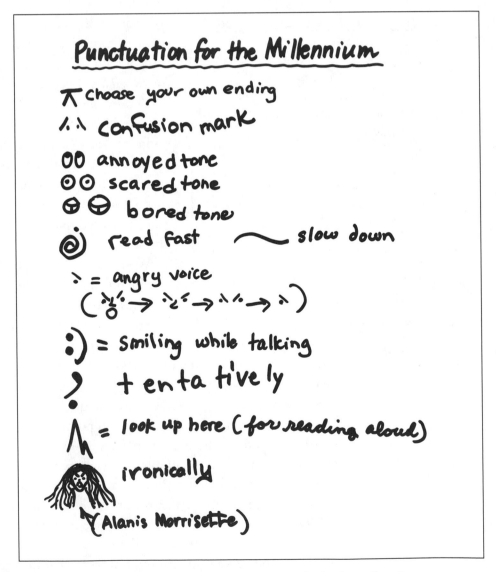

Figure 68–1 A Page of Nancie's Class's Punctuation Marks for the Millennium

tonight is to invent one or two Punctuation Marks for the Millennium. [See Figure 68–1 for some of the marks created by my students.] We ought to be able to signal more to our readers beyond *drop your voice— here's a period*, or *this is a question: raise your inflection*, or *gee, I'm excited*. The mood, inflection, purpose, and appearance of the new mark is up to you. The point is to invent a mark that could be inserted into texts to indicate something brand new about what a writer wants readers to do or understand.

And yes, these can be funny.

We'll gather the new marks on transparencies, starting tomorrow.

FOLLOW-UP

[Over the next several days, I ask a handful of students at the start of class to come up to the overhead projector, draw their invented punctuation marks on a transparency, and explain to the class what they indicate. After each student has had a turn, I photocopy the transparencies, so everyone has a set of their classmates' creations.]

ADDITIONAL FOLLOW-UP

[To help my students understand more about the history and function of punctuation marks, I review with them "Two Kinds of Punctuation," which shows the differences between tone marks, essential back when most writing was read aloud, and refinements, which evolved when readers began to read silently.]

TWO KINDS OF PUNCTUATION

Definition: Punctuation is a device for writers that supplements letters.

1. Tone Marks
These came first, were developed for writing to be read aloud, and show tone of voice, stresses, and pauses.

Declaration (. , ;)	Parenthesis ( )
Interrogation (?)	Elaboration (:)
Exclamation (!)	Borrowing or Quoting (" ")

2. Refinements
These came later and were developed for writing to be read silently.

Brackets ([ ])	Indentation of paragraphs
Capital letters	Ellipsis (...)
Paragraphs	Dash (—)

Food for Thought
The apostrophe (') and hyphen (-) are practically extra letters. Are they part of our spelling system, rather than marks of punctuation?

More Food for Thought
Did you know that . . .

- in Greek writing, the semicolon stands for a question mark, and a raised dot (·) is a semicolon?
- in Spanish writing, inverted ! (¡) and ? (¿) appear at the beginning of a sentence, to cue readers about how to inflect?
- in German writing, all nouns are capitalized?

TWO KINDS OF PUNCTUATION   LESSON 68

Overhead
Two Kinds of
Punctuation

Essential Punctuation Information

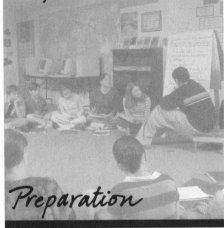

Preparation

✔ Trimmed photocopies of the notes on each of seven punctuation topics for students to tape into their handbooks: "Period Confusions," "Most Common Comma Omissions," "Reasons for a Semicolon," "Colons Signal Readers," "To Dash or to Hyphen," "Apostrophe Headaches," and "Parentheses: Why Not"

✔ Tape dispensers

69 LESSON

MARCH

What I Was Thinking Read any usage handbook and recognize that an English teacher could devote a whole year to lessons about the intricacies of American punctuation. I've narrowed my focus to teach about the punctuation mistakes I find and correct most often when I edit students' writing—their confusions, oversights, misunderstandings, and omissions.

I learned that students will respond to punctuation lessons when the content is relevant—when they need the information to strengthen their writing. So I don't waste time covering old ground—for example, periods at the ends of sentences, question marks after questions, ellipses to show omissions and pauses—and I pull examples of the marks I'm teaching from students' writing, the writing we're reading, and my own drafts.

Principles from these lessons make frequent appearances on individual proofreading lists. The lessons address, in this order: kids' confusions about periods, frequent occasions for omitted commas, reasons to use a semicolon, functions of a colon, differences between a dash and a hyphen, the minutiae of using apostrophes on various kinds of possessive nouns, and why and how to avoid parentheses in nontechnical prose. There are no separate scripts for these lessons, since the reproducibles themselves contain all the relevant information.

In citing this series of lessons as important, student after student wrote comments along the lines of "I finally got what colons and semicolons are good for," or "Now I know the differ-ence between a dash and a hyphen—I just love the dash," or "I've been confused about where a period goes at the end of a quote for as long as I can remember." As their teacher, I took real satisfaction in sweeping away the cobwebs and shedding some light.

Be aware that some of the sentences that exemplify the marks and rules come from my life or my kids'. I hope that wherever the given examples are particular, teachers will invent exam-ples from which to teach their students.

At the end of each lesson, I've found it helpful for kids to create their own examples—phrases or sentences that use the marks—on the bottom of the relevant page in their writing handbooks. Then I ask kids to leave their handbooks turned open to the page in question, col-lect the notebooks, conduct a quick check of their applications of the marks, and write responses and corrections.

69

Troubleshooting: Convention Confusions

70 **How to Correct Comma Splices**

71 **How to Punctuate Dialogue**

72 **Homonyms**

73 **Four Capitalization Confusions**

74 **Writing Numbers**

75 **Indicating Titles**

76 *Me or I?*

What I Was Thinking There are no months indicated for these lessons because I conduct them in response to problems I observe as I edit kids' writing. I keep a few blue 4-by-6-inch file cards in a pocket of my lesson plan binder. At home at night, when I'm editing student drafts and I spot a trouble area, I make a note on a blue card to plan a lesson around the confusion or to retrieve my file folder on that convention and update the information and examples. I'd define a lesson-worthy convention confusion as an error or omission that shows up in three or four kids' pieces in the course of two weeks.

The seven lessons included here were mentioned time and again by students as ones for which they were grateful. Kids want conventionality. They want to feel confident about their writing, and they want to be on the inside when it comes to doing things right. As Meg put it, "I knew there was some system for quoting or underlining titles of books, poems, songs, and things, but I could never get it. Now I do. And when I'm not positive, I just look on that page in my handbook to check. It's one of my most-used pages."

How to Correct Comma Splices

Preparation

✔ Overhead transparency of "Correcting Comma Splices"
✔ Fine-point overhead marker

"Last summer I was cleaning out files at home and came across a folder of papers I'd written in college. It was fun to reread them and try to remember who I was when I wrote them. But it was also discomfiting. I kept finding errors—or, rather, the same error, here, there, and everywhere. Based on what I've learned over the years as an editor of writing, I shouldn't have been surprised. The error I was committing, as a nineteen-year-old, is, for many writers, the last big one to go, the final confusion to be cleared up. Can you guess what it was? . . .

I was connecting my sentences with commas: trying to splice two sentences together by inserting a comma between them. Can someone tell me why this is an error? . . .

As a mark, a comma isn't strong enough to connect two sentences. Remember what we learned about the origins of the word *comma*, how it comes from a Greek word meaning "little knife"? The Greeks wanted to show that a part of a sentence, a phrase or a clause, had been split but not severed from the whole—a comma's not a big knife, but a little one.

A comma *is* strong enough to connect groups of words, like phrases and clauses, to sentences, but it's *not* strong enough to connect two sentences. When a writer attempts to butt two sentences together by inserting a comma between them, the error is called a *comma splice*.

As an editor of your writing, I'm finding comma splices. We'll focus on these today to make you aware of what a comma cannot do and to gear you up to start identifying and correcting the Last Big Convention Error.

Please turn to the next clean page in your writing handbook and record this heading:

Correcting Comma Splices

First, let's define a comma splice. Please copy the definition from the overhead transparency: *A comma splice occurs when a writer attempts to hook two sentences together with a comma.*

Here's an example of a comma splice error for you to record in your handbooks: *The clouds are gathering in the west, it will rain soon.*

Now, there's a test to determine whether a construction is a comma splice, or if it's a legal sentence with a comma in it: can the groups of words on either side of the comma stand alone, as complete and sensible sentences? Read aloud with me the words that precede and follow the comma in the first example on the transparency. . . . Yes, they can stand alone as sentences.

So, how do we correct this comma splice? We have some options. What are they? . . . Please record the alternatives in your handbook as I write them on the transparency.

You could make a new sentence: *The clouds are gathering in the west. It will rain soon.*

You could insert a conjunction after the comma: a word that will cement the two sentences into a compound sentence: *The clouds are gathering in the west, and it will rain soon.* Frankly, this is my least favorite solution. Why stick in extra words, when there's punctuation that will make the splice legal and keep the voice?

What I'm thinking is you could also use a semicolon here, which is what I'd do as a writer. This is the mark I didn't know about yet when I was writing papers in college. When I looked closely at the places where I comma-spliced back then, and when I observe your comma splice errors today, I see a pattern: in most cases, there's a relationship between the two sentences we tried to splice together. In other words, I don't think comma splices are an arbitrary error. Writers are trying to do something, but they don't know the right mark. Often, the semicolon is the right mark.

A writer uses a semicolon to connect two sentences *not* connected by

---

CORRECTING COMMA SPLICES

Definition: A comma splice occurs when a writer attempts to hook two sentences together with a comma.

EXAMPLES:

The clouds are gathering in the west, it will rain soon.

I'm crazy about dogs, English springer spaniels are my favorites.

I dreamed, around me the night shifted and settled.

© 2002 by Nancie Atwell from
Lessons That Change Writers
(Portsmouth, NH: Heinemann)

CORRECTING COMMA SPLICES   LESSON 70

Reproducible
Correcting Comma
Splices

70

and, when he or she wants to show a relationship between the sentences—when there's a closeness in meaning between them.

So, for example: *The clouds are gathering in the west; it will rain soon.* There's a relationship here: clouds in the west mean rain. The semicolon cements the relationship.

A colon is another possibility. Remember how one of the things it does is show a reader that an explanation is coming? *The clouds are gathering in the west: it will rain soon.*

Let's try another example: *I'm crazy about dogs, English springer spaniels are my favorites.*

First, is it a comma splice? Perform the test aloud with me. . . . Yup. Now, how do we correct it? Let's record some possibilities.

I'm crazy about dogs. English springer spaniels are my favorites.
I'm crazy about dogs; English springer spaniels are my favorites.
I'm crazy about dogs, but English springer spaniels are my favorites.

Let's try another. Is this a comma splice? Perform the test with me. . . . *I dreamed, around me the night shifted and settled.*

Yes, this is a comma splice. "I dreamed" is a sentence—a short one, but it does have a subject and a verb, a someone doing something. What are the options for correcting it? Record with me:

I dreamed. Around me the night shifted and settled.
I dreamed; around me the night shifted and settled.
I dreamed, and around me the night shifted and settled.

Observations about comma splices and correcting them? Questions?

Tonight for homework I'd like you to try to find examples of two comma splice errors in pieces of your prose. If you can't find splices, create two. Write the spliced sentences in your writing handbook, beneath your notes on this lesson. Then, under each splice error, write out two or three alternative versions for correcting it, as we did for the spliced sentences in this lesson.

Questions?

FOLLOW-UP

[The next day, at the end of the mini-lesson, I ask students to pass me their writing handbooks, opened to the page on which they recorded the homework. I check their examples and give a √+ if they got the concept; if they didn't, I correct their attempt and ask them to try another one for homework that night, then I check it the next day.]

70

How to Punctuate Dialogue

Preparation

7 1 LESSON

- ✔ Trimmed photocopies of "Punctuating Conversation" for students to tape into their handbooks
- ✔ An overhead transparency and photocopies of "An Editing Exercise: Punctuating and Paragraphing Dialogue"
- ✔ Fine-point overhead marker in red or blue
- ✔ Tape dispensers

" Please take a copy of "Punctuating Conversation" and tape it to the next clean page of your writing handbook. . . .

I realize there's a heck of a lot of information about quotation marks crammed onto this one page. My aim today, in reading and discussing all of it with you, is to hit each of you where you live in terms of what you already understand about punctuating dialogue and what you still don't get. So we'll start at the most basic level, rule-wise, and move up through the various refinements.

However: I'm going to ask that after today, every one of you tries to do everything on this page when you write or edit dialogue. In other words, this is the system. It's straightforward. I expect you to refer to these handy-dandy guidelines when you're writing the words that people say aloud and when you're checking to see if you did it right.

As we read through the list of rules, please keep your pencil handy and highlight anything you didn't realize or understand before about quoting,

PUNCTUATING CONVERSATION

Quotation marks began in ancient Greek texts as two curved lines that represented the lips of a person speaking. One curved line was placed at the beginning, as if the writer were saying, "I'm telling you something someone else said." The other curved line came at the end, to say, "I've finished writing the words that came out of the other person's mouth."

- **Quotation marks are placed before the first word of a quote and after the punctuation that follows the last word.**

  EX: The teacher said, "In this class there will be no talking, chewing, breathing, unnecessary eye movements, or tap dancing."

- **A quoted remark begins with a capital letter: it's the speaker's first word.**

  EX: I questioned, "Are you up on the furniture again, you bad dog?" She was driving me crazy. I hollered, "Get down now!"

- **A quote is separated from the "he said" part or explanatory phrase with a *comma* OR a *question mark* OR an *exclamation point*, but *never* with a period (a period would create two sentences and a full stop).**

  EX: "I just finished reading *I Am the Cheese*," she remarked.
  "So what did you think of it?" I asked.
  "It was excellent!" she effused.
  I agreed, "I loved it, too."

  Note: The punctuation that follows a quoted remark belongs inside the closing quotation marks. It's part of the sentence and shows *how* the speaker said what he or she said. Also note that the first word of the explanatory phrase is *not* capitalized when it follows the quote: "Beggin' Strips® are my favorite snack," she said.

- **In writing dialogue—two or more people having a conversation—begin a new paragraph *each time* you alternate or change speakers.**

  EX: "I wish today were Friday," she said. "I've been looking forward to it for months now."
  "How come?" he asked.
  "Because finally, *finally*, I'm supposed to get my braces taken off. At least that's what my orthodontist promised."

PUNCTUATING CONVERSATION   LESSON 71

Reproducible
Punctuating Conversation

AN EDITING EXERCISE: PUNCTUATING AND PARAGRAPHING DIALOGUE

Within five minutes the snow was falling so hard we couldn't see the streetlights. I went into full panic mode. Where was my father? My mother said don't worry—he's a good driver. He'll be okay. Do you really think so I asked. Yes I do she said. She put her arm around me and hugged me close to her. Together we stood at the window and watched the storm. Have you ever seen it snow like this before I asked like it will never stop? My mother waited a moment before she answered. Never she said never.

AN EDITING EXERCISE: PUNCTUATING AND PARAGRAPHING DIALOGUE   LESSON 71

Reproducible
An Editing Exercise: Punctuating and
Paragraphing Dialog

punctuating, or paragraphing conversation, as well as anything you weren't 100 percent certain of.

Ready? Follow along with me. . . .

What are some of the rules you highlighted? . . . What are your other observations or questions? . . .

Let's put this knowledge into practice. Try your hand as an editor of quotations: take a copy of "An Editing Exercise" and correct this short narrative, which includes dialogue. Where necessary add quotation marks, capital letters, commas, periods, and question marks. Also, indicate where new paragraphs should start by using the paragraph symbol (¶).

A few things here will be judgment calls, but most of it is straightforward. This is an open-book exercise. Use the new page in your writing handbook to help you. Ready? . . .

FOLLOW-UP

[I ask for individual volunteers to come up to the overhead projector, make editorial corrections on the transparency version of "An Editing Exercise," and discuss their decisions, while classmates follow along, ask questions, and make changes and corrections to their own copies.]

71

Homonyms

Preparation

✔ Trimmed photocopies of "Homonyms" for students to tape into their handbooks

✔ Overhead transparencies and photocopies of "Homonym Review: *Their, There,* and *They're*" and "Homonym Review: *Its* and *It's* and *Your* and *You're*"

✔ Fine-point overhead marker in red or blue

✔ Tape dispensers

" Let me be blunt. If I could expunge one error from the writing of everyone in this class with the wave of a magic wand, it would be the MISSPELLING OF HOMONYMS.

I'm being driven mad—*mad*, I tell you—by the number of writers who are confusing *their*, *there*, and *they're*; *your* and *you're*; and *its* and *it's*. These words may sound alike, but they don't mean alike, nor are they spelled alike. Since I've started to edit them in my dreams, this is probably a good time to turn over responsibility for finding them and correcting them to you.

Please tape "Homonyms" onto the next clean page of your writing handbook. As we read through it, pay particular attention to the brief definition I wrote for each homonym, because *I want you to memorize these phrases and use them as mnemonics* when testing to see whether you've used the right word. Ready? . . .

Now, let's drill this for a minute. I'm serious—everybody, out loud. What does *your* mean? . . . *you're*? . . . *their*? . . . *they're*? . . . *there*? . . . *its*? . . . *it's*? . . . I'm drilling the definitions because if you're uncertain

HOMONYMS

Homonyms are words that sound alike but mean and are spelled differently. *Homonym* means, literally, "same name." Improper use of a homonym is a spelling error with extreme consequences (e.g., lashings).

Commonly Misspelled Homonyms: Definitions and Examples

THEIR — Belongs to a *them* (The teacher stole *their* M&M's.)
THEY'RE — They are (*They're* the world's best candies.)
THERE — In that place; as an introductory adverb. (*There* they are: on the teacher's desk. *There* can never be enough M&M's.)

TWO — The number (*Two* or three packages of M&M's provide a nutritious after-school snack.)
TOO — In addition (ALSO) or more than enough (He, *too*, eats *too* many M&M's.)
TO — Preposition meaning "toward" or used with the infinitive of a verb (I'm going *to* M&M heaven, where I'm going *to* eat many M&M's.)

YOUR — Belongs to a *you* (*Your* M&M's are my M&M's.)
YOU'RE — You are (*You're* in my power; hand over your M&M's.)

ITS — Belongs to an *it* (The dog ate *its* M&M's and wanted mine.)
IT'S — It is (*It's* that kind of day when I crave M&M's.)

HOMONYMS   LESSON 72

Reproducible
Homonyms

about whether you've used the right homonym and you have a mnemonic, you can always, easily, check it yourself.

Study these tonight. Tomorrow and the next day, I'll give you a couple of review exercises. If you memorize the definitions, you'll ace the reviews and I'll give you M&M's.

One final note: I'm convinced that the entire English-writing population can be divided, finally, into two camps: people who get the difference between *it's* and *its* and people who never do. Please study this one especially hard tonight, so you can come over to the gets-it camp for good.

FOLLOW-UP

[I start the next two classes with the homonym review exercises on *their*, *there*, and *they're*, *its* and *it's*, and *your* and *you're*. After everyone has finished with his or her paper version of the review, volunteers come up to the overhead, fill in the blanks on the transparency version, and discuss their decisions by reciting the definition of the appropriate homonym.]

72

**HOMO...
THEIR,**

1. _____

2. They

3. _____
poor

4. _____

5. I lik

6. _____

7. _____

8. Don'

9. They
with

10. _____
rat,
Worl

HOMONYM REVIEW: *ITS* AND *IT'S* AND *YOUR* AND *YOU'RE*

ITS or IT'S?

1. The Declaration of Independence draws _____ strength from the writing, most of it Thomas Jefferson's.

2. The hermit crab finished eating _____ dog biscuit.

3. _____ going to be another cold day.

4. I chose this book because I know _____ author.

5. I don't think _____ nice to put your finger in your nose.

6. _____ funny when she gives people the evil eye.

YOUR or YOU'RE?

1. Is that a new sweater _____ wearing?

2. Do you think _____ coming to my house after school?

3. _____ getting on my nerves.

4. Leave _____ attitude outside.

5. This isn't _____ day, is it?

6. I think _____ great.

Now, join the FUN! and write two of your own, one for ITS/IT'S and one for YOUR/YOU'RE.

1.

2.

HOMONYM REVIEW: *ITS* AND *IT'S* AND *YOUR* AND *YOU'RE*   LESSON 72

Reproducibles and Overheads
Homonym Review and More Homonym Review

Four Capitalization Confusions

Preparation

✔ A blank overhead transparency for you to write each capitalization rule, its exceptions, and examples

73 LESSON

"You guys are pretty savvy about capital letters. For example, you understand the basic differences between common nouns and proper nouns—that the names of specific people and places should be capitalized. You recognize that first words of sentences and first, last, and important words in your titles take caps. But there are a few lingering issues of capitalization confusion I'd like to clear up today. As I summarize the conventions on the overhead, please take notes in your handbooks. The heading will be

Four Capitalization Confusions

First, *school subjects, like math and social studies, don't take capitals*: they're general fields of study, not titles of specific courses. *An exception is English*, because it's the name of a language—as are Spanish, French, and German. Later in your academic careers, to write the titles of *specific college courses*, you'll use caps: History 101 or Earth Science 202.

Now, what about *seasons of the year*? The answer is *no caps: It was a beautiful fall day; I love summer best; we're going south for the winter.* However, *specific, seasonal events and occasions do take caps: Spring Prom, Fall Homecoming, Winter Carnival.*

A similar rule applies to directions of the compass: *east, west, north, and south aren't capitalized* unless *the writer is referring to a* specific *place or region: the Northeast, West Southport, the Wild West.*

Finally, what about mom, dad, and grandma? It depends. Here's the rule: *If there's a personal pronoun—my, our, her—in front of the family role, there's not a capital letter.* It's merely an identification, not a name: *my mom, our dad, her grandma*—like his dog, their cat, my barracuda, yes?

But *if there's no personal pronoun, and you're using the word like it's a first name, then do capitalize it: I asked Mom for money; I hollered for Dad to come quickly; she loves Grandma to pieces.*

A good test is to substitute the first name of the relative in question. If your mother's name is Mary, and you can say in your sentence about her, "I asked Mary for money," then *mom* will be capitalized: "I asked Mom for money." But if your original sentence is "I asked my mom for money," when you substitute *Mary* for *mom,* you get "I asked my Mary for money." This should cue you that here *mom* will be lowercase—a common noun, not the proper noun of a person's name.

For homework tonight, I'd like you to try out some of these conventions. On the lines immediately following your notes on the lesson, please write a sentence that uses *mom* as a proper noun or name. Write another sentence that uses *dad* as a common noun or identification. Use the correct capitalization on both. Then invent a third sentence that includes the words *autumn, south,* and *math,* correctly capitalized according to their use. We'll review these around the circle tomorrow at the start of class.

Questions?

73

Writing Numbers

Preparation

✔ Overhead transparency of "Conventions for Writing Numbers"

✔ Trimmed photocopies of "Conventions for Writing Numbers" for students to tape into their handbooks

✔ Fine-point overhead markers in red or blue

✔ Tape dispensers

74 LESSON

CONVENTIONS FOR WRITING NUMBERS

The general rule is to *spell out numerals of one or two words*: three, seventeen, thirty-seven, five hundred, fifty-five hundred, three million, nine-tenths, 101, 250, 5,280, $4\frac{3}{4}$.

EXCEPT: Use numerals to express: decimals (   ), money ($.), percents (percent), time (:   ), telephone numbers (-   ), dates (April   ,   ), book chapters (chapter   ), book pages (page   -   ), addresses (Main Street), ZIP codes (   ), route numbers (Route   ), and big numbers (___.5 billion).

NOTE: When numbers of one or two words *and* numbers of three or more words appear in the same sentence, write all of the numbers as numerals (

).

FURTHER: A sentence can't *ever* begin with a numeral. Either spell out the numeral, or recast the sentence.
   WRONG: 1968 was a momentous year in U.S. history.
   CORRECT: Nineteen-sixty-eight was a momentous year in U.S. history.
   BETTER: The year 1968 marked a momentous time in U.S. history.

© 2002 by Nancie Atwell from *Lessons That Change Writers* (Portsmouth, NH: Heinemann)   CONVENTIONS FOR WRITING NUMBERS   LESSON 74

Reproducible and Overhead
Conventions for Writing Numbers

"There are times when it's legal to write numerals as numerals, and times when numbers must be written out as words. You guys tend to use numerals most of the time, and you need to be aware that often it's not okay—that readers of literature will be surprised if you write, "It was *2* months later," or "When I was *12* years old. . . ."

Think back for a minute to your own experiences as readers of literature. What have you noticed about when it's okay to use numerals, and when they've been spelled out? . . .

Let's build a generalization from your observations. Please turn to the next clean page of your writing handbook and tape in a copy of "Conventions for Writing Numbers."

Follow along with me as I read aloud the first paragraph; then we'll go back and count how many words there are in each of the numerals I cited as examples. . . .

The bracketed blank spaces on the rest of this page are there for you to generate examples. I'll ask volunteers to come up to the overhead projector and illustrate each exception in the space provided. Then, once we agree that it's correct, I'll ask everyone to copy the example in the appropriate blank space in the copy in your handbook. Ready? . . .

74

Indicating Titles

Preparation

✔ Trimmed photocopies of "Indicating Titles" for students to tape into their handbooks

✔ An overhead transparency and photocopies of "Practice with Indicating Titles"

✔ Fine-point overhead markers in colors

✔ Tape dispensers

"How to handle a title when you refer to it in a piece of your writing—whether to quote it, underline/italicize it, or merely capitalize it—is another adventure in conventions. Just when I think I can articulate a hard-and-fast rule, I discover a new permutation.

So, *in general*, the convention is this: put *quotation marks* around the titles of shorter works and the titles of parts of longer works. These include short stories, poems, articles, speeches, essays, book chapters, and one-act plays.

But you should also put quotes around the titles of TV and radio shows and shorter musical compositions, like songs and piano pieces.

As for underlining: now that so many of you are composing on the word processor, when a title calls for underlining, and the word processor gives you the capability of italicizing, please italicize.

So, what do you italicize/underline? In general, the rule says to italicize or underline the titles of long works that are complete unto themselves. Titles that take underlines/italics include books, pamphlets, magazines, journals, newspapers, movies, long poems (e.g., Milton's *Paradise Lost*),

INDICATING TITLES

Capitalize the first word of a title, the last word, and every word in between that conveys meaning. This means that unless they appear at the beginning or end of a title, you won't capitalize articles (*a*, *an*, *the*), prepositions (*about*, *above*, *at*, *before*, *behind*, *down*, *in*, *near*, *of*, *off*, *on*, *out*, *over*, *to*, *with*, etc.), or short conjunctions (*and*, *but*, *or*, *nor*, *for*, *yet*, *also*, *as*, *that*).

Underlined or *Italicized*
WHOLE AND LONGER WORKS

Books	Operas	Paintings, drawings, and
Pamphlets	Full-length plays	sculptures (e.g., Monet's
Magazines	Musicals	*Impression: Sunrise*,
Journals	Record albums, tape	*1872*)
Newspapers	cassettes, and CDs	Names of ships, aircraft,
Movies	Ballets	or spacecraft (e.g., *The*
Long poems	Symphonies	*Bounty*; *Apollo 8*)
(e.g., Homer's *Iliad*)		

"Quoted"
PARTS AND SHORTER WORKS

Poems	Short stories	TV shows
Newspaper articles	Chapters	Radio shows
Magazine articles	One-act plays	References to pieces of
Songs	Speeches	your own writing
Piano pieces	Essays	(unless you write a book)

Just Caps
SACRED SCRIPTURES

Bible	Torah	Koran
Talmud	Book of Genesis	New Testament

SERIES

David Eddings' Belgariad	the Harry Potter books	Berg's Durable Goods trilogy

YOUR OWN TITLES
(i.e., at the top of the first page of a piece of your writing)

INDICATING TITLES   LESSON 75

Reproducible
Indicating Titles

PRACTICE WITH INDICATING TITLES

1. I hope that you'll read Cold Mountain, Charles Frazier's first novel.
2. Our special song is In My Life by John Lennon.
3. Someday I'd like to sail to England on the Queen Elizabeth 2.
4. Does anyone here subscribe to Sports Illustrated?
5. Anne loved the Babysitter's Club books when she was in second grade.
6. I have mixed feelings about the I Am Sam soundtrack.
7. He cut out and saved Frank Rich's column from the Saturday New York Times.
8. The best piece in the exhibit was Picasso's Head of a Woman.
9. The Lottery is recognized as Shirley Jackson's best short story.
10. I memorized Frost's Stopping by Woods on a Snowy Evening.
11. The Book of Daniel appears in the Old Testament of the Bible.
12. They went to Boston to see a performance by the National Ballet Company of Swan Lake.
13. He listens to Fresh Air on National Public Radio on the way home from work.
14. We read Billy Collins' essay The Companionship of a Poem; it was published in The Washington Post.
15. She memorized the complete score and all the dialogue from the Broadway musical Rent.

PRACTICE WITH INDICATING TITLES   LESSON 75

Reproducible and Overhead
Practice with Indicating Titles

plays, symphonies, operas, ballets, record albums, tape cassettes, and CD's.

But you should also underline/italicize the given titles of paintings, drawings, and sculptures and the names of ships, aircraft, and spacecraft. Go figure.

Finally, some literary titles take neither quotation marks nor underlines/italics. These are sacred writings, like the Bible and its books, and the names of series of books.

Please tape these guidelines for indicating titles onto the next clean page of your writing handbook. Then read along with me, starting with the summary at the top of the page of how to capitalize words in titles. . . .

Are you ready to try to apply these conventions? Here's a practice sheet. Take two minutes and decide what to do with each example: put it in quotes, underline it, or leave it alone. This is an open-book practice session, so go ahead and consult the new page in your writing handbook. . . .

Ready? Would a volunteer come on up to the overhead projector, show how you handled the first example, and explain why? . . .

75

Me or I ?

Preparation

✔ Overhead transparencies of "Pronoun Case, or *Me* or *I*?" and "Pronoun Case Review"

✔ Photocopies of "Pronoun Case Review"

✔ Fine-point overhead marker

"You already know that a noun is a word that names a person, place, thing, or idea. A *pronoun* is a word used in place of a noun; so instead of saying *Nancie* all the time, I can say *I* or *me*. When I address *the class*, I can say *you*; when you talk about *the class*, you can say *we* or *us*.

The *case* of a pronoun tells how it relates to other words in sentences. There are two kinds or cases of pronouns, and it's time for some notes. Please turn to the next clean page in your writing handbook and copy these notes from the transparency as I talk you through them. . . .

Reproducible and Overhead
Pronoun Case, or *Me* or *I*?

Pronoun Case, or *Me* or *I*?

Nominative-case pronouns are used as *actors*, as *subjects of sentences*: *I, he, she, we, they, you,* and *it*. They usually come at the beginning of a sentence.

Objective-case pronouns *receive the action*: *me, him, her, us, them, you,* and *it*. They usually come at the middle or end of a sentence.

The purpose of this lesson and all this background about pronouns is to help you with the *me*-or-*I* conundrum. You guys seldom make errors in pronoun case with singular subjects or objects. In other words, I never hear you say, "Me went to the movies," instead of "I went to the movies." And I've never heard any of you announce, "My parents gave I a new CD player."

The trouble with pronouns comes when the subjects or objects are compound—when there are two or more actors or recipients of the action. Back to the transparency and notetaking:

Errors in pronoun case usually occur when the subject or object is compound (more than one person) and a writer confuses the nominative (actor) and objective (recipient of the action) cases.

EXAMPLES: Kyle and me love M&M's (wrong).

Kyle and I love M&M's (correct).

Rachael gave M&M's to Kyle and I (wrong).

Rachael gave M&M's to Kyle and me (correct).

One way to test for case is to determine if the pronoun is the subject of a verb or the recipient of the action. But there's an even simpler test for correct pronoun case, one you can perform when you're confused about *I/me*, *she/her*, *he/him*, *we/us*, and *they/them*. Please copy it into your notes:

To test for the correct case of a pronoun when there's a compound construction, e.g., *(name) and I/me*, drop the *(name) and* part, then ask yourself, is it *I* or *me*? In other words, test the pronoun by itself with the verb.

EXAMPLE: [*Kyle and*] _____ love M&M's. (*I or me?*)

Rachael gave M&M's to [*Kyle and*] _____. (*I or me?*)

Take the next two minutes and write two sentences of your own for practice. Give one sentence a compound *subject*, with one of the words someone's name and the other a pronoun like *I, he, she, we,* or *they*. Give the other a compound *object*, with one of the words a name and the other a pronoun like *me, him, her, us,* or *them*. We'll read your examples around the circle. And yes, these can be funny.

FOLLOW-UP LESSON

[I start the class the next day with the "Pronoun Case Review." After everyone has finished a paper copy, individual volunteers come to the overhead, fill in the blanks on the transparency version, discuss their decisions, and explain how they applied the test for pronoun case.]

PRONOUN CASE REVIEW

Directions: Write the correct pronoun on the line, using the referent(s) in brackets at the end of each sentence.

1. _____ and _____ collect stamps. (Jack and Jill)

2. My grandmaw and _____ watch "Wheel of Fortune." (myself)

3. _____ girls are going to wreck the boys. (*we* or *us*)

4. _____ and _____ have pet weasels. (Tyler and myself)

5. Do you and _____ like Slurpees®? (Molly)

6. Why are _____ and _____ eating David's lunch? (Nick and Marcia)

7. _____ and _____ are having a big basketball rivalry. (*Us and them* or *We and they?*)

8. The Godivas belong to Rosie and _____ (myself); Toby and _____ get the Tootsie Rolls. (Anne)

9. _____ and _____ love opera. (Peter and Nora)

10. The award for rowdiest student was split between _____ and Phaelon. (Ruthie)

11. Please give any extra money to Jonathan and _____ . (myself)

12. Did Audrey or _____ answer the phone? (Michael)

    PRONOUN CASE REVIEW   LESSON 76

Reproducible and Overhead
Pronoun Case Review

ME OR I?

I'm grateful first, foremost, and always to my students, whose writing is the heart of this book, and to the K–6 teachers of CTL who grow, nurture, and inspire our kids as writers.

To Ron Miller, a continent away from Edgecomb, I extend for-the-last-time gratitude for his assistance in preparing the manuscript and for being such a generous first reader.

Thanks to Mary Ellen Giacobbe for telephone conversations and encouragement, to Anne for typing and more encouragement, and to Toby for hand-holding and the blue room.

To the folks at Heinemann, a million thanks for their genius, their insane hard work, and their commitment to teachers. Leigh Peake managed this project with humor, patience, and skill. Lisa Fowler created forty-eight cover designs before she recognized the one that showed the essence of my classroom and the kids. Kelley Hersey's design pulled the diverse elements of the manuscript together and gave them a life. And Louise Richardson took on the challenge of a brand new format and made it classy and beautiful.

Finally, Mike Gibbons, first man of FirstHand, cheered me through each stage of this project. His cards, notes, and phone calls raised my spirits every time, and his responses to my writing showed me how I want to respond to my students. I never had a muse before; now, I don't know how I wrote without one.